A Display of the
ROYAL BANNER *and* STANDARDS,

bore by the Loyalists *in the* GRAND-REBELLION, *begun Anno Dom.* 1641.

with their several curious Devises & Motto's, *together w.th the Names of y.e Lords & principal Gentlemen y.t gave them.*

Never before Publish'd, 1722.

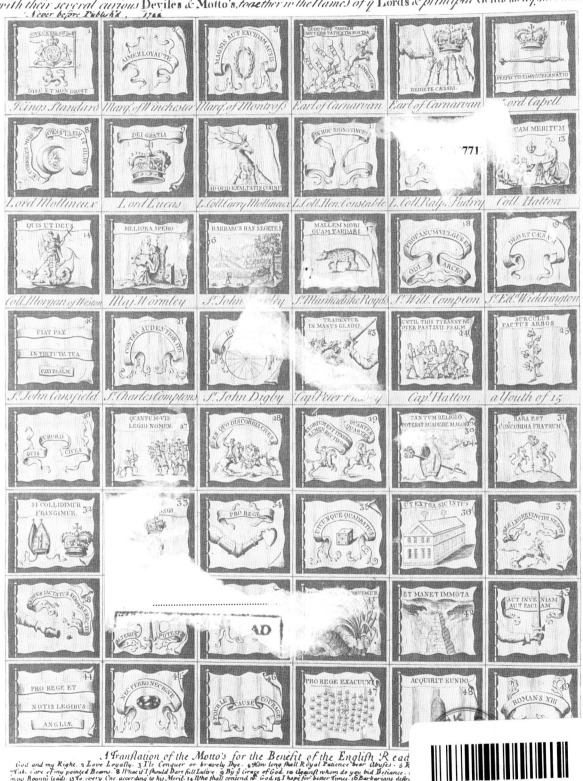

A Translation of the Motto's for the Benefit of the English Reader.

THE ENGLISH CIVIL WAR

At First Hand

THE ENGLISH CIVIL WAR

At First Hand

TRISTRAM HUNT

Weidenfeld & Nicolson
LONDON

First published in Great Britain in 2002 by
Weidenfeld & Nicolson

© Tristram Hunt 2002

A CIP catalogue record for this book is available from the British Library.

ISBN 0 297 82953 X

Printed in Italy by Printer Trento s.r.l

Weidenfeld & Nicolson

The Orion Publishing Group Ltd
Orion House
5 Upper Saint Martin's Lane
London
WC2H 9EA

Picture credit abbreviations
AA   Art Archive
BAL   Bridgeman Art Library
BL   British Library
NPG   National Portrait Gallery
WA   Weidenfeld Archive

Title page: *The Battle of Marston Moor, 2 July 1644, nineteenth-century painting by
Abraham Cooper (BAL, Harris Museum and Art Gallery, Preston)*
Endpapers: *Parliamentarian and Royalist standards and banners (BAL, Ashmolean
Museum, Oxford)*
Opposite: *Cromwell as depicted in The Genealogy of the Anti-Christ Oliver Cromwell.*

The Lord hath done such things amongst us as have not been known in the world these thousand years

OLIVER CROMWELL, 27 January 1654

Acknowledgements

I would like to thank Anthony Cheetham for suggesting the idea for this book and my editors Michele Hutchison and Ion Trewin for making it happen so calmly. At Weidenfeld and Nicolson, Roisin Heycock, Laura Searle, Alex Knights and Victoria Webb were invaluable in marshalling the vast array of documents. For his help in discovering the more obscure texts of the period and for his excellent knowledge of mid-seventeenth century literature and religious heterodoxy, my thanks to Simon Dyton. And for his intricate grasp of seventeenth-century portraiture and iconography, Tom Graves. I would also like to thank my agent, Georgina Capel; Alan Clements at WarkClements for re-igniting my interest in the war of the three kingdoms; Professor John Morrill, University of Cambridge; Professor Blair Worden, University of Sussex; Susan and Richard Griffin; the staff of the Rare Books Room, Cambridge Library; and the Centre for History and Economics, King's College, Cambridge.

Contents

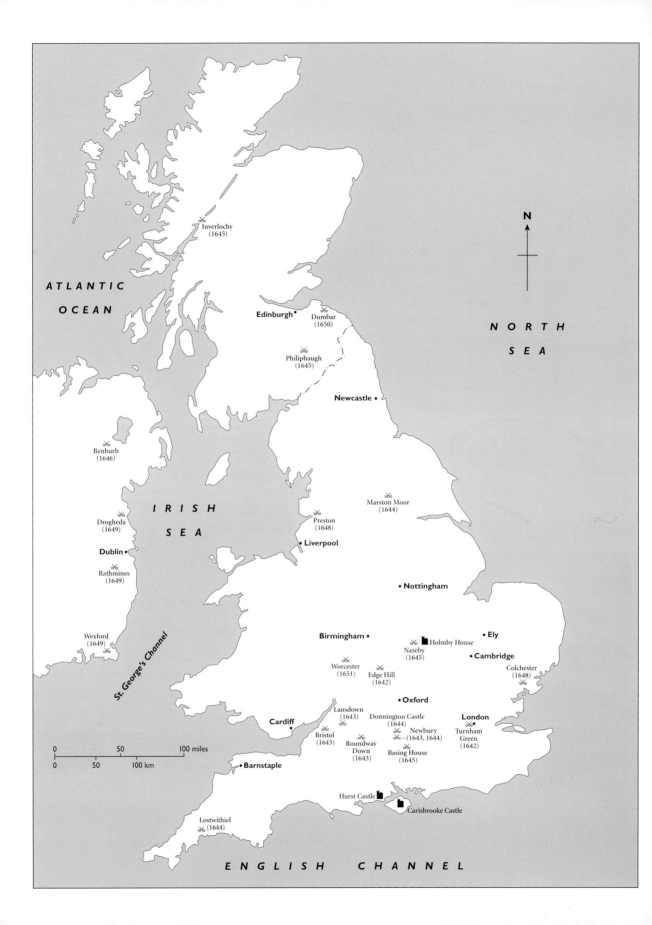

N

ATLANTIC

OCEAN

NORTH

SEA

Inverlochy
(1645)

Edinburgh• Dumbar
(1650)

Philiphaugh
(1645)

Newcastle •

Benburb
(1646)

IRISH

SEA

Drogheda
(1649)

Marston Moor
(1644)

Preston
(1648)

Dublin •

Liverpool

Rathmines
(1649)

• Nottingham

Wexford
(1649)

Birmingham •

Holmby House

• Ely

Naseby
(1645)

St. George's Channel

Worcester
(1651)

Edge Hill
(1642)

• Cambridge

Colchester
(1648)

• Oxford

Lansdown
(1643)

Donnington Castle
(1644)

London

Cardiff

Newbury
—(1643, 1644)

Turnham
Green
(1642)

Bristol
(1643)

Roundway
Down
(1643)

Basing House
(1645)

0   50   100 miles

0   50   100 km

• Barnstaple

Hurst Castle

Carisbrooke Castle

Lostwithiel
(1644)

ENGLISH   CHANNEL

Introduction

The land is weary of our discords, being thereby polluted with our blood.

God has given you great successes in many places against our enemies, and sometimes he is pleased to give our enemies successes against us; in all of them, whether of the one or the other party, the poor English are still sufferers.

Whose goods, I pray sir, are plundered? Whose houses are burnt? Whose limbs are cut or shot off? Whose persons are thrown into loathsome dungeons? Whose blood stains the walls of our towns and defiles our land?

Is it not all English? And is it not then time for us, who are all Englishmen, to be weary of these discords, and to use our utmost endeavours to put an end to them?

I know, sir, you are all here of the same opinion with me in this point; and that it was an unhappy mistake of those who told us in the beginning of our warfare, that it would be only to show ourselves in the field with a few forces, and then all would be presently ended.

We have found it otherwise: let us now again seek to recover these blessings of peace, whereof we are told, that *nihil tam populare quam pax,* that nothing is than peace more gracious to be heard of, more pleasing to be desired, and more profitable to be enjoyed.

So lamented the parliamentarian Bulstrode Whitelocke in a speech to the House of Commons. As early as 1643, he could already sense the terrifying chaos awaiting his countrymen. The civil wars of the 1640s, known historically as the English Civil War, ripped apart England, Ireland and Scotland. Institutions, hierarchies and the very fabric of society were transformed by the most dramatic decade in British history. When King Charles I raised his Royal Standard in August 1642 and declared war against Parliament, he unleashed a revolution. The civil war years would see a king executed, the establishment of a republic, the digging of communes in Surrey, the abolition of the House of Lords, a torrent of religious freethinking, and the creation of a military dictatorship. All on English soil. Meanwhile Ireland would suffer subjugation and sectarian bloodshed while Scotland erupted into brutal clan conflict. By the conclusion of the wars in 1651, the British Isles had become a foreign land. New ideas about political liberty and religious toleration, the balance of power between king and parliament, the justice of private property, and the function of the Church of England had melted away the old belief systems. In the process the country became a vast battlefield: 30,000-strong armies laying waste the country; tortuous sieges gutting medieval towns and country houses; and staggering displays of military bravura that have secured the names of Edgehill, Marston Moor, and Dunbar their place in British history.

This revolutionary epoch came with a terrible human cost. Almost a quarter of a million people lost their lives in a conflict unrivalled for proportionate British casualties until the carnage of World War One. The grim horror of civil war divided families and communities. The country went to war over the rights of parliament against the unfettered power of the monarch as well as the future direction of the Church of England. Such seemingly esoteric issues set father against son and forced brother into battle against brother. The competing pull of king and parliament, Anglican and Puritan scythed through old loyalties and traditional ties. During some nine years of fighting, no corner of the British Isles, no town or village, escaped the gruesome burden of war.

The devastation of those years affected rich and poor, Cavalier and Roundhead alike. In a predominantly rural economy, the chaos of huge armies on the march, working sons press-ganged into combat, and soldiers arbitrarily billeted in houses and farms destroyed the precarious living of millions. Harvests were left to rot, property plundered and generations of work sent up in the flames of war. It was a terrible, bloody time – a warning of the dangers when politics collapse, ideology flares and religious zealotry possesses a people. While few understood the war's roots or reasons, all had to endure the exhaustive search for its resolution.

The consequences of the wars were as fundamental as the Russian or French revolution. It put the English off political upheaval to this day and brought the nation back from the brink in 1688 when the political establishment chose a Glorious Revolution (or Dutch invasion) rather than another bloody civil war. Its intellectual ramifications are equally tangible. With the collapse of the traditional authority of church and state, novel philosophies and eccentric heresies flourished. A free press combined with a messianic fervour to produce some of the most fertile religious and political debate in European history. And for the first time, these debates included the contributions of the lower or middling sorts, the tenant farmers and small tradesmen, traditionally excluded from discussions of power. When we argue today about the value of republicanism, the relationship between capitalism or private property and democracy, and the principle of devolved power within the British Isles, our starting point should be the civil war years.

Yet for me what makes the 1640s and 1650s so utterly gripping is the language of the day. The mental world of early modern Britain is a different place to the secular cynicism of the twenty-first century. Their defining lodestars were biblical and classical history. Whether they were Puritan believers or conservative Anglicans, the supremacy of the Bible was all encompassing. Its books, its psalms, its legends were injunctions and guides to daily conduct in real life. The Book of Revelation was minutely dissected for allegorical significance and taken as a graphic warning of what could happen if England ever fell from favour. Similarly, they looked to the ancient histories of Livy and Tacitus to understand their politics and the signs of tyranny. This rich literary hinterland resulted in a culture of oratory, letters and history that retains a timeless urgency that can still engross the modern reader.

In a dazzling recent book, the historian Blair Worden charted the passionate public controversies that surrounded the history of the civil war through to the early 1900s. Two generations ago, the struggle between Roundhead and Cavalier still seemed to retain a contemporary significance. 'I judge a man by one thing,' the Liberal politician Isaac Foot even remarked, 'which side would he have liked his ancestors to fight on at Marston Moor?' The historian W. E. H. Lecky agreed, declaring that 'We are Cavaliers or Roundheads before we are Conservatives or Liberals.' Over the course of the twentieth century, the relevance of the civil war and its place in public discourse dwindled to nought. While France still discusses the aspirations and ideals of the Revolution and American politics continues to operate in the shadow both of the War of Independence and the Civil War, in Britain the collective memory of the revolutionary decades seems to have been totally jettisoned. By bringing back the contemporary debates, journals and diaries of the day, by resuscitating the lost voices of the English Civil War, I hope that this depressing decline might in some small way be curbed. The purpose of this book is to explain the outlines of the civil war, generate interest in the period and bring to as broad an audience as possible the extraordinary literature of our revolution.

Few periods can lay claim to such a hold on the English language. From Speaker Lenthall's decrial that he had 'neither eyes to see nor tongue to speak except as this House is pleased to direct me', to Milton's optimistic assertion that he saw 'a noble and puissant nation rousing herself like a strong man after sleep, and shaking her invincible locks: methinks I see her as an eagle mewing her mighty youth, and kindling her undazzled eyes at the full midday beam; purging and unscaling her long-abused sight at the fountain itself of heavenly radiance.' From the lowly Colonel Rainsborough's belief that 'the poorest he that is in England hath a life to live, as the greatest he' to Jacob Astley's plaintive prayer as he marched his infantry down Edgehill: 'O Lord! thou knowest, how busy I must be this day: if I forget thee, do not thou forget me.'

The civil war is also unparalleled in its language of pathos and drama. From Ralph Verney's letters sharing the news of his beloved father's death, 'Madam, I never loved to be the messenger of ill news: therefore I forbore to send you this; which is the saddest and deepest affliction that ever befell any poor distressed man; I will not add to your grief by relating my own deplorable condition, neither can my pen express the miseries I am in; God's will be done, and give me patience, to support me in this extremity', to King Charles I on the eve of his execution telling his young son the Duke of Gloucester what was about to happen: 'Sweetheart, now they will cut off thy father's head. Mark, child, what I say, they will cut off my head and perhaps make thee a king. But mark what I say; you must not be a king so long as your brothers Charles and James do live. For they will cut off your brothers' heads, when they can catch them, and cut off thy head too, at the last.'

Then there is Cromwell. No man extorted more meaning and moment from the English language than old Ironside himself. His biblical literalism was joined to an awesomely fiery temper and out it spewed in his letters and speeches. He warned his fellow Roundhead commanders, 'I had rather have a plain russet-coated captain what knows what he fights for, and loves what he knows, than that which you call a gentleman and is nothing else.' After his victory at Marston Moor, he wrote a letter to the father of a dead soldier, mixing divine righteousness with common English matter of fact: 'Truly England and the Church of God hath had a great favour from the Lord, in this great victory given unto us, such as the like never was since the war began….God made them as stubble to our swords, we charged their regiments of foot with our horse, routed all we charged… Give glory, all the glory, to God. Sir, god hath taken away your eldest son by a cannon-shot. It brake his leg. We were necessitated to have it cut off, whereof he died.' And his dismissal of Parliament in 1653 became immortalised in British political history when the same bitter words were used to urge Neville Chamberlain to resign in May 1940: 'You have sat too long here for any good you have been doing. Depart, I say, and let us have done with you. In the name of God, go!'

This is but the tip of a literary culture inspired, revolted and terrified by the civil war years. It includes Cavalier letters from the battlefield, the Puritan memoirs of a Roundhead wife, the speeches of Cromwell, the correspondence of King Charles I, and the sublime account of the 'Great Rebellion' by the Earl of Clarendon. It is primarily a collection of works from England. The enormous cultural breadth of the civil wars, a multifaceted conflict engrossing England, Ireland and Scotland, is not reflected in this purposively Anglo-centric account. Scottish and Irish sources are included but only where they enlighten the English aspect of the narrative. However, there exist many fascinating collections of Irish and Scottish documents as listed in the bibliography. The intent of this book is to place the language of the civil war within popular English cultural and political discourse.

This work does not seek to provide a comprehensive explanation of the many complicated social, political and intellectual causes of the civil war. It is a story of the war's drama, politics, ideas, and battles as told by eyewitnesses to the event. As with any history, it is necessarily subjective in its selection of sources and the course of its analysis. Yet the very fundamentals of its approach are indebted to (but in no way the responsibility of) the decades of research by such eminent civil war scholars as John Morrill, Mark Kishlansky, Conrad Russell, Blair Worden and the late C.V. Wedgwood. For readers who wish to understand the period more fully, and explore its historical significance with greater nuance, it is to their books they should turn.

Portrait of Cromwell, by Robert Walker (WA)

This collection is an opening introduction to the English Civil War through the work of those most suited to describe it. Those who charged into battle at Naseby, those who witnessed the execution of Charles I, those who lost a father, those who sought to build a New Jerusalem, and those who had their worlds turned upside down by the tumultuous, fascinating, awesome years of the mid-seventeenth century. History is always recounted best at first hand.

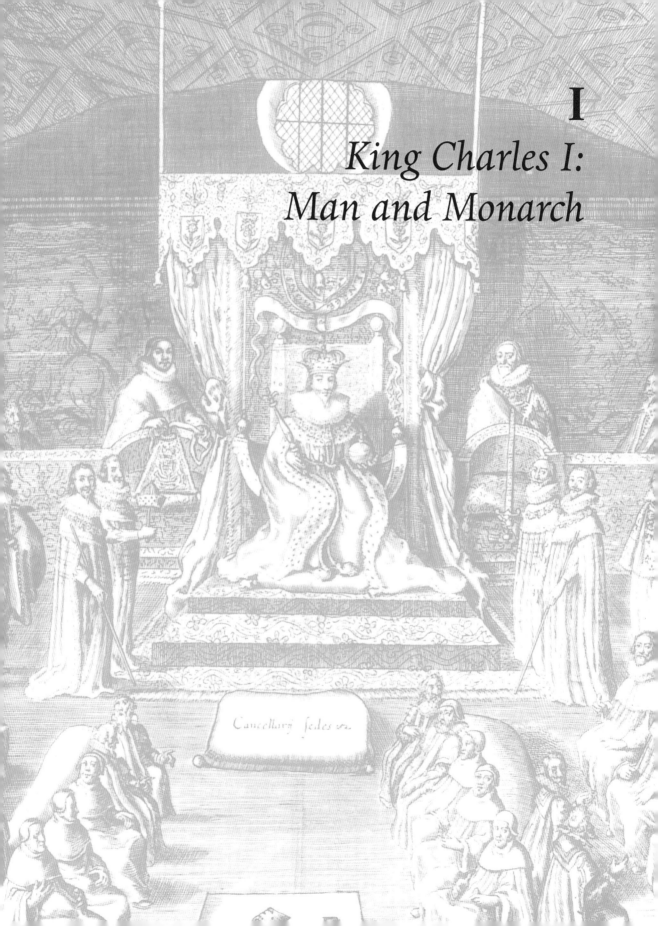

I

King Charles I:
Man and Monarch

Cancellarij sedes va.

1600 *November*	Birth of Charles Stuart, Duke of York
1612 *November*	Death of Henry, Prince of Wales. Charles Stuart becomes heir to the throne
1618 *May*	'Defenestration' of Prague and start of Thirty Years War between Catholic and Protestant armies across Europe
1625 *March*	Death of James I. Succession of Charles I as King of England, Ireland and Scotland
1625 *June*	Marriage of King Charles to Princess Henrietta-Maria
1628 *August*	Assassination of Charles's confidant and close friend, George Villiers, Duke of Buckingham

1629 *March*	Dissolution of Parliament after Speaker is forcibly held in the Chair. Start of eleven years of 'Personal Rule'
1633 *August*	Appointment of high-church cleric William Laud as Archbishop of Canterbury
1634 *October*	Introduction of ship money as an extra source of revenue for King Charles's depleted coffers
1637 *June*	Pillory and mutilation of Puritan activists Prynne, Burton, and Bastwick
1637 *November*	John Hampden's case against ship money heard in Court

BEHIND THE MYRIAD EVENTS OF THE ENGLISH CIVIL WAR LIES ONE MAN – King Charles I. The seventeenth century was an age of personal monarchy when the whims of a king overshadowed all political decisions. The character of a monarch determined the very shape of the kingdom. In the 1640s, it was Charles's arrogance, fastidious sense of monarchy and unshakeable belief in his divine mission as king that time and again prevented an escape from civil war.

As the stammering, shy and sickly younger son of James I, Charles was never meant to be king. He lived his early years as Duke of York, watching in awe the alpha-male exuberance of his handsome elder brother, Henry, Prince of Wales. But following Henry's tragic death from smallpox at the age of nineteen in 1612, the stunted Charles was thrust forward as heir apparent. He immediately set about improving his physical prowess, kingly airs and chivalric skills. Even when he arrived on the throne in 1625, Charles was still trying to prove himself a born king.

King Charles I, after Van Dyck (BAL)

Charles I as Duke of York prior to his brother's death, by Robert Peake the Elder (BAL, City of Bristol Museum and Art Gallery)

The dignity, the majesty of monarchy was always uppermost in his thoughts – as were his fears about his own capacity to fulfil those duties. This nagging insecurity goes some way to explain his extraordinary focus on the image and iconography of kingship. From the famous portraits by Van Dyck to the elaborate masques written by Ben Jonson, the elevation of monarchy was all consuming in Caroline England.

In the absence of his elder brother, the young Charles fell under the malign influence of George Villiers, the Duke of Buckingham. Although he was James I's most loved and loyal courtier, Buckingham understood it made sound political sense to be on equally good terms with the future king. Staggeringly beautiful and a master of court intrigue, he soon had the unsure prince under his sway. Together the two young bucks began to run rings round the ageing and indulgent King James, undermining both his foreign and parliamentary strategy. As James tried to guide Britain through the treacherous waters of European dynastic diplomacy, Charles and Buckingham embarked on extraordinary foreign jaunts which imperilled the entirety of government policy. Their ill-conceived trip to Madrid in the mid-1620s to woo the Spanish infanta was a catastrophe which Charles later tried to dig himself out of by declaring war on Europe's seventeenth-century super-power. When Buckingham was assassinated in 1628 by the disgruntled sailor John Felton, Charles was devastated. He retreated further into himself and away from what he regarded as the ungrateful and malicious politicians at Westminster.

'Staggeringly beautiful and a master of court intrigue'. George Villiers, Duke of Buckingham (National Portrait Gallery)

Beyond their shared passion for the Duke of Buckingham, Charles I and James I had little in common. As king, Charles was in fact the polar opposite of his father – who had been a sensual and profligate ruler with a great love of the discussion and practice of politics. Before he succeeded Elizabeth I in 1603, James had governed Scotland which was a kingdom where the monarch enjoyed far less control over noble elites than in England. James had realised early on that even though you were king, you still had to negotiate to achieve your objectives. Whether it was debating the future of the Church or marrying off his daughter, James loved to haggle. Charles, on the other hand, was aloof and ascetic. He had no taste for compromise. As king, he regarded himself as God's representative on earth and his word was simply to be taken as law. As Charles himself put it:

> A good king acknowledges himself ordained by God for his people. He receives from God the burden of government for which he must be accountable. But a king must rule his people like a father and, like a father, his authority is founded on the immutable decrees of Almighty God. His subjects must therefore respect the sovereign like a father. I alone must answer to God for our exercise of the authority he has vested in me. It is for me to decide how our nation is to be governed, how my subjects are to be ruled and above all how the Church shall be established under the rule of law. These are the Divine Rights of Kings and are ordained by the Almighty. It is not the place of the subject to question the royal prerogative.

Unlike his father, Charles was also deeply spiritual. Where James enjoyed intellectual arguments about religion, Charles was a more private but earnest believer. Few knew or loved the King with such blind devotion as Edward Hyde, Earl of Clarendon. Initially a critic and then loyal courtier of Charles I, he went on to mentor his son Charles II during the 1650s Commonwealth. Here he admiringly describes the King's devotional duties:

> He was very punctual and regular in his devotions, and was never known to enter upon his recreations or sports before he had been at public prayers; so that on hunting days his chaplains were bound to a very early attendance. He was likewise very strict in observing the hours of his private chamber devotions; and was so severe an exactor of gravity and reverence in all mention of religion, that he could never endure any light or profane word in religion, with what sharpness of wit soever it was covered. Though he was well pleased and delighted with reading verses made upon any occasion, no man durst bring before him anything that was profane or unclean; that kind of wit had never any countenance then.

The royalist politician and future combatant, Sir Philip Warwick, paints a similarly reserved picture of the monarch:

> His deportment was very majestic; for he would not let fall his dignity, no not to the greatest foreigners that came to visit him and his Court; for though he was far from pride, yet he was careful of majesty, and would be approached with respect and reverence. His conversation was free, and the subject matter of it was most commonly rational…

The many faces of Charles I, by Carlo Maratti, after Van Dyck (BAL, The Trustees of the Weston Park Foundation)

This attention to the dignity of majesty was extended even to his eating habits:

> His appetite was to plain meats and though he took a good quantity thereof, yet it was suitable to an easy digestion. He seldom eat of above three dishes at most, nor drank above three: a glass of small beer, another of claret wine, and the last of water; he eat suppers as well as dinners heartily; but betwixt meals, he never meddled with anything. Fruit he would eat plentifully; and with this regularity he moved as steadily as a star follows its course.

The Court

The style and character of a monarch was expressed through the court. The distinction between public and private melted away as every action of the monarch was understood in a public, political context. Charles was determined that his court would not endure the same depraved, lustful scenes that marred the Jacobean court of his father. Ironically, in the context of future struggles, the Caroline court was almost puritanical in its style. Where James revelled in the public life of the court, Charles was far more withdrawn. And although as king he built up the foundations

*'Beneath the Rubens and glorious Titians there existed a highly formal and controlled society'.
Ceiling of the Banqueting Hall, Whitehall Palace, painted by Peter Paul Rubens
(BAL, Whitehall)*

of an astounding royal art collection (which the Commonwealth later sold off to Spain), the court was more reserved and less showy than his father's. Behind the sumptuous architecture of Inigo Jones's Banqueting House, beneath the Rubens and glorious Titians there existed a highly formal and controlled society. The Venetian ambassador in London, in one of his many reports back to base, notes the change:

> The King observes a great deal of decorum. The nobles do not enter his apartment in confusion as heretofore, but each rank has its apportioned place, and he has declared that he desires the observance of the rules and maxims of the late Queen Elizabeth, whose rule was so popular and is so vastly famous. The King has also drawn up rules for himself, dividing the day from his very early rising, for prayers, exercises, audiences, business, eating and sleeping. It is said that he will set apart a day for public audience, and he does not wish anyone to be introduced to him unless sent for.

While such abstinence was admirable, it did not engender wide affection for the King. Leading nobles who were used to easy interaction with the monarch were put off by his haughtiness. But the Puritan writer Lucy Hutchinson was impressed by the court's alteration. Writing in the mid-1660s, as the highly educated wife of a leading Roundhead partisan and later signatory to Charles's death-warrant, she was remarkably generous:

> The face of the court was much changed in the change of the king, for King Charles was temperate and chaste and serious, so that the fools and bawds, mimics and catamites of the former court grew out of fashion, and the nobility and courtiers, who did not quite abandon their debaucheries, had yet that reverence to the King to retire into corners to practise them. Men of learning and ingenuity in all arts were in esteem, and received encouragement from the King, who was a most excellent judge and a great lover of paintings, carvings, engravings and many other ingenuities less offensive than the bawdy and profane wit which was the only exercise of the other court.

But many feared that behind the formality of Charles's court, more sinister forces were at play. His authoritarian style, the continental art and culture he patronised, and the high-church faith he encouraged, seemed unsettling. At court, the person who symbolised this hidden agenda was his queen, Henrietta-Maria. The precocious child of the King of France, Henrietta-Maria believed in the untrammelled power of the King. He was God's tribune on earth and that was that. The terms of her marriage treaty were such that the Queen was also allowed to continue to practise as a Roman Catholic. The combination of her forthright belief in the powers of monarchy and her ostentatious Catholic observance made Henrietta-Maria deeply unpopular. But after a tricky start to the marriage, Charles fell utterly in love with his wife, leading political opponents to wonder whether he was being unduly influenced by this Papist cuckoo in the nest. Clarendon describes the scene:

Charles I's loyal historian, The Earl of Clarendon, after Adriaen Hanneman (NPG)

The King's affection to the queen was of a very great extraordinary alloy; a composition of conscience, and love, and generosity, and gratitude, and all those noble affections which raise the passion to the greatest height; insomuch as he saw with her eyes, and determined by her judgement; and did not only pay her this adoration, but desired that all men should know that he was swayed by her; which was not good for either of them…When she was admitted to the knowledge and participation of the most secret affairs, she took delight in the examining and discussing them, and from thence in making judgement of them; in which her passions were always strong…And she so far concurred with the King's inclination, that she did not more desire to be possessed of this unlimited power, than that all the world should take notice that she was the entire mistress of it: which in truth was the foundation upon which the first and the utmost prejudices to the King and his government were raised and prosecuted.

Lucy Hutchinson, never a feminist, was equally angered by her presence in the King's court:

He married a Papist, a French lady of haughty spirit, and a great wit and beauty, to whom he became a most uxorious husband. By this means the court was replenished with Papists, and many who hoped to advance themselves by the change turned to that religion. All the Papists in the kingdom were favoured, and, by the King's example, matched into the best families…

Looking back from the 1660s, the Roundhead commander Edmund Ludlow similarly emphasises the Queen's damaging influence upon the King:

In the beginning of his reign he married a daughter of France, who was not wanting on her part to press him, upon all occasions, to pursue the design of enlarging his power, not omitting to solicit him also to mould the Church of England to a nearer compliance with the See of Rome: wherein she was but too well seconded by corrupt Ministers of State, of whom some were professed Papists; and an ambitious Clergy, whose influence upon the King was always greater than could well consist with the peace and happiness of England.

Queen Henrietta Maria, 'a French lady of haughty spirit, and a great wit and beauty'. Portrait by Van Dyck (BAL)

Seventeenth-century Flemish panel depicting Charles I and Henrietta-Maria, by Van Dyck (BAL, Palazzo Pitti, Florence)

The Catholicism and authoritarianism of the court were particularly resented because they reflected Charles's broader policies. In the 1630s, the King's religious and constitutional reforms were exacerbating barely suppressed tensions which would later provide the kindling for civil war.

Religious Reforms

By the 1630s, the religious settlement established by King Henry VIII at the 1533 Protestant Reformation and later refined by Queen Elizabeth I was falling apart at the seams. The Church of England was created in the 1530s as a political compromise with the monarch as its supreme governor. For most of the sixteenth century, the Church's middle of the road Protestantism and fairly Catholic structure of bishops and clergy was accepted. Yet during the latter years of Queen Elizabeth's reign, a faction of godly or Puritan worshippers became increasingly dissatisfied with the practices and doctrine of the Church. They wanted to dismantle the ecclesiastical structure of bishops and archbishops that led to the sovereign being Supreme Governor. They felt such a governing structure showed the Church had never been fully reformed from its Roman Catholic roots. It was like a badly set bone which needed to be rebroken and then refashioned afresh.

Following the teachings of the Geneva theologian John Calvin, they argued for a Church that adhered far more rigorously to the word of the Bible. They wanted to do away with the man-made artifices of the Church – the institution of bishops, the clerical surplices which many clergy wore and the images and icons (such as stained-glass windows) which littered English churches. The Kidderminster-based

Puritan preacher Richard Baxter describes his fellow believers as:

> religious persons that used to talk of God and heaven and scripture and holiness, and
> to follow sermons and read books of devotion and pray in their families and spent
> the Lord's day in religious exercises, and plead for mortification and serious devotion,
> and strict obedience to God, and speak against swearing, cursing, drunkenness,
> profaneness etc.

Above all, Puritans believed in the individual's direct, personal relationship with
God. Following the teachings of Calvin, many also adhered to the doctrine of predestination whereby God had already elected his chosen saints for heaven. They
were convinced that no amount of good work or taking of the sacrament could
change that. Consequently, they believed the clergy's role should be limited to
preaching and reading scripture and certainly not acting as some kind of interme-
diary to God.

Opposed to the Puritans were the Arminians or high-church clergy who took
their name from the Dutch theologian, Jacobus Arminius. They refuted the idea of
predestination and believed that only through prayer and the sacrament would the
individual gain divine grace. They believed in the vital, ceremonial role of the
clergy and that the glory of God should be reflected through the beauty of
churches. Their vision was shared by Charles I. For Puritans, such beliefs were
nothing short of popery. They could see little difference between the high-church
ceremonial and the practices of the Roman Catholic church. Lucy Hutchinson best
describes this growing battle for the soul of the Church between her own fellow
Puritans, those caught in the middle and the high-church faction:

> When the dawn of the Gospel began to break upon this isle, after the dark midnight
> of Papacy, the morning was more cloudy here than in other places by reason of the
> state interest, which was mixing and working itself into the interest of religion, and
> which in the end quite wrought it out. But even then there wanted not many who dis-
> cerned the corruptions that were retained in the church, and eagerly applied their
> endeavours to obtain a purer reformation, through excess of joy for that which was
> already brought forth or else through a secret love of superstition rooted in their
> hearts, thought this too much, were bitterly incensed, and, hating that light which
> reproved their darkness, everywhere stirred up spirits of envy and persecution against
> them. Upon this great revolution, the nation became divided into three great factions:
> the Papist, the State Protestant, and the more religious zealots who afterward were
> branded with the name of Puritan.

Communities became increasingly divided by this religious discord. Richard Baxter
had a terrible time with his less than godly congregation in Kidderminster. Here he
explains how his views on man's innate sin went down with the rough locals:

> Whilst I was employed between outward labours and inward trials, Satan stirred up a
> little inconsiderable rage of wicked men against me. The town having been formerly
> eminent for vanity, had yearly a show, in which they brought forth the painted forms

Portrait of Lucy and Colonel Hutchinson and family, by Jurgen Ovens (BAL, Noortman, Maastricht, Netherlands)

of giants and such like foolery, to walk about the streets with; and though I said nothing against them, as being not simply evil, yet on every one of those days of riot the rabble of the more vicious sort had still some spleen to vent against me as one part of their game. And once all the ignorant rout were raging mad against me for preaching the doctrine of original sin to them, and telling them that infants before regeneration had so much guilt and corruption as made them loathsome in the eyes of God; whereupon they vented it abroad in the country that I preached that God hated or loathed infants, so that they railed at me as I passed through the streets. The next Lord's-day I cleared and confirmed it, and showed them that if this were not true their infants had no need of Christ, of baptism, or of renewing by the Holy Ghost. And I asked them whether they durst say that their children were saved without a Saviour, and were no Christians, and why they baptised them, with much more to that purpose; and afterwards they were ashamed and mute as fishes.

Archbishop Laud

At the head of the high-church faction was Charles's Archbishop of Canterbury, William Laud. From humble beginnings in Reading, Laud rose to become head of an Oxford college and Bishop of London before he finally succeeded to the see of Canterbury in 1633. Yet through the mid-1620s his career was thwarted by Puritan clerics. It was Charles who rescued him and to the King Laud owed everything. When he finally got into power, he was determined to make his presence felt and purge the Church of his troublesome Puritan enemies. Clarendon, who saw so much damage inflicted on the monarchy by Laud's bellicose personality, put the Archbishop's psychology at the heart of his actions:

> The archbishop had, all his life, eminently opposed Calvin's doctrine in those controversies, before the name of Arminius was taken notice of, or his opinions heard of; and thereupon, for want of another name, they had called him a papist...When he came into great authority, it may be, he retained too keen a memory of those who had so unjustly and uncharitably persecuted him before; and, I doubt, was so far transported with the same passions he had reason to complain of in his adversaries, that, as they accused him of popery, because he had some doctrinal opinions which they liked not, though they were nothing allied to popery; so he entertained too much prejudice to some persons, as if they were enemies to the discipline of the church, because they concurred with Calvin in some doctrinal points...He had, from his first entrance into the world, without any disguise or dissimulation, declared his own opinion of that classis of men; and, as soon as it was in his power, he did all he could to hinder the growth and increase of that faction, and to restrain those who were inclined to it, from doing the mischief they desired to do.

Laud's most controversial reform was to demand the movement of communion tables from the body of the church to the east end and for it then to be cut off from the congregation by a decorative rail. This move was to emphasise the sacerdotal role of the clergy. Puritans were appalled by this change regarding it as a highly aggressive theological innovation. John Milton, the radical Puritan poet and future Cromwellian pamphleteer, saw Laud's reforms coming between the people and their God:

> The table of communion, now become a table of separation, stands like an exalted platform upon the brow of the quire, fortified with bulwark and barricado, to keep off the profane touch of the laics, whilst the obscene and surfeited priest scruples not to paw and mammoc the sacramental bread, as familiarly as his tavern biscuit. And thus the people, vilified and rejected by them, give over the earnest study of virtue and godliness, as a thing of greater purity than they need, and the search of divine knowledge as a mystery too high for their capacities, and only for churchmen to meddle with; which is what the prelates desire, that when they have brought us back to popish blindness, we might commit to their dispose the whole management of our salvation...

William Laud, Archbishop of Canterbury, by Van Dyck (BAL, Fitzwilliam Museum, University of Cambridge)

Above and beyond changes to the fabric of the church, Laud also persecuted Puritan clergy and activists. They were removed from office and through a swathe of judicial commissions harassed for voicing any discontent with the existing structure or doctrine of the Church of England. Lucy Hutchinson melodramatically recalls the hounding which many Puritans hoped to avoid by fleeing to America:

> the Puritans [were] more than ever discountenanced and persecuted, insomuch that many of them chose to abandon their native country and leave their dearest relations, to retire into any foreign soil or plantation, where they might, amidst all outward inconveniences, enjoy the free exercise of God's worship. Such as could not flee were tormented in the bishop's courts, fined, whipped, pilloried, imprisoned and suffered to enjoy no rest, so that death was better than life to them.

Laud's most celebrated and brutal act of repression was against three well-educated Puritans, William Prynne, Henry Burton and John Bastwick. They were hauled before the Court of Star Chamber and prosecuted for having written and published pamphlets denouncing the hierarchy of the Church and institution of bishops. All three had been in trouble before for promoting Puritan opinions and this time Laud was determined to silence them. As he explained at the trial: 'The intention of these men was and is to raise a sedition, being as great incendiaries in the State as they have ever been in the Church.' They were rapidly found guilty and sentenced to heavy fines, imprisonment and a gruesome, public mutilation.

On a hot June day in 1637, the lawyer Prynne, the physician Bastwick and the cleric Burton ascended the public pillory in Westminster yard in front of a large, sympathetic crowd. Much to the fury of Laud, for two long hours the three Puritans preached to their godly spectators:

> Dr Bastwick spoke first, and (among other things) said, had he a thousand lives he would give them all up for this cause. Mr Prynne...showed the disparity between the times of Queen Mary and Queen Elizabeth, and the times then (of King Charles), and how far more dangerous it was now to write against a bishop or two than against a King or Queen: there at the most there was but six months imprisonment in ordinary prisons, and the delinquent might redeem his ears for £200, and had two months' time for payment, but no fine; here they are fined £5,000 a piece, to be perpetually imprisoned in the remotest castles, where no friends must be permitted to see them, and to lose their ears without redemption. There no stigmatising, here must be branded on both cheeks...He said, if the people but knew into what times they were cast, and what changes of laws, religion and ceremonies had been made of late by one man [Laud], they would look about them. They might see that no degree or profession was exempted from the prelates' malice...Mr Burton...spoke much while in the pillory to the people. The executioner cut off his ears deep and close, in a cruel manner, with much effusion of blood, an artery being cut, as there was likewise of Dr Bastwick. Then Mr Prynne's cheeks were seared with an iron made exceeding hot; which done, the executioner cut off one of his ears and a piece of cheek with it; then hacking the other ear almost off, he left it hanging and went down; but being called up again he cut it off.

With the backing of King Charles, Laud's high-church policy was widening the breach in the church and the country. As churches were re-ordered and godly ministers sacked, many traditional Anglicans felt the King was undermining the core Protestantism of the Church of England. They were all the more fearful because across the English Channel, the Protestant religion was fighting for its survival. The Thirty Years War (1618–48) which engulfed the Continent was a pitched battle between the forces of Catholicism, led by Spain, and the Protestantism of the Dutch Republic and various German principalities. It was Catholicism that was winning. Slowly but brutally, the land area controlled by Protestants was receding and this religious rout terrified the English. Since the days of the Spanish Armada, England had always feared a Catholic invasion from the Continent. And since the Gunpowder Plot of Guy Fawkes, they had been equally paranoid about internal popish conspiracies. In such circumstances, the quasi-Catholic reforms of King Charles, with his Papist wife, and Archbishop Laud, with his Arminian background, seemed deliberately provocative if not plain dangerous.

'The King in Parliament': a scene depicting Charles I in the House of Lords, contemporary engraving (BAL)

Cancellarij sedes on

Arte: bee sould in Popes head Ally by George Humble

Personal Rule

The English feared the politics as much as the religion of Catholicism. Across Europe, Catholic monarchs were typically arbitrary rulers. They dispensed with elected assemblies, ruled through a small clique and played fast and loose with the judicial system. Many assumed that given Charles's quasi-Catholic faith he also harboured a similarly absolutist political outlook. Lucy Hutchinson displayed little but rank bitterness for what she regarded as a conniving, Papist King:

> The example of the French king was propounded to him, and he thought himself no monarch so long as his will was confined to the bounds of any law. But knowing that the people of England were not pliable to an arbitrary rule, he plotted to subdue them to his yoke by foreign force…for he was a prince that had nothing of faith or trust, justice or generosity, in him. He was the most obstinate person in his self-will that ever was, and so bent upon being an absolute, uncontrollable sovereign that he was resolved to be such a king or none.

Charles's decision in 1629 to dispense with Parliament only served to confirm this suspicion. Since the Reformation, which King Henry VIII prosecuted through parliamentary statute, an uneasy *modus vivendi* had grown up between King and Parliament. The theory was that the highest form of authority in the state was the King-in-Parliament – that is, the King working in unity with the House of Commons and House of Lords to pass legislation. Yet ultimately Parliament was summoned or dissolved at the monarch's whim and its main purpose was to supply the necessary finances for royal policy. Occasionally, but increasingly, the House of Commons would try to make the passing of taxes contingent on the monarch addressing their various grievances. In the Elizabethan era, MPs tried to dictate the Queen's marital strategy by withholding revenue or supply as it was known. They got short shrift. During James's government the voting of taxes was similarly dependent on reforms. Sometimes the monarch concurred, and other times dismissed Parliament with warnings not to encroach upon royal sovereignty.

During the 1620s, like other monarchs before him Charles grew increasingly frustrated with the constitutional and religious agenda of various MPs. Their ceaseless but disorganised hostility to his foreign and matrimonial policies as well as their intense dislike for the Duke of Buckingham (with many of them openly celebrating his assassination) led to a cooling of relations. This tone of mutual distrust was fuelled by Charles's use of unconstitutional forced loans, his introduction of martial law, the imprisoning of certain of his parliamentary critics, and his promotion of avowedly Arminian clergy. In turn, the House of Commons issued petitions against the power of the monarch, demanded why he was not intervening in the continental struggle against Catholicism (to which he answered that they had not given him the funds) and most crucially they withheld taxation revenues. The final breakdown in relations came when disgruntled MPs physically held down the loyalist Speaker of the Commons, Sir John Finch, as he tried to dissolve the House. Puritan MPs locked the doors of the Chamber and voted through a proclamation against illegal taxation and innovations in religion. Charles was horrified at such *lèse-majesté* and dissolved the Parliament: 'I never came upon so unpleasant an occasion…let Me tell you…that I know that there are many there as dutiful Subjects as any in the World; it being but some few Vipers amongst them that did cast this Mist of Undutifulness over most of their Eyes.' He went on to tell them that 'princes are not bound to give account of their actions, but to God alone'.

Like numerous other continental monarchs, he had decided that as God's representative on earth he could rule alone without counsel from Parliament. Governing without Parliament was by no means unprecedented for a British monarch. Following disputes with their Parliaments, both Elizabeth I and James I had ruled for years without summoning them. But Clarendon, who had been a critic of the King during the 1620s Parliaments, regarded the dissolution as a disaster which only further distanced the King from his country.

> And here I cannot but let myself loose to say, that no man can show me a source, from whence these waters of bitterness we now taste have more probably flowed, than from these unseasonable, unskilful, and precipitate dissolutions of Parliaments; in which, by an unjust survey of the passion, insolence, and ambition of particular persons, the court measured the temper and affection of the country; and by the same standard the people considered the honour, justice, and piety of the court; and so usually parted, at those sad seasons, with no other respect and charity one toward the other, than accompanies persons who never meant to meet but in their own defence. In which the King had always the disadvantage to harbour persons about him, who, with their utmost industry, information, and malice, improved the faults and infirmities of the court to the people; and again, as much as in them lay, rendered the people suspected, if not odious to the King.

By dissolving Parliament, Charles not only alienated the political classes and cemented his authoritarian image, he also painted himself into a financial corner. Without a sitting Parliament he was unable to receive the usual taxation revenue of import and excise duty known as 'Tonnage and Poundage'. This traditionally formed the core of the monarchy's income to which they could then add further revenue from the royal estate. Without this vital income stream, the monarch either had to tighten their belt or discover new methods of raising money. Charles chose the latter.

Through a catalogue of unpopular and legally questionable tax-raising ventures, Charles kept his monarchy afloat through the 1630s. He fined those who infringed on the royal forests, he sold monopoly rights and commercial patents, and he revived an old feudal custom of charging wealthy gentry who had not taken up their rights of knighthood. Yet according to Clarendon, the new revenue brought Charles more unpopularity than income.

And by this ill husbandry the King received a vast sum of money from all persons of quality, or indeed of any reasonable condition throughout the kingdom, upon the law of knighthood; which, though it had a foundation in right, yet, in the circumstances of proceeding, was very grievous. And no less unjust projects of all kinds, many ridiculous, many scandalous, all very grievous, were set on foot; the envy and reproach of which came to the King...

Then in 1635 Charles upped the stakes with an even more unpopular tax.

Ship Money

Traditionally the charge known as ship money had been levied on all coastal counties to fund the upkeep of the navy. As maritime areas were thereby protected from piracy and raiders it seemed only fair for them to pay. However, Charles decided that since the whole country gained from having a strong navy the whole country should pay for it and he made the tax a national levy. He set out his case in a letter to the Mayor and citizens of the City of London.

To the Mayor, commonalty, and citizens of our city of London...Because we are given to understand that certain thieves, pirates, and robbers of the sea, as well Turks, enemies of the Christian name, as others, being gathered together, wickedly taking by force and spoiling the ships, and goods, and merchandises, not only of our subjects, but also the subjects of our friends in the sea, which have been accustomed anciently to be defended by the English nation, and the same, at their pleasure, have carried away, delivering the men in the same into miserable captivity: and forasmuch as we see them daily preparing all manner of shipping farther to molest our merchants, and to grieve the kingdom, unless remedy be not sooner applied, and their endeavours be not more manly met withal; also the dangers considered which, on every side, in these times of war do hang over our heads, that it behoves us and our subjects to hasten the defence of the sea and kingdom with all expedition or speed that we can; we willing by the help of God chiefly to provide for the defence of the kingdom, safeguard of the sea, security of our subjects, safe conduct of ships and merchandises to our kingdom of England coming, and from the same kingdom to foreign parts passing; forasmuch as we, and our progenitors, Kings of England, have been always heretofore masters of the aforesaid sea, and it would be very irksome unto us if that princely honour in our times should be lost or in any thing diminished.

Charles went on to demand from the city of London funding for a number of new warships complete with men and munitions to be delivered to Portsmouth. Those without a ship to donate or unwilling to serve on a ship were to be taxed.

Also we have assigned you, the aforesaid Mayor and aldermen of the city aforesaid, or any thirteen, or more of you, within thirteen days, after the receipt of this writ, to assess all men in the said city, and in the liberties in the same, not having a ship, or any part of the aforesaid ship, nor serving in the same, to contribute to the expenses, about the necessary provision of the premises; and to assess and lay upon the aforesaid city, with the liberties and members thereof, viz. upon every of them according to their estate and substance, and the portion assessed upon them; and to nominate and appoint collectors in this behalf…and to commit to prison all those whom you shall find rebellious and contrary in the premises, there to remain until we shall give further order for their delivery.

In Northamptonshire, Oxfordshire and Buckinghamshire leading Puritan nobles opposed the tax and led subvert campaigns of non-payment until at last, one of them, John Hampden of Great Missenden in Buckinghamshire, contested the very principle of the tax in the court. In 1637, Hampden argued that a tax levied without the approval of Parliament was illegal. If the King could simply levy new taxes at will, then the rule of law and the very principle of private property was in danger. He

Portrait of John Hampden, nineteenth-century engraving (BAL)

also contended that while in the case of national emergencies it might be right for the King quickly to raise new taxes for the defence of the realm, there was no such new emergency in the mid-1630s. It was simply an excuse to raise revenue without calling Parliament. Hampden's case was put to the Court of Exchequer by the Puritan lawyer Oliver St John.

And as without the assistance of his Judges, who are his settled counsel at law, His Majesty applies not the law and justice in many unto his subjects; so likewise in other cases: neither is this sufficient to do it without the assistance of his great Council in Parliament;…My Lords, the Parliament, as it is best qualified and fitted to make this supply for some of each rank, and that through all the parts of the kingdom being there met, His Majesty having declared the danger, they best knowing the estates of all men within the realm, are fittest, by comparing the danger and men's estates together, to proportion aid accordingly.

And secondly, as they are fittest for the preservation of that fundamental propriety which the subject has in his lands and goods, because each subject's vote is included in whatsoever is there done; so that it cannot be done otherwise, I shall endeavour to prove to your Lordships both by reason and authority.

My first reason is this, that the Parliament by the law is appointed as the ordinary means for supply upon extraordinary occasions, when the ordinary supplies will not do it: if this is in the writ therefore may, without resorting to that, be used, the same argument will hold as before in resorting to the extraordinary, by exclusion of the ordinary, and the same inconvenience follow.

My second reason is taken from the actions of former Kings in this of the defence.

The aids demanded by them, and granted in Parliament, even for this purpose of the defence, and that in times of imminent danger, are so frequent, that I will spare the citing of any of them: it is rare in a subject, and more in a prince, to ask and take that of gift, which he may and ought to have of right, and that without so much as a *salvo*, or declaration of his right....

My Lords, it appears not by anything in the writ [for ship money] that any war at all was proclaimed against any State, or that if any His Majesty's subjects had taken away the goods of any prince's subjects in Christendom, but that the party might have recovered them before your Lordships in any His Majesty's Courts; so that the case in the first place is, whether in times of peace His Majesty may, without consent in Parliament, alter the property of the subject's goods for the defence of the realm.

Despite many of the judges having deep concerns about the legality of ship money, Hampden lost his case. Sir Robert Berkeley, Justice of the King's Bench, gave judgement which declared that *rex* was *lex* – that whatever the King said had force of law solely because it came from the King. The views of Parliament were neither here nor there compared to the unassailable rights of majesty. These opposing views concerning the inherent rights of monarchy *versus* the power of Parliament to govern the nation were central to the coming struggle.

Where Mr Holbourne [another of John Hampden's lawyers] supposed a fundamental policy in the creation of the frame of this kingdom, that in case the monarch of England should be inclined to exact from his subjects at his pleasure, he should be restrained, for that he could have nothing from them, but upon a common consent in Parliament.

He is utterly mistaken herein. I agree the Parliament to be a most ancient and supreme court, where the King and Peers, as judges, are in person and the whole body of the Commons representatively. There Peers and Commons may, in a fitting way, *parler lour ment* and show the estate of every part of the kingdom; and amongst other things, make known their grievances (if there be any) to their sovereign, and humbly petition him for redress.

But the former fancied policy I utterly deny. The law knows no such king-yoking policy. The law is of itself an old and trusty servant of the King's; it is his instrument or means which he uses to govern his people by...

There are two maxims of the law of England, which plainly disprove Mr Holbourne's supposed policy. The first is, 'That the King is a person trusted with the state of the commonwealth.' The second of these maxims is, 'That the King cannot do wrong.' Upon these two maxims the *jura summae majestatis* [highest rights of majesty] are grounded, with which none but the King himself (not his high court of Parliament without leave) has to meddle, as, namely, war and peace, value of coin, Parliament at pleasure, power to dispense with penal laws, and divers others; amongst which I range these also, of regal powers to command provision (in case of necessity) of means from the subjects, to be adjoined to the King's own means for the defence of the commonwealth, for the preservation of the *salus reipublicae* [well-being of the state]. Otherwise I do not understand how the King's Majesty may be said to have the majestical right and power of a free monarch…the King of mere right ought to have, and the people of mere duty are bound to yield unto the King, supply for the defence of the kingdom. And when the Parliament itself does grant supply in that case, it is not merely a benevolence of the people, but therein they do an act of justice and duty to the King.

The case meanwhile had become a *cause célèbre*, and though Hampden might have lost in court he won the greater battle for public opinion. Across the country collection levels for ship money collapsed as ever greater numbers refused to pay. What was even more worrying for the King than the loss of income was how Hampden's case indicated the level of distrust that now existed between Charles and the country's leading gentry. Men such as Hampden were the backbone of the English political and judicial system. That leading county figures were in a state of civil unrest should have set alarm bells ringing in the Whitehall. Clarendon gives an indication of the case's political consequences.

> It is notoriously known that pressure was borne with much more cheerfulness before the judgement for the King than ever it was after; men before pleasing themselves with doing somewhat for the King's service, as a testimony of their affection, which they were not bound to do; many really believing the necessity, and therefore thinking the burden reasonable; others observing that the access to the King was of importance, when the damage to them was not considerable; and all assuring themselves that when they should be weary, or unwilling to continue the payment, they might resort to the law for relief and find it. But when they heard this demanded in a court of law as a right, and found it by sworn judges of the law adjudged so, upon such grounds and reasons as every stander-by was able to swear was not law, and so had lost the pleasure and delight of being kind and dutiful to the King; and instead of giving were required to pay, and by a logic that left no man anything which he might call his own; they no more looked upon it as the case of one man but the case of the kingdom, nor as an imposition laid upon them by the King but by the judges; which they thought themselves bound in conscience to the public justice not to submit to.

Religious divisions, the growing estrangement between King and gentry, and a residual fear of the Popish and authoritarian Caroline court were all prevalent in late 1630s England. Yet none of them were seismic problems. Compared to what Elizabeth I and James I endured as monarchs – the Spanish Armada; Mary Queen of Scots; the Earl of Essex's attempted coup; the Gunpowder Plot; military fiascos – none of the tensions in Charles's reign were insurmountable. A monarch with just a modicum of political nous would have been able to chart their way through such waters. Unfortunately, Charles lacked any such ability.

What made the situation more fraught was that Charles was King not only of England, but also of Scotland and Ireland. And whilst England might have been governable, the single-minded pursuit of his policies across the three kingdoms opened up far more serious political difficulties. As the civil war historian John Morrill has written, while the stability of early Stuart *England* made civil war unlikely it was the instability of early modern *Britain* that made it possible.

In one of the most beautiful passages written by Clarendon, he gives a benign but foreboding account of the conditions King Charles faced in 1637.

> Of all the princes of Europe, the king of England alone seemed to be seated upon that pleasant promontory, that might safely view the tragic sufferings of all his neighbours about him, without any other concernment than what arose from his own princely heart and Christian compassion, to see such desolation wrought by the pride, and passion, and ambition of private persons, supported by princes who knew not what themselves would have. His three kingdoms flourishing in entire peace and universal plenty, in danger of nothing but their own surfeits; and his dominions every day enlarged, by sending out colonies upon large and fruitful plantations; his strong fleets commanding all seas; and the numerous shipping of the nation bringing all the trade of the world into his ports; nor could it with unquestionable security be carried any whither else; and all these blessings enjoyed under a prince of the greatest clemency and justice, and of the greatest piety and devotion, and the most indulgent to his subjects, and most solicitous for their happiness and prosperity...
>
> In this blessed conjuncture, when no other prince thought he wanted any thing to compass what he most desired to be possessed of, but the affection and friendship of the king of England, a small, scarce, discernible cloud arose in the north, which was shortly after attended with such a storm, that never gave over raging till it had shaken, and even rooted up, the greatest and tallest cedars of the three nations; blasted all its beauty and fruitfulness; brought its strength to decay, and its glory to reproach, and almost to desolation; by such a career and deluge of wickedness and rebellion, as by not being enough foreseen, or in truth suspected, could not be prevented.

II

Charles I and Scotland:
Kingdoms in Collision

1637 *July*	Rioting in St Giles' Cathedral, Edinburgh, over the introduction of the Laudian prayer book into the Scottish church	**1640** *May*	Charles dissolves Parliament as it refuses to grant him unconditional subsidies
1638 *March*	Scottish assembly adopts National Covenant rejecting religious innovation	**1640** *August*	Second Bishops' War between the Covenanters and King Charles
1639 *April*	First Bishops' War between the Scottish Covenanters and King Charles's reluctant English army	**1640** *August*	English army defeated by the Covenanters at the Battle of Newburn
1639 *June*	Pacification of Berwick concludes First Bishops' War	**1640** *October*	Treaty of Ripon concludes the Second Bishops' War on highly unfavourable terms for King Charles
1640 *April*	Short Parliament is called to debate crisis in Scotland. End of eleven year 'Personal Rule'		

IN 1637, CHARLES I EXTENDED HIS UNPOPULAR RELIGIOUS REFORMS TO HIS KINGDOM NORTH OF THE BORDER. With typical insensitivity, he imposed a new prayer book upon the Scottish church with little or no debate. Its introduction heralded riots across Scotland. They began in Edinburgh and were led by the mythical, stool-throwing figure of Jenny Geddes. The royalist dean of Durham, William Balcanquall, gives this account:

> On the twenty third day of July 1637, being Sunday, according to the public warning given the Sunday before, the service book was begun to be read in Edinburgh in Saint Giles's church where were present many of our council, both the archbishops and divers other bishops, the lords of the sessions, the magistrates of Edinburgh, and a very great auditory of all sorts of people. Amongst this great multitude there appeared no sign of trouble: but, no sooner was the book opened by the dean of Edinburgh, but a number of the meaner sort, most of them women, with clapping of their hands, cursings, and outcries, raised such a barbarous hubbub in that sacred place, that not anyone could either hear or be heard: the bishop of Edinburgh, who was to preach, stepped into the pulpit intending to appease the tumult but he was entertained with as much irreverence as the dean, and with more violence; in so much, that if a stool, aimed to be thrown at him, had not by the providence of God been diverted by the hand of one present, the life of that reverend bishop had been endangered, if not lost: the archbishop of Saint Andrews lord chancellor, and divers others offering to appease the multitude, were entertained with such bitter curses and imprecations, as they not being able to prevail with the people, the provost, bailiffs, and divers others of the council of that city were forced to come down from the gallery in which they do usually sit, and with much ado thrust out of the church these disorderly people, making fast the church doors: after all which, the dean devoutly read service, assisted by our councillors, bishops and many other persons of quality there present: yet the outcries, rapping at the church doors, throwing of stones at the church windows by the tumultuous multitude without, was so great as the bailiffs of the city were once more put to forsake their places, and use their best endeavours for the appeasing of the rage and fury of those who were without.

Across Scotland, congregations reacted with similar fury to the new prayer book. In Glasgow a minister was almost torn to pieces when he read from the new service and in Brechian, the Bishop had to protect himself from his congregation with a pair of loaded pistols. The events in Scotland during the summer of 1637 would produce just as dramatic consequences south of the border. It is the great irony of the 'English Civil War' that it began with events in Scotland.

Both Charles I and Archbishop Laud had long resented the independence of the Church of Scotland. Their ambition was to bring it more into line with the Arminian, or Laudian, Church of England. Yet the Scottish people were proud of

Depiction of the Prayer Book Rebellion, St Giles' Cathedral, Edinburgh, seventeenth-century engraving (BAL, British Library)

their Presbyterian brand of Protestantism. Since John Knox had led a more radical Reformation in Scotland, the country adhered to a stricter creed of worship than their English brethren. Presbyterians believed there was no place in organised religion for bishops or any other part of the hierarchy that governed the Church of England. Apart from an annual national assembly, the Scottish church was governed simply at parish level by presbyteries. Like the Puritans, Presbyterians believed in a simple liturgy combined with an active role for ministers as preachers and expounders of scripture. They were deeply opposed to the kind of high-church doctrine expounded by Archbishop Laud.

Having reformed the Church of England, Charles and Laud regarded the Scottish church as unfinished business. In 1636 Laud published his 'Canons for the Scottish Church' which aimed to undermine the power of local presbyteries and affirm royal supremacy over religion. By the time of their official introduction in July 1637 at St Giles' Cathedral, discontent had been brewing for well over a year. In Scotland's power circles, there was also a broader discontent with a king who rarely visited and seemed to have little affection for the country. The Presbyterian minister Robert Baillie described the mood:

> What shall be the event, God knows: there was in our Land ever such an appearance of a stir; the whole people thinks Popery at the doors; the scandalous pamphlets which comes daily new from England, add oil to this flame; no man may speak any thing in public for the King's part, except he would have himself marked for a sacrifice to be killed one day. I think our people possessed with a bloody devil far above any thing that ever I could have imagined, though the mass in Latin had been presented. The Ministers who has the command of their mind, does disavow their unchristian humour, but are no ways so zealous against the devil of their fury, as they are against the seducing spirit of the Bishops. For myself, I think, God, to revenge the crying sins of all estates and professions…is going to execute his long denounced threatenings, and to give us over unto madness, that we may every one shoot our swords in our neighbours hearts.

Clarendon loyally declared that Charles was 'always an immoderate lover of the Scottish nation, having not only been born there, but educated by that people, and besieged by them always, having few English about him until he was king'. Yet even in this passage, Clarendon gives the game away – for once King, Charles had little to do with Scottish lords at his Whitehall court. While James I had surrounded himself with his old clan and Edinburgh allies, Charles distanced himself from the Scottish nobles. In an act of classic political mismanagement, the King actually undercut their power in Scotland by strengthening the Scottish church and increasing the wealth and power of the bishops. He introduced an Act of Revocation which returned to the Church land and money taken by the nobility. The historian Mark Kishlansky describes the process: 'the compulsory transfer of wealth from the nobility to the episcopacy drove a wedge between two groups that had been drawing closer together. The last thing Charles needed was an alliance between nobility and the leaders of the Presbyterian kirk, yet this was the result of policies which isolated the bishops, who were blamed by the nobility for attacks upon their wealth and by the clergy for attacks upon their doctrine.' The Scottish gentleman, Sir James Balfour, was more succinct. He called the Act of Revocation 'the ground-stone of all the mischief that followed'.

The National Covenant

The trouble surrounding the prayer book gave the Scottish nobles the opening they needed to put some pressure on their absentee king. When Charles declared enemies of the prayer book guilty of treachery they knew they would garner enough popular support to act. In February 1638, the King's opponents came together at Greyfriars Kirk in Edinburgh to sign a National Covenant drafted by the Fife minister Alexander Henderson and the militant Presbyterian lawyer Archibald Johnston of Wariston. The Covenant urged the King to stop any further religious innovations and instead adhere to the Confession of Faith defending the principles of Calvinist worship and organisation which his father had signed up to as King of Scotland in 1580:

> The confession of faith of the Kirk of Scotland, subscribed at first by the king's majesty and his household in the year of God 1580; thereafter by persons of all ranks in the year 1581; subscribed again by all sorts of persons, in the year 1590...and now subscribed in the year 1638, by us nobleman, barons, gentlemen, burgesses, ministers, and commons under subscribing; together with our resolution and promises of the causes after specified, to maintain the said true religion, and the king's majesty, according to the confession afore-said, and acts of parliament; the tenure whereof here follows.
>
> We all, and everyone of us under written, do protest, that after long and due examination of our own consciences in matters of true and false religion, are now thoroughly resolved of the truth, by the word and spirit of God; and therefore we believe...that this only is the true Christian faith and religion, pleasing God, and bringing salvation to man. And received, believed, and defended by many sundry and notable kirks and realms, but chiefly by the Kirk of Scotland, the king's majesty, and three estates of this realm, as God's eternal truth, and only ground of our salvation; as more particularly expressed in the confession of our faith, established and publicly confirmed by sundry acts of parliament; and now of a long time hath been openly professed by the king's majesty, and whole body of his realm, both in burgh and land...and therefore we abhor and detest all contrary religion and doctrine, but chiefly all kinds of papistry in general and particular heads....But in special, we detest and refute the usurped authority of that Roman Antichrist upon the scriptures of God, upon the kirk, the civil magistrate and consciences of men...
>
> We noblemen, barons, gentlemen, burgesses, ministers, and commons under subscribing...do hereby profess, and before god, his angels and world solemnly declare,

The signing of the National Covenant at Greyfriars Kirk, Edinburgh, eighteenth-century lithograph (BAL)

that with our whole hearts we agree and resolve all the days of our life constantly to adhere unto, and to defend the foresaid true religion, and forbearing the practice of all innovations already introduced in the matters of the worship of God, or approbation of the corruptions of the public government of the kirk, or civil places and powers of kirkmen, till they be tried and allowed in free assemblies, and in parliaments, to labour by all means lawful to recover the purity and liberty of the gospel, as it was established and professed before the aforesaid innovations: and because after due examination we plainly perceive, and undoubtedly believe, that the innovations and evils…have no warrant of the Word of God, are contrary to the articles of the aforesaid confessions, to the intention and meaning of blessed reformers of religion to this land…

And in like manner with the same heart we declare before god and men, that we have no intention or desire to attempt anything that may turn to the dishonour of God or the diminution of the king's greatness and authority; but on the contrary we promise and swear, that we shall do the utmost of our power, with our means and lives, stand to the defence of our dread sovereign of the king's majesty, his person and authority, in the defence and preservation of the aforesaid true religion, liberties and laws of the kingdom; as also to the mutual defence and assistance, everyone of us of another, in the same cause maintaining the true religion and his majesty's authority, with our best counsels, our bodies, means and whole power, against all sorts of persons whatsoever. So that whatsoever shall be done to the least of us for that cause, shall be taken as done to us all in general, and to everyone of us in particular...

Neither do we fear the foul aspersions of *rebellion, combination,* or what else our adversaries from their craft and malice would put upon us, seeing what we do is so well warranted, and arises from an unfeigned desire to maintain the true worship of God, the majesty of our king, and the peace of the kingdom, for the common happiness of ourselves and posterity.

In witness thereof we have subscribed with our hands all the premises, etc.

The Covenant, a copy of which can still be seen upstairs today in Greyfriars Kirk, then travelled across Scotland gaining signatures and rallying opposition to the King's reforms. On the face of it, the Covenant was simply a plea to respect Scotland's religious traditions as sanctified in 1580. Yet the document was more, much more. It signalled a determination by the country's leading aristocrats to wrest back control and a refusal to be part of a unitary Great Britain. In London, Charles was outraged.

For the Scottish people to reject the prayer book was bad enough, but for them to rebel through the Covenant against his monarchical authority was unforgivable. It was a direct affront to his sovereignty. Unfortunately, Charles chose as his adviser in these matters one of the grandest but most ineffectual Scottish lairds, James, Marquis of Hamilton. Hamilton had long since given up his Scottish roots to be a favoured courtier – a career choice symbolised by toadyingly naming his children James and Henrietta-Mary (not quite being able to go so far as the ultra-Catholic Henrietta-*Maria*). Charles appointed Hamilton his Commissioner in Scotland, allowing him extensive leeway to negotiate with the Covenanters. While Hamilton pursued his clumsy diplomacy, Charles made clear his real intent in a series of letters.

<u>To The Marquess of Hamilton</u>

Greenwich, June 11 1638

Though I answered not yours of the 4th, yet I assure you that I have not been idle; so that I hope that by the end of next week I shall send you some good assurance of the announcing of our preparations. This I say, not to make you precipitate anything (for I like all you have hitherto done, and over, of that which I find you mind to do): but to show you that I mean to stick to my grounds, and that I expect not anything can reduce that people to obedience, but only force.

I thank you for the clearness of your advertisements, of all which none troubles me so much as that (in a manner) they have possessed themselves of the castle of Edinburgh, and likewise I give Stirling as good as lost...In the meantime, your care must be how to dissolve the multitude; and, if it be possible, to possess yourself of my castles of Edinburgh and Stirling (which I do not expect) and to this end, I give you leave to flatter them with what hopes you please, so you engage me not against my grounds (and, in particular, that you consent neither to the calling of Parliament nor General Assembly, until the covenant be disavowed and given up). Your chief end being now to win time, that they may not commit public follies, until I be ready to suppress them. And that it is (as you well observe) my own people, which by this means will be for a time ruined; so that the loss must be inevitably mine; and this if I could eschew (were it not with a greater) were well. But, when I consider that not only now my crown, but my reputation for ever, lies at stake, I must rather suffer the first that time will help, than this last, which is irreparable.

This I have written to no other end than to show you that I will rather die than yield to these impertinent and damnable demands (as you rightly call them), for it is all one, as to yield to be no king in a very short time. So wishing you better success than I can expect, I rest,

Your assured, constant friend,
Charles R

The King's signature (WA)

Nine days later, Charles wrote again to Hamilton showing even more bellicose intentions towards the Covenanter traitors.

To The Marquess of Hamilton

Greenwich, June 20 1638

…What I now write is, first to show you in what state I am, and then to have your advice in some things. My train of artillery consisting of 40 pieces of ordnance (with the appurtenances) all drakes (half and more of which are to be drawn with one or two horses apiece), is in good forwardness, and I hope will be ready within six weeks; for I am sure there wants neither money, nor materials to do it with. I have taken as good order as I can for the present, for securing of Carlisle and Berwick; but of this you shall have more certainly by my next. I have sent for arms to Holland, for 14,000 foot and 2,000 horse: for my ships they are ready, and I have given order to send three for the coast of Ireland immediately, under pretence to defend our fishermen.

Thus you may see, that I intend not to yield to the demands of those traitors the Covenanters, who I think will declare themselves so by their actions, before I shall do it by my Proclamation; which I shall not be sorry for, so that it be without the personal hurt of you, or any other of my honest servants, or the taking of any English place. This is to show you, that I care not for their affronting or disobeying my Declaration, so that it got not to open mischief, and that I may have some time to end my preparations. So I rest

Your assured, constant friend,
Charles R

The Marquis of Hamilton, Charles's Commissioner in Scotland, contemporary engraving after Van Dyck (BAL)

First Bishops' War

Although Charles agreed to the calling of a General Assembly of the Scottish Church, he refused to accept the Covenant. A military solution to the situation now seemed inevitable. After importing arms from Holland, the King called upon his Lord-Lieutenants, his governors in the counties, to provide him with troops from the county militia for battle against the Covenanters.

<u>To Theophilus, Earl of Suffolk,</u>
<u>Lord-Lieutenant of Cambridge, Suffolk and Dorset</u>

Palace at Westminster, February 18, 1639

The great and considerable forces lately raised in Scotland, without order or warrant from us, by the instigation of some factious persons ill affected to monarchical government, who seek to cloak their too apparent rebellious designs under pretence of religion, albeit we have often given them good assurance of our resolution constantly to maintain the religion established by the laws of that kingdom, have moved us to take into our Royal care to provide for the preservation and safety of this our kingdom of England, which is by the tumultuous proceedings of these factious spirits in apparent danger to be annoyed and invaded; wherefore, upon serious debate and mature advice with our Privy Council we have resolved to repair in person to the northern parts of our kingdom with a Royal army. And this being for the defence and safety of this kingdom, unto which all our good subjects are obliged, we have appointed that a select number of foot shall be presently taken out of our trained bands, and brought to our city of York, or such other rendezvous as the General of our army shall appoint, there to attend our person and standard; of which number we require and command that you cause to be forthwith selected out of the trained bands in our county of Cambridge 400, in our county of Suffolk 1,500, and in our county of Dorset 700, of the most able men, which, together with their arms complete, you are to cause to be presently put in readiness, and to be weekly exercised....And our will and command is that you cause to be forthwith selected out of the troop of horse in Cambridge 40 horse, in Suffolk 150 horse, and in Dorset 50 horse, to be armed, and exercised weekly, so as to be ready to march to the rendezvous.

The royalist Governor of Scarborough, Sir Hugh Cholmley, recorded in his idiosyncratic Memoirs his preparations for the campaign:

In preparation to the King's march against the Scots, I had much business about mustering and training the soldiers of the Train-bands, and many journies to York, to consult with the Vice-president and rest of Deputy-lieutenants...The Earl of Northumberland was General, from whom I had a commission. Divers of the Colonels of the Train-bands, with their regiments, were called to march with the King into Northumberland; amongst which I had been one, but that at that time I had caught cold and a dangerous sickness, in viewing and training my whole regiment together on Paxton-Moor, near Thornton; where one Hallden, a stubborn fellow of Pickering, not obeying his Captain, and giving me some unhandsome language, I struck him with my cane, and felled him to the ground. The cane was tipped with silver, and hitting just under the ear, had greater operation than I intended.

Whether through malice or incompetence, most Lord Lieutenants of England did not provide their King with the 'most able men'. The troops who joined Charles on his march from London to York in March 1639 were a dispirited, ramshackle lot.

Sir Edmund Verney, the King's Knight Marshall (NPG)

The country's leading noblemen, whose retainers traditionally provided the backbone of any English army, were highly critical of the King's invasion plans. Why, they asked, is the King of England fighting his fellow Protestants in Scotland while he refuses to fight the Catholic menace rampaging on the Continent? Charles it seemed would rather have an unnecessary war over a prayer book in Scotland than support the broader struggle for the Protestant religion abroad. Edmund Ludlow, the future Roundhead commander, attributed the nobles' hesitation to a more subtle fear that if Charles beat the Scots then his authoritarian style would know no bounds.

> The nobility and gentry were likewise required to further this expedition; in which, though divers of them did appear, yet was it rather out of compliment than affection to the design, being sensible of the oppressions they themselves lay under; and how dangerous to the people of England a thorough success against the Scots might prove.

Under the strategic guidance of Archibald Campbell, the Earl of Argyll, and the military leadership of the Thirty Years War veteran Alexander Leslie, the Covenanters fielded a highly impressive fighting force. The Covenanter soldiers believed they were fighting for their religious and political liberty – two of the surest incentives to military success. 'We are busy preaching, praying, drilling,' wrote their army chaplain Alexander Baillie. Charles's army, on the other hand, endured a divided command between the Earls of Arundel, Essex and Holland, and suffered from low morale. One soldier not looking forward to the fight was the King's Knight-Marshall and close but critical courtier, Sir Edmund Verney. He wrote affectionately to his son Ralph from the royalist base at York in April 1639.

> Since Prince Henry's death I never knew so much grief as to part from you; and truly, because I saw you equally afflicted with it, my sorrow was the greater. But, Ralph, we cannot live always together. It cannot be long ere by course of nature we must be severed, and if that time be prevented by accident, yet we must resolve to bear it with that patience and courage as becomes men and Christians; and so the great God of heaven send us well to meet again, either in this world or the next...
>
> Our army is but weak; our purse is weaker; and if we fight with these forces and early in the year we shall have our throats cut; and to delay fighting long we can not for want of money to keep our Army together. I dare say there was never so raw, so unskilful and so unwilling an Army brought to fight...truly here are many brave Gentlemen that for point of honour must run such a hazard. For my own part I have lived till pain and trouble has made me weary to do so; and the worst that can come shall not be unwelcome to me; but it is a pity to see what men are like to be slaughtered here.
>
> I am infinitely afraid of the gout, for I feel cruel twinges, but I hope to starve it away, for God willing, I will drink but once a day. I pray put your mother in mind to send me those papers of powder I gave her to keep for me, for they are excellent to prevent the gout.
>
> ...When my pot is done let it be quilted and lined, and sent to me, for here is no hope at all of peace, and we are like to have the worst of the war which makes the Scots insufferably proud and insolent, insomuch that every Englishman's heart is ready to break with rage against them here.

Ralph wrote to his father's doctor pleading with him to persuade the (gout-ridden) old man to return.

> Oh Dr if my father goes to the Borders he is lost, I know his courage will be his destruction; no man did ever so willfully ruin himself and his posterity; God forgive him and grant me patience; certainly his heart is more than stone, or else he could not so soon forget both friends and wife and children and all to get (that which he can never lose) honour, should he spend all his time in contriving which way he might make us more miserable, he could not invent a readier course than this. Did he beget us to no other end but to make us the sad spectacles of the world? Will nothing move him? Dear Dr: try, and try again and set all his friends upon him, be more than earnest, night and day persuade him, give him no rest till he hath yielded to stay. I can say no more, this grief's too great to be expressed by your unhappy kinsman.

He then wrote to Sir Edmund himself accusing him of a wilful disregard for the interests of his family.

> Sir you know your years, your charge, your distracted fortune, your former life, were privileged enough to keep you back, without the least stain to your reputation; But when I see you thus hastily run to your own ruin, and as it were purposely to lose that life that is so much dearer to me then my own, how can I think you love me? Has the vain hope of a little fading honour swallowed up all your good nature? Are your compassions quite shut up? Will neither the numberless sighs of your dearest friends, nor the incessant cries of your forlorn widow, nor the mournful groan of your fatherless brood prevail to stay you?

But Sir Edmund wouldn't be moved.

> My design of going to the Borders with my Lord of Holland had only matter of kindness, none of danger in it. Yet because it might seem so to my friends I was desirous they might not know it, but that design was put off and now we are all going thither where I desire you to put so much trust in me as to believe that I will not wilfully thrust myself in danger, nor will I think you could wish me to leave any thing undone when it falls to my turn to be in action. Ralph, I thank you for your good advice; it has both expressed your judgement and affection and I pray let me entreat you to believe I will neither seek my ruin nor avoid any hazard when that little honour I have lived in may suffer by it, but truly I think we are not in much danger of fighting...
>
> Commend me to Dr Cragg and tell him he is a churl for not writing all this while, I will never write above a letter or two hereafter for upon my credit it is now almost three of the clock...Commend me to your wife...God bless you both.

One Royal officer at least had a more positive attitude to the coming fight. Thomas Windebank, son of the King's Secretary of State Francis Windebank, wrote how:

> We have had a most cold, wet and long time of living in the field, but kept ourselves warm with the hope of rubbing, fubbing and scrubbing those scurvy, filthy, dirty, nasty, lousy, itchy, scabby, shitten, stinking, slovenly, snotty-nosed, logger-headd, foolish, insolent, proud, beggarly, impertinent, absurd, grout-headed, villainous, barbarous, beastial, false, lying, roguish, devilish, long-eared, short-haired, damnable, atheistical, puritanical, crew of the Scottish Covenant.

In June 1639, Windebank, Verney and another 18,000 English troops marched to the Scottish lowlands to face a far superior Covenanter force. Whereupon King Charles, realising that he was outgunned and outmanoeuvred by a Covenanter army which now controlled all of Scotland, dropped his military plans and agreed to sign a peace treaty at Berwick – the border town where the two armies faced each other across the River Tweed. The Pacification of Berwick disbanded both armies with Charles agreeing to travel to Scotland to soothe out remaining differences with the General Assembly of the Kirk and Scottish Parliament. But he did no such thing. Instead, the King reneged on the deal and returned to London, furious at his inability to crush the Covenanter army. In this time of trouble, Charles sought advice from an old adversary turned *eminence grise*.

The iconography of the Bishops' War, contemporary engraving (Art Archive, London)

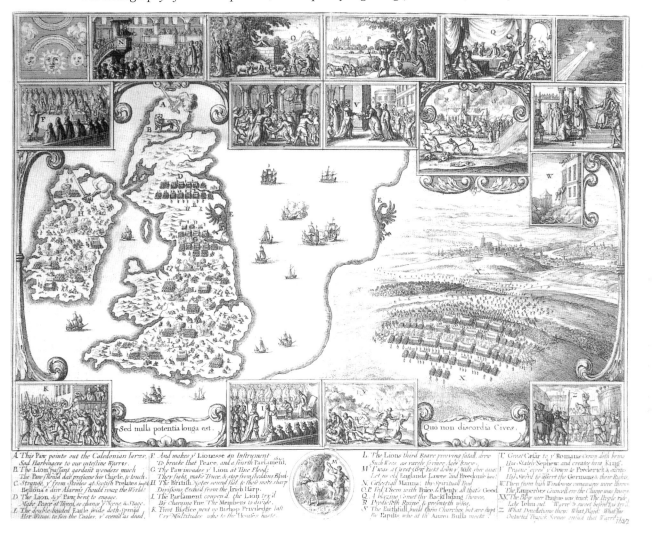

The Earl of Strafford

Sir Thomas Wentworth, Earl of Strafford, had been a thorn in the side of Charles's monarchy throughout the 1620s. As a Member of Parliament, he passionately supported the rights of the House of Commons and opposed the King's extra-parliamentary forced loans. But during the 1630s, Wentworth effortlessly changed sides to join the royalist clique. He earned his spurs as the King's enforcer in the North where his vigorous collection of ship money secured him the sobriquet 'Black Tom Tyrant'. As a reward for his loyalty in the North, Charles appointed him his Lord Lieutenant in Ireland (the King's third kingdom). There he enjoyed equal success playing off the native Gaelic Irish against the burgeoning Scottish and

Thomas Wentworth, Earl of Strafford, and his Secretary, Philip Mainwaring, by Van Dyck (BAL)

'Black Tom Tyrant': the Earl of Strafford, King Charles's Lord Lieutenant in Ireland, by Van Dyck (BAL)

English settler communities. His policy was known as 'Thorough' and it brought both a degree of peace to the island's tempestuous relations and generated revenue for the royal Exchequer. Crucially, he had also managed a session of the Dublin Parliament with consummate skill.

While few doubted Strafford's bully-boy political nous, he unfortunately lacked any redeeming personal characteristics. He was vindictive, spiteful, aggressive, and now blindly committed to the ideal of strong monarchical government. But he also stood out as efficient and intelligent in a royal circle brimming with mediocrity. Clarendon (who was not a friend) gave a typically bitter-sweet judgement:

> He was a man of great parts, and extraordinary endowments of nature; not unadorned with some addition of art and learning, though that again was more improved and illustrated by the other; for he had a readiness of conception, and sharpness of expression, which made his learning thought more than in truth it was.

Strafford told the King that the Covenanters needed to be crushed for their rebellion against royal authority. But to do so would require a larger army and far greater resources than the King currently possessed. It was essential to recall Parliament and gain their financial and political support. As a former MP himself as well as successful convenor of the Dublin Parliament, Strafford thought he could manage a Parliament to the King's best wishes. 'Thereupon', wrote Ludlow, 'hoping that a Parliament would espouse his quarrel, and furnish him with money for the carrying on of his design, he summoned one to meet at Westminster on the 3d of April, 1640, which, sitting but a little time, thereby obtained the name of the Short Parliament.'

John Pym and the Short Parliament

The first Parliament to be called after eleven years of personal rule met in fact on 13 April 1640. For Charles, the sole purpose of the session was to furnish him with the resources he needed to challenge the Scottish rebels. In his mind, it was Parliament's duty at this time of war to offer up all proper revenues. Many MPs, however, had a different agenda. As soon as Parliament opened it was flooded with angry petitions complaining of religious innovations, ship money and a myriad of other fines and royal taxes. In the Commons, politicians linked the passage of royal subsidies with action on their religious and financial grievances. More intractably, a substantial part of the Commons had some sympathy with the stance of the Covenanters and were not necessarily keen to vote funds for their suppression. Sir Henry Slingsby, the royalist MP for Knaresborough, watched first hand these Westminster machinations:

> The 13th of April anno 1640 began the court of parliament to sit which was so unfortunate that it lasted but three weeks without having anything done to content either king or country. The House of Commons sat to advise how to have their grievances redressed, and the King by my lord keeper, whom he had lately created baron [the loyalist Speaker of 1629, Lord Finch] did signify to both Houses the great need he had of supplies to maintain his wars against his rebellious subjects of Scotland; this held the House of Commons in debate whether they should not represent unto the King their grievances, and to obtain a redress thereof, before their giving of subsidy, or that they should supply the King first and take his word for the latter, which he did largely promise by my lord keeper, that he would reform all their just grievances. These they had drawn into three principal heads. That is 1st grievances concerning matter of religion. 2ndly property of goods. 3rdly privilege of parliament. But chiefly they insist upon that of ship money, which the House had voted to be absolutely against the law…

The man who emerged as leader of the opposition grouping in the House of Commons was John Pym. He was a West Country lawyer of modest means but part of a circle of powerful and wealthy Puritan nobles. Centred around a business of merchant adventurers called the Providence Island Company, the circle included such influential figures as the Earl of Bedford, Lord Saye and Sele, the Earl of Essex, the Earl of Warwick, and John Hampden. These men would soon be at the heart of the campaign against the King. They resented Charles's religious policies, which they saw undermining English Protestantism, and his foreign policy flirtations with Spain which threatened their commercial interests in the West Indies. In John Pym they found a skilful political strategist and ruthless operator ready to ditch any principles in the struggle against the King.

On 17 April 1640, John Pym rose in the Commons to make a two-hour speech drawing together all the grievances against the King. Sir Thomas Peyton, a Kent

*The 'Short Parliament',
contemporary engraving (AA)*

John Pym (WA)

baronet, described him as

> An ancient and stout man of the parliament, that ever zealously affected the good of
> his country, who as yet only made the full complaint of the Commons, for he left not
> anything untouched, ship-money, forests, knight-hood, recusants, monopolies, the
> present inclination of our church to popery, and more than my memory can suggest
> to me, and in the close desired the Lower House to move the Upper in an humble
> request that they would be pleased to join with them in a petition to the King for
> redress of all those grievances.

Surprisingly, Charles took such objections in fairly good form. He agreed to give
up ship money for twelve subsidies (effectively, a short-term wealth tax). The
House of Lords concurred with the compromise, but the Commons wanted its
grievances addressed before it gave any new funds. Charles was infuriated by such

impunity at a time of war. Strafford urged further negotiations, but with the Commons still resisting his demands Charles dissolved the 'Short Parliament' in a fury on 5 May 1640. As Parliament dissolved, Charles searched the offices of Pym, Hampden and Lords Warwick and Saye suspecting to find some evidence of collusion with the Covenanters. Tension began to mount in the streets of London. Pym published his speech against the King, while bishops were attacked in the streets by anti-Catholic mobs that even tried to storm the hated Archbishop Laud in his Lambeth Palace residence. That vast majority of the gentry, apolitical and religiously conservative, who hoped for a resolution between King and Parliament after eleven years of separation, were bitterly frustrated by the dissolution. But Clarendon saw other forces who were not so disappointed:

> There could not a greater damp have seized upon the spirits of the whole nation, than this dissolution caused; and men had much of the misery in view, which shortly after fell out. It could never be hoped, that more sober dispassionate men would ever meet together in that place, or fewer who brought ill purposes with them; nor could any man imagine what offence they had given, which put the King to that resolution. But I was observed, that in the countenances of those who had most opposed all that was desired by his majesty, there was a marvellous serenity; nor could they conceal the joy of their hearts: for they knew enough of what was to come, to conclude that the King would shortly be compelled to call another parliament; and they were as sure, that so many grave and unbiased men would never be elected again.

Undeterred by Parliament's refusal of funds, and with a promise by Strafford of 8,000 troops from Ireland, the King marched back to York in August 1640 to take on the Covenanters once again. It was even more of a fiasco. The Covenanters stole a march on the King, crossed the border, routed the English forces at Newburn and took Newcastle by the end of the month. Charles had little support from his noble kinsmen who both disapproved of war with the Covenanters and were even more horrified by Strafford's plans for an invasionary force of Irish Catholics. The so-called Second Bishops' War ended with an ignominious treaty at Ripon with the King agreeing to pay the Covenanters maintenance costs during their occupancy of northern England. At an emergency meeting of the country's leading peers in a Great Council at York, Charles agreed to peace with the Covenanters, to return to London and recall Parliament. It was a Parliament Charles would not live to see the end of.

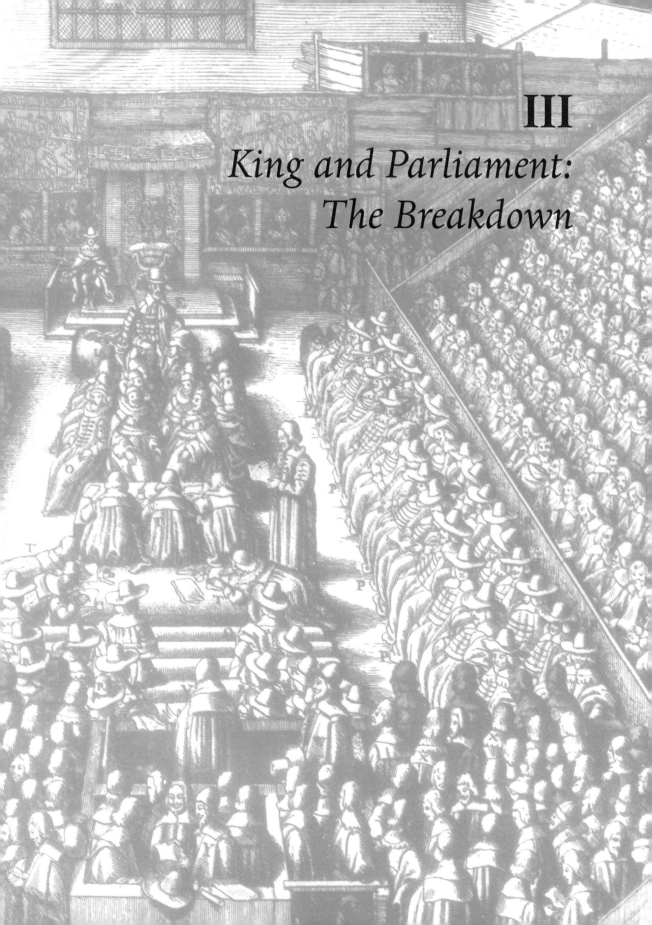

III

King and Parliament: The Breakdown

1640 *November*	Charles is forced to summon the Long Parliament
1640 *December*	The Earl of Strafford is impeached on charges of high treason and Archbishop Laud is imprisoned
1641 *February*	Parliament passes the Triennial Act requiring the regular calling of Parliament
1641 *March*	The Earl of Strafford's trial begins in Westminster Hall
1641 *April*	London mobs attack Portuguese and Spanish embassies. Anti-Catholic sentiments grips London
1641 *May*	The Earl of Strafford is executed on Tower Hill. Catholics rumoured to have razed the House of Commons

1641 *July*	The much hated High Commission and Star Chamber are abolished
1641 *August*	Charles travels to Scotland to negotiate a lasting peace with the Scottish Covenanters
1641 *October*	News of rebellion of indigenous Catholics against Protestant settlers in Ireland reaches London, inflaming anti-Catholic hysteria
1641 *November*	Grand Remonstrance criticising Royal policy is passed by 11 votes
1641 *December*	Charles rejects the Grand Remonstrance and attempts to gain control of the Tower
1642 *January*	Charles fails to arrest the Five Members and abandons London for Hampton Court

ON A VISIT TO LONDON IN AUTUMN 1640, the diarist John Evelyn spotted the King's carriage returning from York:

> Octob: 15. I went to the Temple, it being Michaelmas Tearme: and Oct:30, I saw his Majestie (coming from his Northern expedition) ride in pomp, and a kind of Ovation, with all the markes of an happy Peace restor'd to the affections of the People; being conducted through London, with a most splendid Cavalcade; and on November following, the third (a day never to be mention'd without a curse) to that long, ungrateful, foolish and fatal Parliament, the beginning of all sorrows for twenty yeares after, and the period of the most happy Monarch in the World.

The Long Parliament opened with a speech from King Charles denouncing the Scottish Covenanters for their treachery and demanding yet more funds to quash the rebellion. Charles had no understanding of the grievous political situation he faced. It was only because the Covenanters were occupying the north of England that Parliament had been summoned. Unsurprisingly, a growing body of MPs saw no benefit in giving Charles the resources to attack an army which had secured their assembly. Puritan MPs also hoped the Covenanters might help to persuade the King to drop his Laudian reforms and bring the Church of England more into line with Scottish Presbyterianism.

Trial of Strafford

The faction centred around John Pym, the unofficial leader of opposition to the King, had a clear agenda for the Parliamentary session. Realising Charles was under duress, they aimed to achieve a sizeable ceding of power from King to Parliament. With the King weakened by the Scottish humiliations and lacking any proper resources, now was their chance. Yet in an era when it was believed a king could do no wrong, they were unable to criticise the monarch directly. Instead, they went for his 'evil counsellors'. And no one was more feared and loathed in parliamentary circles than the Earl of Strafford. His urging of force against the Covenanters, his plans to use Catholic troops, and his general tenor of support for unbridled monarchy left the Earl wide open to attack. On 11 November 1640 Pym led the assault. Sitting as the MP for Saltash, Clarendon watched in shock at this brazen political offensive:

> The very first day they met together, in which they could enter on business, Mr. John Pym, in a long, formed discourse, lamented the miserable state and condition of the kingdom, aggravated all the particulars which had been done amiss in the government,

as 'done and contrived maliciously and upon deliberation, to change the whole frame, and to deprive the nation of all the liberty and property which was their birthright by the laws of the land, which were now no more considered, but subjected to the arbitrary and power of the privy council, which governed the kingdom according to their will and pleasure; these calamities falling upon us in the reign of the pious and virtuous king, who loved his people, and was a great lover of justice...We must inquire from what fountain these waters of bitterness flowed; what persons they were who had so far insinuated themselves into his royal affections, as to be able to pervert his excellent judgement, to abuse his name, and wickedly apply his authority to countenance and support their own corrupt designs. Though he doubted there would be found many of this classis, who had contributed their joint endeavours to bring this misery upon the nation; yet he believed there was one more signal in that administration than the rest, being a man of great parts and contrivance, and of great industry to bring what he designed to pass; a man, who in the memory of many present had sat in that house an earnest vindicator of the laws, and a most zealous assertor and champion for the liberties of the people; but that it was long since he turned apostate from those good affections, and, according to the custom and nature of apostates, was become the greatest enemy to the liberties of his country, and the greatest promoter of tyranny that any age had produced.'; and then named 'the earl of Strafford, lord lieutenant of Ireland, and lord president of the council established in York, for the Northern parts of the kingdom; who', he said, 'had in both places, and in all provinces wherein his service had been used by the king, raised ample monuments of his tyrannical nature'; and that he believed, 'if they took a short survey of his actions and behaviour, they would find him the principal author and promoter of all those counsels, which had exposed the kingdom to so much ruin'.

Before Strafford had time to react, he was impeached on charges of high treason, had his sword removed and was led away to the Tower of London. Charles had expected trouble from the Parliament, but this level both of hostility and organised opposition was beyond his worst fears. The Commons were beginning to flex their muscles. The Puritan martyrs Prynne, Bastwicke and Burton were released from jail with a triumphant procession. Ship money was declared illegal. And a new Bill was introduced for triennial parliaments to put an end to the practice of personal rule. Throughout the sitting, Puritan militants in London, encouraged by MPs in Parliament, kept the pressure on. On 11 December 1640, a rowdy 1,500-strong crowd brought the so-called 'root and branch petition' to the Commons demanding the fundamental reform of the Church of England:

The same morning a petition was brought by the citizens of London subscribed by fifteen thousand hands in a schedule annexed to the petition...The petition was read in the House, it was much to this purpose against innovations of the clergy in point of ceremonies, concerning bowing at the name of Jesus at the alter, against coming up to the rails to receive the sacrament, they require the [communion] table to be set again in the midst of the chancel, they require they may be no more enjoined to receive the sacrament kneeling, and some other old ceremonies they would have abolished, they complain also against the high commission and the bishops' courts in their dioceses, and against the insolency of the clergy of late years, which they cannot undergo, and they allege the clergy to have been the causes of the divisions of the two kingdoms of England and Scotland, they therefore desire episcopacy may be absolutely taken away root and branches…

Pym used the momentum provided by the petition to attack Archbishop Laud. One week later, he too was impeached on charges of high treason and followed Strafford into the Tower. The court party, those loyal to the King in Parliament, were being systematically outmanoeuvred. After the impeachment of Strafford and Laud, many royal aides saw the writing on the wall and simply fled the country. According to the Puritan lecturer Richard Baxter, Pym's supporters on the back-benches were made up of two groups:

The triumphant return to London of Prynne, Bastwicke and Burton, the Puritan Martyrs, contemporary engraving (Weidenfeld Archives, BL)

The Parliament consisted of two sorts of men, who by the conjunction of these causes were united in their votes and endeavours for a reformation. One party made no great matter of these alterations in the church; but they said that if parliaments were once down and our propriety gone, and arbitrary government set up, and law subjected to the Prince's will, we would then all be slaves; and this they made a thing intolerable, for the remedying of which, they said, every true Englishman should think no price too dear. These the people called good Commonwealth's Men. The other sort were the more religious men, who were also sensible of all these things, but were much more sensible of the interest of religion; and these most inveighed against the innovations in the Church, the bowing to alters, the Book for Sports on Sundays, the casting out of ministers, the troubling of the people by the High Commission Court, the pillorying and cutting off mens' ears (Mr. Burton's, Mr. Prynne's and Dr. Bastwick's) for speaking against the bishops, the putting down lectures and afternoon sermons and expositions on the Lord's-days, with such other things as they thought of greater weight than ship money.

Both factions supported the legal proceedings against Strafford which were now coming to court. On 22 March 1641, his trial on the charge of high treason began in Westminster Hall – a venue which would come forever to be associated with show trials. The proceedings gripped the nation with the drama only heightened by the verbal jousting between Pym and Strafford. From the King and Queen down, anyone who was anyone attended the proceedings. The Scottish Presbyterian, Robert Baillie, watched as the flower of English nobility came to gawp. But for the dour Baillie, the fashion of the court was an unwarranted irritation.

A number of ladies were in boxes, above the rails, for which they paid much money. It was daily the most glorious assembly the isle could afford; yet the gravity not such as I expected; often great clamour without about the doors; in the intervals, while Strafford was making ready for answers, the Lords got always to their feet, walked and clattered; the Lower House men too loud clattering; after ten hours, much public eating, not only of confections, but of flesh and bread, bottles of beer and winegoing thick from mouth to mouth without cups, and all this in the King's eye...All being set, as I have said, the Prince in his robes on a little chair at the side of the throne, the Chamberlain and Black-Rod went and fetched in my Lord Strafford; he was always in the same suit of black, as in doole. At the entry he gave a low courtesy, proceeding a little, he gave a second, when he came to his desk a third, then at the bar, the fore-face of his desk, he kneeled: rising quickly, he saluted both sides of the Houses, and then sat down. Some few of the Lords lifted their hats to him: this was his daily carriage.

At the heart of Pym's case were notes written by Sir Henry Vane of a speech made by Strafford to the Council for Scottish Affairs. The transcript was 'discovered' by Vane's Puritan son and handed over to his co-conspirator Pym. The influential lawyer and MP for Marlow, Bulstrode Whitelocke, describes the murky history of this note:

Sir Henry Vane the Elder, author of the minutes that brought Strafford down (NPG)

Secretary Vane being out of town sent a letter to his son Sir Henry Vane the younger, then in London, with the key of his study, for his son to look into his cabinet for some papers there, to send to his father.

The son looking over many papers, among them lighted upon those notes, which being of so great concernment to the public, and declaring so much against the earl of Strafford, he held himself bound in duty and conscience to discover them.

He showed them to Mr. Pym, who urged him, and prevailed with him, that they might be made use of in the evidence against the earl of Strafford, as being most material and of great consequence in relation to that business.

Accordingly they were now produced to the house of commons, and in the afternoon at a conference with the lords, and the next day, the earl being brought to Westminster, and both houses being met, the notes were openly read; the title of them was, 'No danger of a war with Scotland, if offensive not defensive.'

King Charles. How can we undertake offensive war, if we have no more money?

Lord Lieutenant of Ireland [Strafford]. Borrow of the city £100,000 go on vigorously to levy shipmoney; your majesty having tried the affection of your people, you are absolved and loose from all rule of government, and to do what power will admit.

Your majesty having tried all ways, and being refused, shall be acquitted before God and man. And you have an army in Ireland that you may employ to reduce this kingdom to obedience; for I am confident the Scots cannot hold out five months.

For Pym here were any number of tell-tale signs pointing to tyranny. Strafford's suggestion that the King was 'absolved and loose from all rule of government' was an invitation for Charles to ignore any restraints on monarchical power. But the crucial point was whether when Strafford advised using an Irish army to reduce 'this kingdom' he meant England and not just Scotland. Pym's sly implication was that Strafford was urging the King to launch a military coup against Parliament:

> These articles have expressed the character of a great and dangerous treason, such a one as is advanced to the highest degree of malice and mischief. It is enlarged beyond the limits of any description and definition, it is so heinous in itself as that it is capable of no aggravation; a treason against God, betraying his truth and worship; against the king, obscuring the glory and weakening the foundations of his throne; against the Commonwealth, by destroying the principles of safety and prosperity. Other treasons are against the rule of the law: this is against the being of the law. It is the law that unites the king and his people, and the author of this treason has endeavoured to dissolve that union even to break the mutual, irreversible, indissoluble bond of protection and allegiance whereby they are, and I hope ever will be, bound together.
>
> If this treason had taken effect our souls had been enthralled to the spiritual tyranny of Satan, our consciences to the ecclesiastical tyranny of the Pope, our lives, our persons and estates, to the civil tyranny of an arbitrary, unlimited, confused government.

Strafford was no fool. He put up a stalwart defence, countering all charges of treason and constitutional misdemeanour:

> My Lords, I have all along my charge watched to see that poisoned arrow of treason, that some men would fain have to be feathered in my heart, and that deadly cup of wine, that has so intoxicated some petty misalleged errors, as to put them in the elevation of high-treason, but in truth it has not been my quickness to discern any such monster yet within my breast; though now perhaps, by a sinister information, sticking to my clothes: They tell me of a two fold treason, one against statute, another by the Common-Law; this direct, that consecutive; this individual, that accumulative; this in itself, that by way of construction...
>
> My Lords, give me leave here to pour forth the grief of my soul before you, these proceedings against me seem to be exceeding rigorous, and to have more of prejudice then equity...These gentlemen tell me they speak in defence of the Common-wealth, against my arbitrary laws, give me leave to say it, I speak in defence of the Commonwealth, against their arbitrary-treason, for if this latitude be admitted, what prejudice shall follow to King and country, if you and your posterity, be by the same, disenabled from the greatest affairs of the Kingdom; for my poor self, were it not for your Lordships' interest, and the interest of a saint in heaven who has left me here two pledges on Earth [At this his breath stopped, and he shed tears abundantly, in mentioning his wife, which moved his very enemies to compassion] I should never take the pains to keep up this ruinous cottage of mine, it is loaded with such infirmities, that in truth I have no great pleasure to carry it about with me any longer: Nor could I ever leave it in a better time then this, when I hope that the better part of the world would perhaps think, that by this my misfortune I had given a testimony of my

The trial of Strafford, contemporary engraving. 'These Gentlemen tell me they speak in defence of the Common-wealth, against my Arbitrary Laws, give me leave to say it, I speak in defence of the Common-wealth, against their arbitrary Treason.' (WA, BL)

Integrity to God, my King and country: my Lords, something more I had to say, but my voice and spirits fail me, only I do in all humility and submission cast myself down before your Lordships' feet, and desire that I might be a Pharos to keep you from ship-wrack; do not put such rocks in your own way, which no prudence, no circumspection can eschew or satisfy, but by your utter ruin…

By early April 1641, the case against Strafford was collapsing as he managed to disprove the charge of urging the Irish troops to invade England. So Pym changed tack and introduced an Act of Attainder – this was a ruthless form of attack which paid no heed to the rule of law. It simply decreed treason on the basis of a general presumption of guilt. The Act was passed by the House of Commons and then, following a well-timed revelation by Pym of a suspected army plot, voted through the House of Lords. While many Westminster politicians had policy differences with Strafford, a far larger proportion simply disliked his rapid rise to power, his brusque manner and history of vindictiveness. They saw their opportunity and finished him off. But it was a dangerous precedent.

The King's Betrayal

One thing was clear. King Charles was going to stick by his man. For the Act of Attainder to become law, it needed the Royal Assent and the King was adamant that he would not be forced into it by Parliament. On 23 April 1641, Charles wrote to Strafford in the Tower:

> STRAFFORD,
>
> The misfortune that is fallen upon you by the strange mistaking and conjecture of these times, being such that I must lay by the thought of employing you hereafter in my affairs; yet I cannot satisfy myself in honour or conscience without assuring you (now in the midst of your troubles), that upon the word of a king you shall not suffer in life, honour or fortune. This is but justice, and therefore a very mean reward from a master to so faithful and able a servant as you have showed yourself to be; yet it is as much as I conceive the present times will permit, though none shall hinder them from being
>
> > Your constant, faithful friend,
> > Charles R.

But the pressure was on. Violent crowds began to pour into Whitehall and Westminster demanding 'justice'. Those brave politicians who voted against the Act of Attainder had their names pinned up in public; bishops and suspected papists were again molested in the street. One of these demonstrators was the Puritan turner from Little Eastcheap, Nehemiah Wallington. His *Historical Notes* give a brilliant insight into the world view of a truly godly believer. Here he describes demanding Strafford's head on his visit to Westminster with all the gleeful enthusiasm of a day-tripper.

> And on the 3rd of *May*, a many citizens went up to *Westminster* to petition the Lords for justice on this traitor; and it is to be thought that there were about fifteen thousand people, and I myself was there, and surely I never did see so many together in my life. And when they did see any Lords coming, they all cried with one voice, 'Justice! Justice!' and the next day there went a many more, but I think not so many as before.
>
> On *Monday*, the 3rd of *May*, early in the morning, there met about *Westminster* Hall a great number of citizens, some do think about fifteen thousand (being for the most

part men of good fashion), who as the Lords and other Parliament men came by, made them a lane to pass with their coaches, calling upon them for justice against the Earl of *Strafford* and others, complaining that they were undone through the want of the due execution thereof, and that trading was so decayed thereby, that they could scarce get bread to maintain their families.

Holed up in his secure Whitehall palace, Charles continued to resist the mob. Though safe within the confines of the vast, Tudor-built riverside palace, which sprawled along Whitehall where many of today's modern government ministries now stand, London was becoming more dangerous for the King. The London mob of apprentices and radical tradesmen despised Strafford and the seditious court he symbolised; Parliament was against him; and now even his Privy Council, many of whom had little love for Strafford, said the King was endangering his rule because of misplaced loyalty to one man. In the end, according to Clarendon, it was Strafford who forced the pace:

> During these perplexities, the Earl of Strafford, taking notice of the straits the king was in, the rage of the people still increasing, writ a most pathetical letter to the king, full of acknowledgement of his favours; but lively presenting 'the dangers, which threatened himself and his posterity, by his obstinacy in those favours'; and therefore by many arguments conjuring him 'no longer to defer his assent to the bill, that so his death might free the kingdom from the many troubles it apprehended.'
>
> The delivery of this letter being quickly known, new arguments were applied; 'that this free consent of his own clearly absolved the king from any scruple that could remain with him'; and so in the end they [the privy council] extorted from him, to sign a commission to some lords to pass the bill: which was as valid as if he had signed it himself; though they comforted him even with that circumstance, 'that his own hand was not in it'.

Though Strafford might have given the King an excuse, he was still taken aback when Charles used it. Bulstrode Whitelocke describes how Strafford, imprisoned in the Tower, received the news:

> After he had signed these bills, the King sent Secretary Carleton to the Earl, to acquaint him with what was done, and the motives of it, especially the Earl's consent, who seriously asked the secretary, whether his majesty had passed the bill or not; as not believing without some astonishment that the King would have done it.
>
> And being again assure that it was passed, he rose up from his chair, lift up his eyes to heaven, laid his hand on his heart, and said, *Put not your trust in princes, nor in the sons of men, for in them there is no salvation.*

Charles agreed to the Attainder on 10 May 1641. Two days later Strafford was led from his cell, passing by his old ally Archbishop Laud, to his place of execution on Tower Hill. Clarendon describes the final hour of a man he never liked, but gained deep admiration for during his harrowing trial:

> All things being thus transacted, to conclude the fate of this great person, he was on

*Two depictions of the execution of
Strafford, English and German engravings
(British Museum – right; BAL, Ashmolean
Museum, Oxford – above)*

the twelfth day of May brought from the Tower of London (where he had been a
prisoner nearly six months) to the scaffold on Tower-hill; where, with a composed,
undaunted courage, he told the people, 'he was come here to satisfy them with his
head; but that he much feared, the reformation which was begun in blood would not
prove so fortunate to the kingdom, as they expected, and he wished': and after great
expressions 'of his devotion to the church of England, and the protestant religion,
established by law, and professed in that church; of his loyalty to the king, and affec-

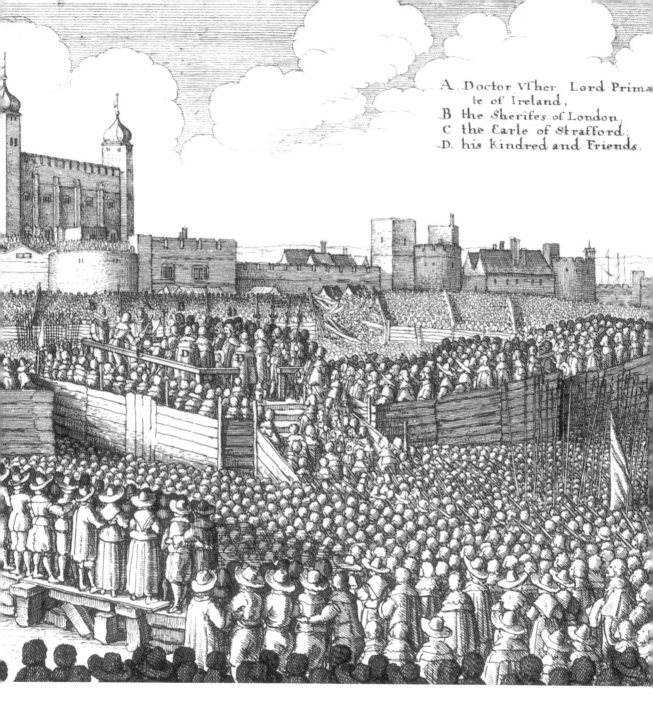

A. Doctor Vſher, Lord Prima
    te of Ireland,
B the Sherifes of London,
C the Earle of Strafford,
D. his Kindred and Friends.

tion to the peace and welfare of the kingdom'; with marvellous tranquillity of mind, he delivered his head to the block, where it was severed from his body at a blow: many of the standers by, who had not been over charitable to him in his life, being much affected with the courage and Christianity of his death.

Among the tens of thousands of spectators was John Evelyn, who saw: 'the fatal Stroake, which sever'd the wisest head in England from the Shoulders of the Earle of Strafford, whose crime coming under the cognizance of no human-Law, a new one was made, not to be precedent, but his destruction, to such exorbitancy were things arrived.'

Charles's betrayal of Strafford was a monumental mistake which he never forgave himself for. When the King later faced his turn on the scaffold, he placed responsibility for his fall with this fateful decision to throw Strafford to the wolves. 'I only say this, that an unjust sentence that I suffered to take effect, is punished now by an unjust Sentence upon me, that is, so far I have said to show you that I am an innocent man.' It was a personal betrayal which always rankled with him. But more importantly at the time it revealed to Parliament that the King could be pushed around. After this, Charles was determined to cede no more ground. Yet events were not running in the King's favour. As political dissent quieted in England and Scotland following the elimination of Strafford, new and terrible events were engulfing Charles's third kingdom.

Irish Rebellion

In November 1641 London learnt of a rebellion sweeping Ireland from letters smuggled out by fleeing Protestants:

> All I can tell you is the miserable estate we continue under, for the rebels daily increase in men and munitions in all parts except the province of Munster, exercising all manner of cruelties, and striving who can be most barbarously exquisite in tormenting the poor Protestants, wheresoever they come, cutting of the privy members, ears, fingers and hands, plucking out their eyes, boiling the heads of the little children before their mothers' faces, and then ripping up their mothers' bowels, stripping women naked, and standing by them being naked, whilst they are in travail, killing the children as soon as they are born, and ripping up their mothers' bellies, as soon as they are delivered; driving men, women and children, by hundreds together upon bridges, and from thence cast them down into rivers, such as drowned not, they knock their brains out with poles, or shoot them with muskets, that endeavour to escape by swimming out; ravishing wives before their husbands' faces, and virgins before their parents' faces, after they have abused their bodies making them renounce their religion, and then marry them to the basest of their fellows.
>
> Oh that the Lord, who hath moved the kingdoms of England and Scotland, to send relief to those afflicted Protestants, would likewise stir them to affect their undertaking, with all possible expedition, lest it be too late.

After years of rising tension between the indigenous population of Gaelic Catholics and the rising tide of Protestant Scottish and English settlers, violence erupted on 22 October 1641. Worried that King Charles, under pressure from Presbyterians in Scotland and Puritans in England, might be forced to curb Catholicism in Ireland, and upset that the Dublin Parliament had failed to address any of their grievances against the settlers, a party of Irish Catholics supported by

Old English families led an assault on Dublin castle. They failed in the attempt but managed to secure Dungannon and Charlemont castles. Across Ulster, this originally tight-knit rebellion began to spiral out of control as the native Irish vented their anger against Protestant neighbours. Decades of resentment at settlers taking the most fertile land, of having their religion and culture undermined, combined with broader fears for their economic future to spark the bloodbath. Over 15,000 Protestants and then Catholics were murdered or left to die of exposure in the harsh Irish winter.

Nehemiah Wallington, writing from first-hand accounts reaching England, gives some taste of how Puritans took news of the rising:

> The rebels did rove extraordinarily up and down in *Ireland* on *Thursday*, the third of *December*, 1641, and did much hurt in divers places of the country. They came to a town called *Rockall*, and then went to the English inhabitants, to one *William Clarke*, and slew him, and his wife, children, and family, seven persons in number, cruelly murdered them.
>
> From thence they marched the next day ten miles, and came to a town of *Puckingell*, inhabited of English, where they fell upon the inhabitants thereof, and slew them in a cruel manner without mercy, to the number of above twenty families, men, women, and children. One woman above the rest they hanged at her own door with her children, and afterward burnt up the whole town with fire. Having made that place desolate, they marched some three miles further. They came to an Englishman's house, where they slew the man at the door, and afterward they entered the house, where they found the woman and her maid a-brewing. The maid they took, and they threw her into the boiling cauldron or pan of wort that was over the fire, and her mistress they slew, and cut off her head, and afterward fired the house....Then they took Mr. *Dabnet*...and when they saw...he was resolved to die protestant, they pulled open his mouth, and cut out his tongue, and run an hot iron down his throat, and so he died.

The rebels then turned on Wallington's wife's brother, Zachariah Rampain, and his family:

> Captain *Adkinson*, (which was kin to my Brother's first wife) being in *Castlecoule*, in the county of *Fermanagh*, knowing of the Rebels coming, sent to speak to my Brother, and cause him to bring his family and goods into the Castle...and on *Monday*, *Brian Maguire* came with his army against it, and took the Castle; and the next day my Brother and his family had a pass under *Brian's* hand to depart the kingdom, and they sent a guard along with them, and then sent another company out with them to murder them. So when they were gone about six miles off, they stripped them all, and bid them say their prayers, for they would kill them all. Then they first did kill my brother *Zachariah*, stabbing their skenes [small swords] into him which his wife beholding did on her knees beg for his life, as also his children, crying pitifully, 'O do not kill my Father, O do not kill my Father,' being much distracted, pulling their hair, being content and desiring to die with him. But these bloody rebels did drive them from him, saying they would reserve them for a worse death, even to starve him to death.

Mr Ffordes house rifled, and to make her Confesse where her mony lay, they tooke hot tonges clapping them to the Soules of her feete & to the Palmes of her handes so tormented her that with the paine thereof shee died.

N

They haue set men & women on hot Grideorns to make them Confesse where there money was.

O

Pulling them about the streetes by the haire of the head, dashing the Childrens braines against the postes saynge, these were the pigges of the English Sowes.

T

Droghedah so bloked up that a bushell of wheate was sold for 23 Shill: & meate scarce to be had at any rate. Ian: 4 . 1641

Drogheda

V

Then my sister, and her four children, and her maids, and a Gentlewoman (whose Husband they then had hewed to pieces before their faces) they went all naked on a mount, and sat starving there; then came the Irish Rebels, and said they would kill them all, and as they were about it, another Rebel kept them from it. So the next day they went some two or three miles in the Frost and Snow, and two days after, other Rebels held three skeins at her breast, the children crying pitifully for her, and some were about to kill the children, and yet God kept them.

The reception of the rebellion in England was as important as the rebellion in Ireland. In the words of Mark Kishlansky, 'The Catholic conspiracy, so long imagined and so exquisitely dreaded, had finally occurred.' Stories of atrocities in Ireland escalated with each account. Graphic woodcuts gloried in the intimate

A Woman mangled in so horred a maner that it was not possible shee should be knowne & after the Villaine washed his handes in her bloode, was taken by the Troopers adiuged to be hanged leaped of the lader & haged Himselfe like a Bloodey Tiger.

W

Companyes of the Rebells meeting with the English flyinge for their liues falling downe before them cryinge for mercy thrust theire into their Childrens bellyes & threw them into the water.

X

11

Contemporary propaganda depicting the slaughter of Protestant settlers by Irish Catholics in October 1641 (BAL)

detail of children butchered, men castrated and women invariably defiled in ever more sadistic ways. Richard Baxter reflected contemporary thinking when he put the number of settlers dead at 200,000. Of particular notoriety was the murder of settlers in Portadown, where they were herded naked onto the bridge over the River Bann, thrown into the freezing waters and then killed on the river banks if they attempted to escape. Protestants today still commemorate this terrible slaughter in Orange Order parades on the 4 July.

Across England, fears of popish plots took on a new urgency. According to Baxter, the rebellion: 'filled all England with a fear both of the Irish and of the Papists at home, for they supposed that the priests and the interest of their religion were the cause.' Joseph Lister, a young Puritan from Bradford, describes one Popish panic:

I think about three o'clock in the afternoon, a certain man that I remember well – (his name was John Sugden) – came and stood up in the chapel door, and cried out with a lamentable voice, 'Friends', said he, 'we are all as good as dead men, for the Irish rebels are coming; they are come as far as Rochdale, and Littleborough, and the Batings, and will be at Halifax and Bradford shortly'; he came, he said, out of pity and good will, to give us this notice…Upon which the congregation was all in confusion, some ran out, others wept, others fell to talking with friends, and the Irish massacre being but lately acted, and all circumstances put together, the people's hearts failed them with fear; so that the reverend Mr. Wales desired the congregation to compose themselves as well as they could, while he put himself and them into the Almighty God by prayer, and so he did, and so dismissed us. But O what a sad and sorrowful going home had we that evening, for we must needs go to Bradford, and knew not but incarnate devils and death would be there before us, and meet us here.

Well we got home, and found friends and neighbours in our case, and expecting the cut-throats coming. But at last some few horsemen were prevailed with to go to Halifax, to know how the case stood. They went with a great deal of fear, but found matters better than when they came there, it proving only to be some Protestants that were escaping out of Ireland for their lives into England; and this news we received with great joy, and spent the residue of that night in praisings and thanksgivings to God. And I well remember what sad discourses I heard about this time, the papists being desperate, bloody men; and those that were put into offices and places of trust were such as would serve the king and his design.

Engraving depicting the notorious killing of Portadown's Protestant community, eighteen-century (BAL)

For this was the point. In many Puritan circles, there were those who thought that somehow the King *was* involved in the rebellion. Accusations about his latent Catholicism had stuck and this Catholic rising was assumed to have his silent contrivance. The King's case wasn't helped by the rebels' ardent protestations of loyalty and regret for rebellion against such a good monarch as Charles I.

Grand Remonstrance

Yet still the majority of the country rallied round the King. After a fairly conciliatory visit to Scotland, he had by now managed to secure a degree of peace with the Covenanters and at this time of crisis English residual loyalty towards the monarch shone through. Charles was himself, like every Protestant Englishman, appalled by the atrocities in Ireland. He had had no connection or common cause with the rebels and now used the groundswell of favourable opinion to demand resources from Parliament for a full-scale offensive in Ireland. But in the bowels of the House of Commons, John Pym had other ideas. He was already disturbed by the public enthusiasm for the King. Fearing what might happen if Charles got hold of an army, Pym blocked moves to supply military resources. Instead, he cynically revived all the historical grievances against Charles's rule and brought them together in a 'Grand Remonstrance'. The petition accompanying the Remonstrance hid its real agenda behind a language of impeccable loyalty.

> The duty which we owe to your Majesty and our country, cannot but make us very sensible and apprehensive, that the multiplicity, sharpness and malignity of those evils under which we have now many years suffered, are fomented and cherished by a corrupt and ill-affected party, who amongst others their mischievous devices for the alteration of religion and government, have sought by many false scandals and imputations, cunningly insinuated and dispersed amongst the people, to blemish and disgrace our proceedings in this Parliament, and to get themselves a party and faction amongst your subjects, for the better strengthening themselves in their wicked courses, and hindering those provisions and remedies which might, by the wisdom of your Majesty and counsel of your Parliament, be opposed against them.
>
> For preventing whereof…we have been necessitated to make a declaration of the state of the kingdom, both before and since the assembly of this Parliament, unto this time, which we do humbly present to your Majesty, without the least intention to lay any blemish upon your royal person, but only to represent how your royal authority and trust have been abused, to the great prejudice and danger of your Majesty, and of all your good subjects.

Frontispiece to Parliamentary pamphlet depicting John Pym (WA/BL)

Master PYM

HIS SPEECH

In *Parliament*, on *Wednesday*, the fifth of *January*, 1641,

Concerning the Vote of the House of *Commons*, for his discharge upon the Accusation of High Treason, exhibited against himselfe, and the Lord *Kimbolton*, Mr. *Iohn Hampden*, Sr. *Arthur Haslerig*, Mr. *Strowd*, M. Hollis, by his Maiesty,

The true Effigies of Mr. *Iohn Pym*, Esquire

London Printed for I. W, 1641.

We, your most humble and obedient subjects, do with all faithfulness and humility beseech your Majesty,-

1. That you will be graciously pleased to concur with the humble desires of your people in a parliamentary way, for the preserving the peace and safety of the kingdom from the malicious designs of the Popish party:-

   For depriving the Bishops of their votes in Parliament, and abridging their immoderate power usurped over the clergy, and other your good subjects, which they have perniciously abused to the hazard of religion, and great prejudice and oppression to the laws of the kingdom, and just liberty of your people:-

   For the taking away such oppressions in religion, church government and discipline, as have been brought in and fomented by them:-

   For uniting all such your loyal subjects as join in the same fundamental truths against the Papists, by removing some oppressive and unnecessary ceremonies by which divers weak consciences have been scrupled, and seem to be divided from the rest, and for the due execution of those good laws which have been made for securing the liberty of your subjects.

2. That your Majesty will likewise be pleased to remove from your council all such as persist to favour and promote any of those pressures and corruptions wherewith your people have been grieved; and that for the future your Majesty will vouchsafe to employ such persons in your great and public affairs, and to take such to be near you in places of trust, as your Parliament may have cause to confide in..

3. That you will be pleased to forbear to alienate any of the forfeited and escheated lands in Ireland which shall accrue to your Crown by reason of this rebellion, that out of them the Crown may be the better supported, and some satisfaction made to your subjects of this kingdom for the great expenses they are like to undergo [in] this war.

The 'Grand Remonstrance' demanded a massive increase in the powers of Parliament. It requested a reversal of the Laudian religious agenda, a veto over key royal appointees, and control of the military campaign in Ireland. But the Remonstrance split the Commons, with some MPs thinking Pym had gone too far – especially at a time of national crisis when Protestant brethren were being murdered in Ireland. According to Clarendon, the document did not receive the easy passage Pym had hoped for:

> For the next morning, the debate being entered upon about nine of the clock in the morning, it continued all that day; and candles being called for when it grew dark, (neither side being very desirous to adjourn it till the next day; though it was evident, very many withdrew themselves out of pure faintness and disability to attend the conclusion,) the debate continued, till after it as twelve of the clock, with much passion; and the house being then divided; upon the passing or not passing it, it was carried for the affirmative, by nine voices, and no more [in fact, it passed at 2 a.m. with a majority of eleven]; and as soon as it was declared, Mr. Hampden moved, 'that there might be an order entered for the present printing it'; which produced a sharper debate than the former. It appeared then, that they did not intend to send it up to the House of Peers for their concurrence, but that it was upon the matter an appeal to the people, and to infuse jealousies into their minds… there was after scarce any quiet and regular debate. But the house after degrees being quieted, they all consented, about two of the clock in the morning, to adjourn till two o'clock of the next afternoon. And as they went out of the house, the Lord Falkland asked Oliver Cromwell, 'Whether there had been a debate?' to which he answered, 'that he would take his word another time'; and whispered him in the ear, with some asseveration, 'that if the remonstrance had been rejected, he would have sold all he had the next morning, and never have seen England more; and he knew many men of the same resolution'. So near was the kingdom at that time to its deliverance.

Presented to the King on 1 December 1641, Charles was appalled at the document's presumption. At last, he began to realise the enormity of Pym's agenda. The arrogant tone and outrageous demands spurred the King to resist any further encroachments on his royal prerogative. Instead of allowing Parliament a say in his appointments, he instead purged his Privy Council of any Westminster-friendly politicians and placed a loyal lieutenant in charge of the Tower of London. The King also hatched a plan to cut out the canker of opposition from the House of Commons. On 3 January 1642, Charles's Attorney General in the House of Lords accused John Pym along with Lord Mandeville, Arthur Haselrig, Denzil Holles and William Strode of High Treason for their history of collusion with the Scottish Covenanters. The following day, Charles himself, in a moment of frenzy, stormed into Westminster to try and arrest the five members accused of treason. It was an act of total folly which irreversibly split King from Parliament. The antiquarian and MP for Sudbury Sir Simond D'Ewes was there:

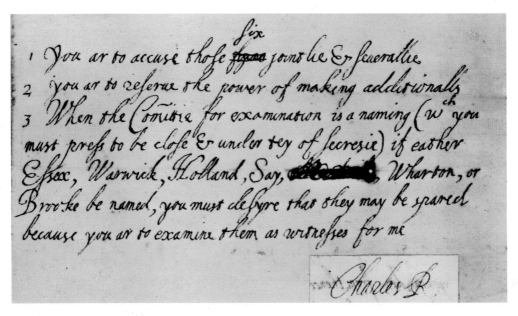

Impeachment of the Five Members: Charles I's instructions to Sir Edward Herbert, Attorney General, 3 January 1642 (WA, BL)

About 3 of the Clock we had notice that his Majesty was coming from Whitehall to Westminster with a great company of armed men....Mr. Pym and the other 4 members of our house who stood accused by his Majesty's Attourney of high Treason knowing that his Majesty was coming to the house of Commons did withdraw of it. The house leaving it to their own liberty whither they would withdraw or stay within, and it was a pretty while before Mr. Strode could be persuaded to it. His Majesty came into the house with Charles Prince Elector Palatine [the King's nephew] with him a little after three of the clock in the afternoon, who all stood up and uncovered our heads and the Speaker [William Lenthall] stood up just before his Chair. His Majesty as he came up along the house came for the most part of the way uncovered also bowing to either side of the house and we all bowed again towards him and so he went to the Speakers Chair on the left hand of it coming up close by the place where I sat between the South end of the Clerks' table and me; he first spoke to the speaker saying *Mr. Speaker I must for a time make bold with your Chair...*

The parliamentarian chronicler, John Rushworth, takes up the story:

whereupon the Speaker came out of the Chair, and his Majesty stept up into it; after he had stood in the Chair a while, casting his eyes upon the members as they stood uncovered, but could not discern any of the five members to be there...Then his Majesty made this Speech, *Gentlemen, I am sorry for this Occasion of coming*

The Speaker William Lenthall, possibly by Henry Paert (NPG)

The Hon: William Lenthall
the Hon: House of Commons
January 4th 1642.

unto you: Yesterday I sent a Sergeant at Arms upon a very important occasion, to apprehend some that by my Command were accused of High Treason; whereunto, I did expect Obedience and not a Message. And I must declare unto you here, that albeit no King ever was in England, shall be more careful of your privileges, to maintain them to the uttermost of his power, than I shall be; yet you must know that in cases of treason, no person has a privilege. And therefore I am come to know if any of these persons that were accused are here…Well, since I see all the birds are flown, I do expect from you, that you shall send them unto me, as soon as they return hither. But I assure you, on the Word of a King, I never did intend any Force, but shall proceed against them in a legal and fair Way, for I never meant any other.…When the King was looking about the House, the Speaker standing below by the Chair, his Majesty asked him, whether any of these persons were in the House? Whether he saw any of them? And where were they? To which the Speaker [William Lenthall] falling on his Knee, thus answered. May it please your Majesty. *I have neither eyes to see nor Tongue to speak in this Place, but as the House is pleased to direct me, whose servant I am here; and humbly beg your Majesty's Pardon, that I cannot give any other Answer than this, to what your Majesty is pleased to demand of me.*

The King having concluded his Speech, went out of the House again, which was in great Disorder, and many members cried out aloud, so as he might hear them, *Privilege! Privilege!* And forthwith adjourned till the next Day at One of the Clock.

Tipped off by Lady Carlyle, a sympathetic female courtier, Pym and his accomplices had long since fled, scurrying through Westminster and onto a barge ready to take them down river to the safety of the City. When Charles later tried to pursue them he was met with more cries of 'Privilege! Privilege!' from the angry mobs. London was turning against him. Many in Parliament saw Charles's fumbled coup as the work of a tyrant who certainly could not be trusted with control of an army.

Charles had never once thought his assault might fail. There was no plan B. And now rather than facing down the opposition, he chose to flee his capital for the safety of Hampton Court. Bulstrode Whitelocke was astounded by the stupidity of the move.

This was another and great wonder to many prudent men, that the King should leave this city, the place of his and his predecessors' usual residence; where most of his friends and servants were about him, the magazine of all provisions both for war and peace, the place for intelligence and supplies, and betake himself to the country, where these things were not to be had, and by his leaving the town bring great disadvantages upon himself and his affairs; this was thought not to have been done advisedly.

But the fears of those with him, and his own fears for them, occasioned by the tumults, and his hopes that by his absence the heat of the House of Commons might in some measure be cooled, were alleged in excuse for this action.

The King would never see London again as a free man.

IV
King or Country?: Choosing Sides

1642 February	Queen Henrietta-Maria flees to Holland with crown jewels to raise Continental support for the King
1642 March	Parliament issues Militia Ordinance calling up county troops. Charles refuses to recognise the Ordinance and orders non-compliance
1642 April	Sir John Hotham denies the King entry to Hull castle with its large magazine
1642 June	Parliament puts the unrealistic Nineteen Propositions to the King
1642 June	Charles rejects the Nineteen Propositions and begins issuing Commissions of Array to call up troops

THE CIVIL WAR SPARKED AS MUCH OF A CULTURAL AND RELIGIOUS UPHEAVAL AS A POLITICAL REVOLUTION. The fraught relations between King and Parliament during 1641 were confined to Westminster, but the growing power of the House of Commons had consequences across the country. Not least in Richard Baxter's Kidderminster parish:

> About that time the parliament sent down an order for the demolishing of all statues and images of any of the three Persons in the Blessed Trinity, or of the Virgin Mary, which should be found in the churches, or on the crosses in churchyards. My judgement was for the obeying of this order, thinking it came from just authority; but I meddled not in it, but left the churchwarden to do what he thought good. The churchwarden (an honest, sober, quiet man,) seeing a crucifix upon the cross in the churchyard, set up a ladder to have reached it but it proved too short; whilst he was gone to seek another, a crew of the drunken riotous party of the town (poor journeymen and servants) took the alarm, and run together with weapons to defend the crucifix and the church images (of which there was divers left since the time of Popery). The report was among them that I was the actor, and it was me they sought; but I was walking almost a mile outside of town, or else I suppose I had there ended my days; when they missed me and the churchwarden both, they went raving about the streets to seek us.

On 8 September 1641 the Commons had indeed passed a motion requiring the removal of railed altars and the stripping of icons and images from churches. With Archbishop Laud in the Tower and King Charles preoccupied by political events in Westminster, there was little to stop the Puritans cleansing churches of popish affectations. Nehemiah Wallington, the devout turner who had so vocally called for Strafford's execution, could not have been happier:

> On the beginning of *October*, 1641, at *Leonard's*, *Eastcheap*, being our church, the idol in the wall was cut down, and the superstitious pictures in the glass was broken in pieces, and the superstitious things and prayers for the dead in brass were picked up, broken, and the picture of the Virgin *Mary* on the branches of candlesticks was broken. And some of those pieces of broken glass I have, to keep for a remembrance to show to the generation to come what God hath done for us, to give us such a reformation that our forefathers never saw the like; His name ever have the praise!

In Nottingham, Lucy Hutchinson's husband Colonel Hutchinson was equally compliant in enforcing Parliament's wishes:

> Within two miles of his house was a church where Christ upon the cross, the virgin and John had been fairly set up in a window over the altar, and sundry other superstitious paintings of the priest's own ordering were drawn upon the walls. When the

order for razing out these relics of superstition came, the priest only took down the heads of the images and laid them carefully up in his closet, and would have had the church officers to have certified that the thing was done according to order. Whereupon they came to Mr. Hutchinson, and desired him that he would take the pains to come and view their church, which he did, and upon discourse with the parson, persuaded him to blot out all the superstitious paintings and break the images in the glass; which he consented to, but being ill-affected, was one of those who began to brand Mr. Hutchinson with the name of Puritan.

Some in the Commons thought things were going too far. The MP and antiquarian scholar Sir Simonds D'Ewes certainly had some qualms about the vandalous iconoclasm they had unleashed:

> There was petition read from one [Michael] Herring one of the church-wardens of Woolchurch in London in which he showed that in obedience to the order of the House of Commons of 8 September last past for the removing of idolatrous pictures he had taken up divers brass inscriptions which tended to idolatry: and defaced some statues on tombs which were in the posture of praying and the like, and desired direction how he should raise to defray the charge with other particulars to the same effect. I desired after Mr. Pym had read the petition that all might withdraw: and so all strangers did.
>
> Then I spoke in the effect following. That this man's indiscretion had brought a great scandal upon the House of Commons as if we meant to deface all antiquities. That when we had prepared a statut to pass to this end and purpose for the removing of all offensive pictures yet we had specially provided that no tombs should be meddled withall…I conceived the man who had done this, to have been an honest man and to have done it with a good intention, and therefore I would wish we might have the tombs again repaired and the matters so compounded as he might come into no further danger for this, his indiscreet act.
>
> Others spoke after me and at last the said Mr. Herring and divers others of the parish were called in, and we declared openly our disapproving of this indiscreet act, and so advised them to agree the matter amongst themselves, and that the brass might be again laid on upon the tombs: and so they departed.

Roundheads and Cavaliers

The rampant iconoclasm in London churches was symbolic of a deeper disorder. The chaotic capital was becoming dangerous. Suspected Catholics or courtiers were assaulted and even killed. Rumours of Irish invasions, Spanish plots, and (a perpetual favourite) Parliament on fire made for a deeply jumpy city. With the King absent in Hampton Court and then at Windsor, the atmosphere was even more febrile. According to Clarendon, rabble-rousing preachers and a scurrilous press only added to the frenzied atmosphere.

And from this time the license of preaching and printing increased to that degree that all pulpits were freely delivered to the schismatical and silenced preachers, who till then had lurked in corners or lived in New England; and the pressed were at liberty for the publishing of the most invective, seditious, and scurrilous pamphlets that their wit and malice could invent.

With frightening crowds of apprentices swarming around Westminster and Whitehall, the nobility began to retreat to their estates. During the winter of 1641–1642, in this atmosphere of panic, the terms 'Roundhead' and 'Cavalier' were first used. The peerless civil war historian Dame Veronica Wedgwood ascribed their provenance as follows: 'Roundhead was an easy word of contempt for the shorn, bullet-headed apprentices, but Cavalier, which so soon acquired its gay and gallant associations, had when it was first angrily hurled at the King's men an ugly sound – "cavaliero", "cabalero", Spanish trooper – brutal oppressor of Protestants and national enemy.' Lucy Hutchinson gives the tag a slightly different pedigree:

> When Puritanism grew into a faction, the zealots distinguished themselves, both men and women, by several affectations of habit, looks, and words, which, had it been a real declension of vanity and embracing of sobriety in all those things, had been most commendable in them…Among other affected habits, few of the Puritans, whatever degree soever they were of, wore their hair long enough to cover their ears, and the ministers and many others cut it close round their heads…From this custom of wearing their hair, that name of 'roundhead' became the scornful term given to the whole Parliament party.

'To Him Pudel, Bite Him Peper': satirical woodcut of civil war divide (BAL)

Yet, the loyal wife of Colonel Hutchinson continues, the term:

> was very ill applied to Mr. Hutchinson, who having a very fine thickset head of hair,
> kept it clean and handsome without any affectation, so that it was a great ornament
> to him, although the godly of those days, when he embraced their party, would not
> allow him to be religious because his hair was not in their cut nor his words in their
> phrase, nor such little formalities altogether fitted to their humour;

Richard Baxter offers a third take on the Roundhead and Cavalier label:

> When the war was beginning the parties set names of contempt upon each other, and
> also took such titles to themselves and their own cause as might be the fittest means
> for that which they designed. The old names of Puritans and Formalists were not
> now broad enough nor of sufficient force. The King's party, as their serious word,
> called the Parliament's party rebels, and as their common ludicrous name, the
> Roundheads (the original of which is not certainly known: some say it was because
> the Puritans then commonly wore short hair, and the King's party long hair; some say
> it was because the Queen, at Strafford's trial, asked who that *round-headed* man was,
> meaning Mr. Pym, because he spoke so strongly).
>
> The Parliament's party called the other side commonly by the name of Malignants,
> as supposing that the generality of the enemies of serious godliness went that way in
> a desire to destroy the religious out of the land. (And the Parliament put that name
> into their mouths) and the soldiers they called Cavaliers, because they took that name
> to themselves; and afterwards they called them Dammes, because "God damn me"
> was a common curse, and as a byword among them.

Yet, as Dame Veronica remarked, within a very short time the label Cavalier had
gained the peculiarly raffish connotations that it has held to this day. Much of this
was down to the swash-buckling arrogance of Charles's nephew and General of
Horse, Prince Rupert of the Rhine. His bravado, womanising and great military
skill transformed the Cavalier into the brave but dandyish figure with which we
now associate it. A contemporary Puritan scribbler poked fun at the debauched
image:

PICTURE OF AN ENGLISH ANTIC
with a list of his ridiculous Habits and apish Gestures

MAIDS, WHERE ARE YOUR HEARTS BECOME? LOOK YOU WHAT HERE IS!

1. His hat in fashion like a close-stoolepan.
2. Set on the top of his noddle like a coxcombe.
3. Banded with a calves tail, and a bunch of riband.
4. A feather in his hat, hanging down like a Fox taile.
5. Long haire, with ribands tied in it.
6. His face spotted.
7. His beard on the upper lip, compassing his mouth.
8. His chin thrust out, singing as he goes.

9. His band lapping over before.
10. Great band strings, with a ring tied.
11. A long wasted dubblet unbuttoned half way.
12. Little skirts.
13. His sleeves unbuttoned.
14. In one hand a stick, playing with it, in the other side his cloke hanging.
15. His breeches unhooked ready to drop off.
16. His shirt hanging out.
17. His codpiece open tied at the top with a great bunch of riband.
18. His belt about his hips.
19. His sword swapping between his legs like a Monkeys taile.
20. Many dozen points at knees.

Prince Rupert of the Rhine, who embodied the ideal of the Cavalier, contemporary oil painting (BAL, Bolton Museum and Art Gallery)

Call to Arms

Behind the humorous name-calling there stood a nervous country being forced to choose sides. In February 1642, the King placed his wife Queen Henrietta-Maria on a boat to Holland with their daughters and the crown jewels. He wanted her out of harm's way, and to engage in some royal diplomacy on the Continent with the hope of raising troops (by pawning the crown jewels) and securing an invasionary force. Despite endless protestations of friendship towards each other and mutual hopes of an end to discord, King and Parliament were now involved in a furious race to gain control of the country's armed forces. Parliament struck first by issuing the Militia Ordinance on 5 March 1642. It was originally brought forward as a Parliamentary Bill for the raising of the county forces against unnamed, malignant threats. Charles didn't trust Parliament's motives and refused to sign it. So in a prophetic exercise of sovereign power over the King's will, Parliament simply issued the Bill as a legally enforceable Ordinance without Royal Assent:

Whereas there has been of late a most dangerous and desperate design upon the House of Commons, which we have just cause to believe to be an effect of the bloody councils of papists and other ill-affected persons, who have already raised a rebellion in the Kingdom of Ireland; and by reason of many discoveries we cannot but fear they will proceed not only to stir up the like rebellion and insurrections in the kingdom of England, built also to back them with the forces from abroad;

For the safety therefore of his Majesty's person, the Parliament and Kingdom in this time of imminent danger; it is ordained by *the king's most excellent Majesty and* the Lords and Commons now in Parliament assembled, that Henry Earl of Holland shall be Lieutenant of the county of Berks, Oliver, Earl of Bolingbroke shall be Lieutenant of the county of Bedford, ...and *shall* severally and respectively have power to assemble and call together his Majesty's subjects within the said several and respective counties and places, as well within the liberties as without, that are meet and fit for the wars, and them to train and exercise and put in readiness, and them after their abilities and faculties well and sufficiently from time to time to cause to be arrayed and weaponed, and to take the muster of them in places most fit for that purpose, and the aforesaid Henry Earl of Holland...[etc.] shall severally and respectively have power within the several and respective counties and places aforesaid to nominate and appoint such persons of quality as to them shall seem meet to be their deputy lieutenants, to be approved of by both Houses of Parliament.

And the said Henry Earl of Holland...[etc.], their deputy or deputies in their absence or by their command, shall have power to lead, conduct and employ the persons aforesaid arrayed and weaponed, for the suppression of all rebellions, insurrections and invasions that may happen within the several and respective counties and places; and shall have further power and authority to lead, conduct and employ the persons aforesaid arrayed and weaponed, as well within their several and respected counties and places, as within any other part of this realm of England or dominion of

Puritan preachers inciting Roundheads, Victorian depiction by Sir John Everett Millais (BAL, Forbes Magazine Collection, New York)

Wales, for the suppression of all rebellions, insurrections and invasions that may happen...And it is further ordained, that such persons as shall not obey in any of the premises, shall answer to their neglect and contempt to the Lords and Commons in a parliamentary way, and not otherwise or elsewhere, and that every the powers granted as aforesaid shall continue until it shall be otherwise ordered or declared by both Houses of Parliament, and no longer.

Though Parliament might protest it was acting for the safety of 'his Majesty's person', in reality it was raising an army to wage war against the King. Charles responded by issuing the Commissions of Array demanding fealty and troops from the country's Lord Lieutenants. He was adamant that Parliament's Militia Ordinance was both an illegal usurpation of royal authority and an unnecessary provocation. To counter Parliament's demands, he published a proclamation 'for-

Queen Henrietta-Maria arriving in Holland with the intention of raising troops for an invasionary force, Dutch engraving (WA, British Library)

bidding all His Majesty's Subjects, belonging to the Trained Bands or Militia of this Kingdom, to rise, march, muster, or exercise by virtue of any Order or Ordinance of one or both Houses of Parliament':

> Whereas, by the statute made in the seventh year of King Edward the First, the Prelates, Earls, Barons, and commonality of this realm, affirmed in Parliament, that to the King it belongs…straightly to defend wearing of armour, and all other force against the peace, at all times when it should please him, and to punish them which do the contrary according to the laws and usages of the realm; and hereunto all subjects are bound to aid the King, as their sovereign lord: And whereas we understand that, expressly contrary to the said statute, and other good laws of this our kingdom, under colour and pretence of an ordinance of Parliament, without our consent, or any commission or warrant from us, the trained bands and militia of this kingdom have been lately, and are intended to be put in arms, and drawn into companies, in a warlike manner, whereby the peace and quiet of our subjects is, or may be, disturbed: we, being desirous…to prevent that some malignant persons in this our kingdom do not by degrees seduce our good subjects from their due obedience to us and the laws of this our kingdom, subtly endeavouring…to hide their mischievous designs and

intentions against the peace of this our kingdom, and, under a specious pretence of putting our trained bands into a posture, draw and engage our good subjects in a war-like opposition against us,…

When he discovered that Parliamentarians in Boston, Lincolnshire were mustering troops under the terms of the Militia Ordinance, he immediately fired off a letter to the town's mayor.

> CHARLES R.
>
> Trusty and well-beloved, we greet you well. Whereas we understand that, contrary to our proclamation and the laws of the land, divers of the trained bands, and others belonging to that our town, do frequently assemble, train, and exercise, in a warlike manner, without any order from us, or delivered from any authority given by us; our will and command is, that presently upon sight hereof, you take effectual order, not only to suppress and hinder any such meeting, training, or exercising; but that you punish, according to law, such as you shall find are refractory and disobedient to this our command, and certify their names to us, or one of our principal Secretaries of State, together with the particulars of such their offences; and of the due performance of this our command, we expect a speedy account of you; for which this shall be your warrant.

With the Militia Ordinance on the one hand and the Commissions of Array on the other it was decision time for the combatants of this civil war. With King and Parliament both demanding loyalty, neutrality was no longer an option. The committed Puritan and future Roundhead commander, Edmund Ludlow, had no hesitation over which side to join:

> I thought it my duty, upon consideration of my age and vigorous constitution, as an Englishman, and an invitation to that purpose from my father [another Parliamentarian], to enter into the service of my country, in the army commanded by the Earl of Essex under the authority of the Parliament. I thought the justice of that cause I had engaged in to be so evident, that I could not imagine it to be intended with that much difficulty. For though I supposed that many of the clergy, who had been the principle author of our miseries, together with some of the courtiers, and such as absolutely depended upon the King for their subsistence, as also some foreigners would adhere to him; yet I could not think that many of the people, who had been long oppressed with heavy burdens, and now with great difficulty had obtained a Parliament, composed of such persons as were willing to run all hazards to procure a lasting settlement for the nation, would either be such enemies to themselves, or so ungrateful to those they had trusted, as not to stand by them to the utmost of their power: at least that they would not be so treacherous and unworthy, to strengthen the hands of the enemy against those who had the laws of God, nature and reason, as well as those of the land on their side.

For another Roundhead soldier, Captain John Hodgson, it was the question of constitutional propriety that drove him into the arms of Parliament:

That the safety of the people is the supreme law both of nature and nations, and that there was a people before there were rulers and governors chosen and set over them; and when these turned the Government, laid down by law, into an armed force, then did the people betake themselves to thoughts of reformation. This has been an old practice, whether the Government hath been monarchy, aristocracy, or democracy: the fountain has been from the agreement of the people; and that rulers and governors are accountable to the people for their misgovernment, when they transgress the laws and rules by which the people did agree they would be governed (that is, the people assembled in parliaments or chief councils).

In Hodgson's eyes, the King had broken his contract with the people and in such a situation it was necessary and legitimate to take up arms. Meanwhile on the King's side, one of his closest lieutenants was filled with angst. Sir Edmund Verney, the loyal aristocrat who had had such a miserable time fighting the Covenanters (or not) in Scotland, revealed his concerns to the far less complicated Clarendon:

'I will willingly join with you the best I can, but I shall act it very scurvily. My condition,' said he [Verney], 'is much worse than yours, and different, I believe, from any other man's; and will very well justify the melancholic that, I confess to you, possesses me. You have satisfaction in your conscience that you are in the right; that the king ought not to grant what is required of him; and so you do your duty and your business together: but for my part I do not like the quarrel, and do heartily wish that the king would yield and consent to what they desire; so that my conscience is only concerned in honour and in gratitude to follow my master. I have eaten his bread, and served him near thirty years, and will not do so base a thing as to forsake him; and choose rather to lose my life (which I am sure I will do) to preserve and defend those things which are against my conscience to preserve and defend: for I will deal freely with you, I have no reverence for the bishops, for whom this quarrel subsists.'

One gentleman even more confused that Sir Edmund was the Norfolk squire, Sir Thomas Knyvett. Both sides commanded his loyalty and in an emotional letter to his wife in May 1642, he gives an indication of the reluctant decisions many had to face:

I would to god I could write thee any good news, but that is impossible so long as the spirit of contradiction reigns between King and Parliament higher still than ever, and 'tis to be feared this threatening storm will not be allayed without some showers (I pray God not a deluge) of blood. The only party now grows as resolute as the other is obstinate...Oh, sweetheart, I am now in a great straight what to do. Walking this other morning at Westminster, Sir John Potts...saluted me with a commission from the Lord of Warwick to take upon me, by virtue of an ordinance of parliament, my company and command [as a captain in the Norfolk county militia] again. I was surprised what to do, whether to take or refuse. 'Twas no place to dispute, so I took it and desired some time to advise upon it. I had not received this many hours, but I met with a Declaration point blank against it [the militia ordinance] by the King. This distraction made me to advise with some understanding men what condition I stand in, which is no other than a great many men of quality do. What further commands we shall receive to put ordinance in execution, if they run in a way that trenches upon my obedience against [to] the King, I shall do according to my conscience; and this is the resolution of all honest men that I can speak with. In the meantime I hold it good wisdom and security to keep my company as close to me as I can in these dangerous times, and to stay out of the way of my new masters till these first musterings be over…I wish myself in thy arms every night most cordially, and all the Potts in Christendom shall not keep me from thee long.

After much agonising, Knyvett would eventually declare for the King.

By the Sword Divided

The most painful aspect of civil war is that it turns not only neighbour against neighbour, but also brother against brother and father against son. Numerous families were divided between supporting the King or fighting for Parliament. In June 1642, the royalist Richard D'Ewes wrote from the King's court now at York to his parliamentarian brother, Sir Simonds D'Ewes, still sitting in the Long Parliament at Westminster:

> Dear Brother,
>
> I was in good hopes to have seen you here before the arrival of these will come into your hands: but I should think this or any other pains awarded, if I could be the happy inducement to bring you hither. I daily understand how you stand affected, and what your opinions are, and out of that sincere affection I bear you, I heartily wish you fortunate in their continuance.
>
> If your other occasions will dispense and give place to my hopes, I can in some measure accommodate you with horses for your journey…
>
> 'Tis worth your journey to be an eyewitness of the justice and equity of the King's Proceedings.
>
> Sir, if you be affected to this journey, I have said enough: if your time and business permit not, then I shall but trouble you. I wish you all health and your own desires, and am,
> > Your affectionate brother and servant,
> > D'EWES

Sir Simonds responded regretfully but firmly:

> Dear Brother,
>
> …For mine own part I have often repented my being of this Parliament…But now, being called into it by his Majesty's wit, I have no other resolution but to continue here where I shall persist, as I have done hitherto, *procule amore, procul livore, procule partium studio*, to discharge my duties to God, his sacred Majesty, and the kingdom, without fear or favour.

I have said or done nothing for vindication of the King's just rights, or the upholding of that reverence due to him, but what my conscience dictated to me to speak in respect of that little knowledge I have in the municipal laws and ancient records of the State, and, therefore, there is no service of mine that deserves either to be taken notice of in the least measure by his Majesty or any at York.

'Tis true I might, perhaps, have escaped some unjust censures by an unseasonable silence: but I bless that higher Providence that gave me courage to speak freely, and if my own heart deceive me not, I could be willing to redeem the re-union of his Majestie and the Two Houses with my dearest blood; that so religion might be established in that power and purity amongst us, and preaching so settled in those places where atheism, profaneness, and ignorance now reigns, as that all men might know their duties to God and the King, so as his Majesty might reign many and many years over us with much honour and grace. For, doubtless, by a civil war he will be the greatest loser, whosoever gains; that being true which Gaspar, Earle of Schomberg told Henry the Fourth of France, that the people who were slaine were his people, the towns and cities which were burnt were his cities and towns, and the kingdom which was harassed was his kingdom. Let your prayers and endeavours be, as mine are, for peace, in which resolution you shall ever oblige,

Your affectionate brother,
SIMONDS D'EWES

A family split upon even more fractious lines was the Verneys. Sir Edmund's son Ralph, who had written such tender letters to his father during the Covenanter campaign, had decided as the MP for Aylesbury to ally himself with Parliament. The father was devastated as he realised he might have to face his son across the field of battle in a war which he himself had no great enthusiasm for. Here a family friend, Lady Sussex, writes to Ralph explaining that she had just received a letter from his father, Sir Edmund:

It was a very sad [one] and his words were this of you; 'madam he hath ever lane near my heart and truly he is there still'; that he had many afflictions upon him, and that you had used him unkindly; this was the effect of it. The paper you sent of is [his] letter to you I bornt presently; I shall never open my lips of that nor any thing else you trust me with; he is passionate, and much troubled I believe that you declared yourself for the Parliament: a little time will digest all I am confident…Now let me intreat you as a friend that loves you most heartily, not to write passionately to your father, but over come him with kindness; good man I see he is infinitely melancholy, for many other things I believe besides the difference betwixt you.

In a further letter, Lady Sussex bravely tries to patch the relationship up:

I see you as much apprehend this unhappy difference bewixt your father and self; I am very confident a little time will make all well again and his affection to you as dear and hearty as ever. I pray be not sad; that will do you a great deal of hurt I am sure. If it please God your father return, I hope one discourse or two, will make all well again bewixt you…If you had failed in anything of duty or love to him it had been some just case of exception, but in going the way your conscience tells you to be right, I hope he hath more goodness and religion then to continue in displeasure with you for it.

Sir Edmund's other son, Mun, was also a royalist and was equally disgusted by Ralph's treacherous ingratitude:

Brother, what I feared is proved too true, which is your being against the King: give me leave to tell you in my opinion tis most unhandsomely done, and it grieves my heart to think that my father already and I, who so dearly love and esteeme you, should be bound in consequence (because in duty to our king) to be your enemy. I hear tis a great grief to my father...I am so much troubled to think of your being of the side you are that I cannot write no more, only I shall pray for peace with all my heart that you may so express your duty to your King that my father may still have cause to rejoice in you.

Ralph didn't reply and so Mun wrote again in slightly more conciliatory terms:

I beseech you let not our unfortunate silence breed the least distrust of each other's affections, although I would willingly lose my right hand that you had gone the other way, yet I will never consent that this dispute shall make a quarrel between us, there be too many to fight with besides ourselves. I pray God grant a sudden and firm peace that we may safely meet in person as well as in affection. Though I am tooth and nail for the King's cause, and endure so to the death, whatsoer his fortune be, yet sweet brother, let not this my opinion (for it is guided by my conscience), nor any report which you can hear of me, cause a diffidence of my dear love to you.

The split between parent and child was the most tortuous. Susan Villiers was a lady-in-waiting to Queen Henrietta-Maria in Holland. Her son, Basil, Lord Feilding, had declared for Parliament. It was breaking his mother's heart:

I cannot but refrain from writing to you and withal to beg of you to have care of yourself and of your honour, and as you have ever professed to me and all your friends that you would not be against the person of the King, and now it is plainly declared what is intended to him and his royal authority, so now is the time to make yourself and me happy by letting all the world see who have been deluded all this time and by them that pretend to be [a word here illegible] of the commonwealth. It is now seen what their aim is, but I hope you will leave them and go to the King to gain the reputation you have lost. Being with them you shall be well received by the King, only let it be in time for I do believe the King will have the better of his enemies.

Not for the first time, a mother's advice was roundly ignored:

MY DEAR SON, – I have so often written to you to alter your course that I may out of all hope of persuading, yet my tender and motherly care cannot abstain from soliciting of you to get to the King before it be too late. All that party will be able to make of their peace, when you will be left out to your ruin and my sorrow. I have not language to express my grief that daily comes more and more into my thoughts, your overthrow presents itself so apparently before my eyes, have pity upon me your poor mother. I have so great part in you that you are cruel to deny me any longer. Look up to Heaven, the Great God of Heaven commands you obey me, this my first desire and commands. You cannot be so void of reason but to see the unjust and valiant actions of that part of the Parliament which are against the King. All the world sees it plainly, the mask is taken off their faces.

The statistics bear out this horrible truth of families divided by the sword of civil war. According to work carried out by the historian Charles Carlton, of the gentry who participated in the hostilities 6 per cent in both Lancashire and south-east Berkshire, 7 per cent in Suffolk, and 16 per cent in Yorkshire were divided, as compared to 15 per cent of the aristocracy, and 20 per cent of the 159 eminent families listed in the Dictionary of National Biography. The most tragic case of family warring took place during a battle at Wardour Castle. As he lay dying from his wounds the Roundhead soldier, Private Hillsdeane, confirmed that it was his own royalist brother who had fired the fatal shot.

Patterns of Allegiance

The civil war divided families and it divided communities. No two areas were the same with allegiances dependent upon varying economic, social and religious motives. Old rivalries and jealousies were often conveniently pursued through the prism of civil war. Lucy Hutchinson describes the tense, fractious atmosphere in the run up to the conflict:

> Before the flame of war broke out in the top of the chimneys, the smoke ascended in every county…in many places, there was fierce contests and disputes, almost to blood, even at the first; for in the progress every county had more or less the civil war within itself. Some counties were in the beginning so wholly for the Parliament that the King's interest appeared not in them; some so wholly for the King, that the godly, for those generally were the Parliament's friends, were forced to forsake their habitations and seek other shelters: of this sort was Nottinghamshire.

Whether the deciding factor in the civil war was class, with a rising gentry fighting on the Roundhead side against a decaying, Cavalier aristocracy, has long exercised historians of the period. It used to be argued that the civil war was the result of a wealthy gentry, enriched from the proceeds of the dissolution of the monasteries and rising commerce, now demanding greater political power through the House of Commons. In the county of Somerset, Clarendon certainly saw a class element in the division of supporters:

> For though the gentlemen of ancient families and estates in that country were, for the most part, well affected to the King, and easily discerned by what faction of the Parliament was governed; yet there were a people of an inferior degree, who, by good

husbandry, clothing, and other thriving arts, had gotten very great fortunes; and, by degrees, getting themselves into the gentlemen's estates, were angry that they found not themselves in the same esteem and reputation with those whose estates they had; and therefore, with more industry than the other, studied all ways to make themselves considerable. These, from the beginning, were fast friends to the parliament; and many of them were now entrusted by them as deputy lieutenants in their new ordinance of the militia...they had always this advantage of the King's party and his counsels, that their resolutions were no sooner published, than they were ready to be executed, there being an absolute implicit obedience in the inferior sort to those who were to command them; and their private agents, with admirable industry and secrecy, preparing all persons and things ready against a call.

From his Kidderminster parish, Richard Baxter also saw splits in the community along economic lines:

On the Parliament's side, were (besides themselves) the smaller part (as some thought) of the gentry in most of the counties, and the greatest part of the tradesmen and freeholders and the middle sort of men, especially in those corporations and countries which depend on clothing and such manufactures...

Yet Baxter goes on to suggest what many historians believe today – that allegiance cut across class and the deciding factor was often religion:

But though it must be confessed that the public safety and liberty wrought very much with most, especially with the nobility and gentry who adhered to the Parliament, yet was it principally the differences about religious matter that filled up the Parliament's armies and put the resolution and valour into the soldiers, which carried them on in another manner than mercenary soldiers are carried on. But the generality of the people through the land (I say not all or every one) who were then called Puritans, precisians, religious persons, that used to talk of God, and heaven, and scripture and holiness...I say the main body of this sort of men, both preachers and people, adhered to the Parliament. And on the other side, the gentry that were not so precise and strict against an oath, or gaming, or plays, or drinking, nor troubled themselves so much about the matters of God and the world to come, and the ministers and people that were for the King's book, for dancing and recreations on the Lord's-days, and those that made not so great a matter of every sin, but went to church and heard common prayer, and were glad to hear a sermon which lashed the Puritans...

The historian Mark Kishlansky concludes that the motivation to join either side was religious and constitutional, 'Royalists fought for the traditions of religion and monarchy that their ancestors had preserved. They believed in bishops and the divine right of kings...as the moorings of a hierarchy in church and state. Parliamentarians fought for true religion and liberty. They feared for their souls, and felt that salvation was too important an individual matter to be left in the hands of the church. Their fundamental principle was consent – an ingrained belief in the cooperation between subject and sovereign.'

London gripped by Puritan fervour, contemporary engraving (BAL)

Ultimatums

By spring of 1642, the country was careering towards war. King Charles had set up a royalist court in York where loyalist courtiers with deep pockets had rushed to pledge fealty. Yet Charles's first military strike ended in failure after he unsuccessfully attempted to storm the country's largest arms magazine at Hull. Parliament meanwhile controlled not only Hull, but also the vitally important Tower of London as well as the Royal Navy. This was a devastating blow for Charles. With the navy under the command of the old Puritan sea-dog the Earl of Warwick, there was little hope of Charles ever receiving support troops from sympathetic continental monarchs.

In June 1642, Parliament issued an ultimatum to the King at York. The Roundheads styled the so-called 'Nineteen Propositions' as a chance to step back from the folly of war, but their demands were so ludicrous there was no chance of the King accepting them. As ever, the document began with the usual otiose protestations of loyalty:

> Your Majesty's most humble and faithful subjects, the Lords and Commons in Parliament…do in all humility and sincerity present to your Majesty their most dutiful petition and advice, that, out of your princely wisdom, for the establishing of your own honour and safety, and gracious tenderness of the welfare and security of your subjects and dominions, you will be pleased to grant and accept these our humble desires and propositions, as the most necessary effectual means, through god's blessing, of removing those jealousies and differences, which have unhappily fallen betwixt you and your people, and procuring both your Majesty and them a constant course of honour, peace and happiness.

Then the demands began:

1. That the Lords and others of your Majesty's privy council and such great officers and ministers of state may be put from your Privy Council, and from those offices and employments, excepting those that shall be approved of by both Houses of Parliament;
2. That the great affairs of the Kingdom may not be concluded or transacted by the advice of private men, or by any unknown or unsworn councillors, but that such matters as concern the public, and are proper for the high court of Parliament, which is your Majesty's great and supreme council, may be debated, resolved and transacted only in parliament and no elsewhere…
5. That no marriage shall be concluded or treated, for any of the King's children, with any foreign prince, or other person whatsoever, abroad or at home, without the consent of Parliament.
6. That the laws in force against Jesuits, priests, and popish recusants, be strictly put in execution, without any toleration or dispensation to the contrary:
7. That the votes of the popish Lords in the House of Peers may be taken away, so

long as they continue papists; and that his Majesty would consent to such a bill as shall be drawn for the education of the children of papists by Protestants, in the Protestant religion.

8. That your Majesty would be pleased to consent, that such a reformation be made of the church government and liturgy, as both Houses of Parliament shall advise.

9. That your Majesty will be pleased to rest satisfied with that course that the Lords and Commons have appointed, for ordering the militia, until the same shall be further settled by a bill; and that your Majesty will recall your declarations and proclamations against the ordinance made by the Lords and Commons concerning it....

13. That the justice of Parliament may pass upon all delinquents, whether they be within the Kingdom or fled out of it; and that all persons cited by either House of Parliament may appear and abide the centure of Parliament....

15. That the forts and castles of this Kingdom may be out under the command and custody of such persons as your Majesty shall appoint with the approbation of your Parliament:

16. That the extraordinary guards and military forces now attending your majesty may be removed, and discharged; and that, for the future, you will raise no such guards or extraordinary forces, but according to the law, in case of actual rebellion or evasion....

18. That your Majesty will be pleased, by act of Parliament, to clear the Lord Kimbolton, and the five Members of the House of Commons, in such manner that future parliaments may be secured from the consequence of that evil precedent.

19. That your Majesty will be graciously pleased to pass a bill for restraining Peers made hereafter from sitting or voting in Parliament, unless they be admitted thereunto with the consent of both Houses of Parliament.

The propositions requested near total parliamentary sovereignty and Charles took no time in rejecting it. With money and arms pouring in, the momentum towards conflict seemed unstoppable. For the parliamentarian lawyer, Bulstrode Whitelocke, the speed and severity of the crisis had an air of unreality:

> It is strange to note how we have insensible slid into this beginning of a civil war by one unexpected accident after another, as waves of the sea, which have brought us thus far; and we scarce know how, but from paper combats, by declarations, remonstrances, protestations, votes, messages, answers, and replies, we are now come to the question of raising forces, and naming a general and officers of an army.

V

Country in Conflict:
This War Without
An Enemy

1642 *August*	Charles raises his royal standard at Nottingham and declares war on Parliament	**1643** *August*	Cavaliers waste precious time laying siege Gloucester
1642 *September*	Oxford becomes Cavaliers' capital	**1643** *September*	Parliament signs the Solemn League and Covenant in a new alliance with the Scottish Covenanters. The Earl of Ormond, the King's Lord Lieutenant of Ireland, signs a truce with the Irish rebels known as the 'Confederates'
1642 *October*	The Battle of Edgehill ends in stalemate but road is left open for King to march on London		
1642 *November*	Cavaliers are turned away from London at the Battle of Turnham Green	**1643** *September*	Cavaliers defeated at the Battle of Newbury
1643 *July*	Cavaliers are victorious at the Battle of Lansdown Hill and Roundway Down. Prince Rupert goes on to capture Bristol	**1643** *December*	John Pym dies of cancer

ON 22 AUGUST 1642, THE KING OF ENGLAND DECLARED WAR ON PARLIAMENT. Charles chose the strategically vital town of Nottingham, with its statuesque castle and intersecting trade routes, to raise his royal standard against the Westminster rebels. John Rushworth describes the scene:

> Not long after the King's coming to Town, the *Standard* was taken out of Castle, and carried into the field, a little on the backside of the Castle-Wall. The likeness of the *Standard* was much of the fashion of the City Streamers used at the Lord-Mayors Show, having about twenty supporters, and was carried after the same way; on the top of it *hangs a Flag*, the *King's Arms quartered, with a Hand pointing to the Crown*, which stands above with the Motto, *Give Caesar his due*.
>
> Likewise there were three Troops of Horse to wait upon the *Standard*, and to bear the same backward and forward, with about 600 Foot Soldiers. It was conducted to the field in great state, His Majesty, the Prince, Prince *Rupert*, (whom His Majesty had lately made Knight of the Garter) going along with it, with divers other Lords and Gentlemen of His Majesty's Train, besides a Great Company of horse and Foot, in all to number of about 2000.
>
> So soon as the *Standard* was set up, and His Majesty, and the other Lords placed about it, a *Herald* at Arms made ready to publish a Proclamation, declaring the Ground and Cause of the His Majesty's setting up of his *Standard*, namely, to suppress the Rebellion of the Earl of *Essex*, in raising forces against him, to which he required the Aid and Assistance of all his loving Subjects; but before the Trumpeters could be found to make Proclamation, His Majesty called to view the said Proclamation, which being given him, he privately read the same over to himself, and seeming to dislike some Passages therein, called for Pen and Ink, and with his own hand crossed out and altered the same in some places, and then gave it to the Herald, who proclaimed the same to the People, tho' with some Difficulty, after His Majesty's Corrections: after reading whereof, the whole Multitude threw up their Hats, and cried, *God save the King*, with other such like Expressions. Not long after the reading of the said Proclamation, it being towards Night, the *Standard* was taken down, and again carried into the Castle, with the like State as it was brought into the Field; and the next day it was set up again, and His Majesty came along with it, and made Proclamation as the day before, and the like was also done on *Wednesday*, his Majesty being also present: but after that it was set up with less Ceremony,

Behind the pomp and circumstance of the ceremony, the King's condition was far from encouraging. He was having trouble raising funds and troops – not least because in August working men were more keen to bring in the harvest than go to war. Clarendon found the scene deeply inauspicious:

> melancholy men observed much ill presages about the time. There was not one regiment of foot yet levied and brought thither; so that the trained bands, which the

The raising of the Royal Standard outside Nottingham Castle, 22 August 1642, by Henry Dawson (BAL, Castle Museum and Art Gallery, Nottingham)

sheriff had drawn together, was all the strength the King had for his person, and the guard of the standard. There appeared no conflux of men in obedience to the proclamation; the arms and ammunition were not yet come from York, and a general sadness covered the whole town, and the King himself appeared more melancholic than he used to be. The standard itself was blown down, the same night it had been set up, by a very strong and unruly wind, and could not be fixed again in a day or two, till the tempest was allayed. This was the melancholy state of the King's affairs, when the standard was set up.

Amongst the loyal troops stood Sir Edmund Verney. He had been promoted from Knight-Marshal to the more gallant role of 'Standard-Bearer' entrusted to carrying the royal standard into battle. He accepted the charge with an outward display of Cavalier steel: 'That by the grace of God they that would wrest that standard from his hand, must first wrest his soul from his body.'

Contemporary engraving of the raising of the Royal Standard (BAL)

A true and exact Relation of the manner of his Maiesties setting up of His Standard at *Nottingham*, on Munday the 22. of August 1642.

First, The forme of the Standard, as it is here figured , and who were present at the advancing of it

Secondly, The danger of setting up of former Standards , and the damage which ensued thereon.

Thirdly, A relation of all the Standards that ever were set up by any King.

Fourthly, the names of those Knights who are appointed to be the Kings Standard-bearers. With the forces that are appoynted to guard it.

Fifthly, The manner of the Kings comming first to *Coventry*.

Sixtly, The *Cavalieres* resolution and dangerous threats which they have uttered, if the King concludes a peace without them. or hearkens unto his great Councell the Parliament : Moreover how they have shared and divided *London* amongst themselves already.

As Charles rallied support in the Midlands, the Roundhead army left London in hot pursuit under command of the Earl of Essex. Robert Devereux, the third Earl of Essex, had thus far suffered a rather traumatic life. His father was the infamously hot-headed and ultimately treacherous Earl of Essex who Elizabeth I had been forced to execute. The third Earl had himself endured repeated public humiliations at the court of James I. In a messy power struggle, he was forced to cede his wife to James I's current Court favourite on the trumped up charges of impotence. Essex sought to transcend these troublesome personal difficulties by vigorous combat on the Continent during the Thirty Years War and he returned to England a battle-hardened soldier. Yet he was aloof and arrogant with a greater sense of his own military prowess than was strictly due. Nonetheless, as Lord General of the Parliamentary forces, at the end of August Essex headed north to engage the King.

Robert Devereux, Third Earl of Essex, Lord General of the Parliamentary Army, contemporary engraving (WA, BL)

The Battle of Edgehill

Charles had already left Nottingham heading west for Derby (where he was joined by a large troop of royalist miners) and then Shrewsbury and the Welsh Marches. At the beginning of October 1642, with a force approaching 14,000 men, the King turned back to reclaim his capital. Essex's army was at Worcester and on hearing of the King's march rushed eastward to block the Cavalier advance. The two forces were to meet for their first full-scale battle – the first encounter of Englishmen fighting Englishmen since the War of the Roses 200 years earlier – on the road from Kineton to Banbury at a dramatic escarpment known as Edgehill. It was the moment when diplomacy and politics finally collapsed and King and Parliament went to war over their competing visions of church and state.

The Cavaliers took the high ground. The soldier-turned-courtier, Lord Wilmot, commanded the cavalry on the left wing; the Earl of Lindsey, Colonel Henry Wentworth and Sir Jacob Astley commanded infantry in the middle; and on the right wing sat Prince Rupert with four cavalry regiments and the King's lifeguards. With battle set to commence, Sir Richard Bulstrode, a royalist cavalry officer, describes how King Charles processed among his troops:

The King was that Day in a black Velvet Coat lined with Ermine, and a Steel Cap covered with Velvet. He rode to every Brigade of Horse, and to all the Tertia's of Foot, to encourage them to their Duty, being accompanied by the great Officers of the Army; His Majesty spoke to them with great Courage and Chearfulness, which caused Huzza's thro' the whole Army.

Facing the Cavaliers below the 300-foot escarpment was a very disgruntled Essex who had been led to believe he would be fighting a far smaller force. Yet his army had the advantage of a clear chain of command and a more disciplined officer class. At 3 p.m. on 23 October 1642, Essex gave the order to open fire. Edmund Ludlow was there:

> My Lord General did give the first charge, presenting them with pieces of ordinance, which killed many of their men, and then the enemy did shoot one to us, which fell twenty yards short in ploughed land and did no harm. Our general having commanded to fire upon the enemy, it was done twice upon that part of the army wherein, as it was reported, the King was. The grape shot was exchanged on both sides for the space of an hour or thereabouts.

Engraved portrait of Prince Rupert, after Van Dyck (BAL)

Having made the propaganda point that the Roundheads had fired the first shots of the civil war, Prince Rupert's cavalry got ready to charge. Among those careering down the hill into the Roundheads was Bulstrode:

> Just before we began our March, Prince Rupert passed from one Wing to the other, giving positive Orders to the Horse, to march as close as was possible, keeping their Ranks with Sword in Hand, to receive the Enemy's Shot, without firing either Carbin or Pistol, till we broke in amongst the Enemy, and then to make use of our Fire-Arms

as need should require: which Order was punctually observed. The Enemy stayed to receive us, in the same Posture as was formerly declared; and when we came within Cannon Shot of the Enemy, they discharged at us three Pieces of Cannon from their left Wing, commanded by Sir James Ramsey; which Cannon mounted over our Troops, without doing any Hurt, except that their second Shot killed a Quarter-Master in the Rear of the Duke of York's Troop. We soon after engaged each other, and our Dragoons on our Right beat the Enemy from the Briars, and Prince Rupert led on our right Wing so furiously, that, after a small Resistance, we forced their left Wing, and were Masters of their Cannon…

Rupert's cavalry had smashed through the Roundhead force by riding tight together, coming in hard on the angle with pistols firing. On the left wing Lord Wilmot was inflicting similar punishment. It looked like a rout and the infantry were sent in to mop up. At their front stood Sir Jacob Astley who, according to the royalist officer Sir Philip Warwick:

made a most excellent, pious, short and soldierly prayer: for he lifted up his eyes and hands to heaven, saying, 'O Lord! thou knowest, how busy I must be this day: if I forget thee, do not thou forget me.' And with that, rose up, crying out, March on Boys!

With their fifteen-foot pikes, the Cavalier foot ploughed into the beleaguered Roundhead troops. But all was not as it seemed. Prince Rupert's enthusiasm had got the better of him and instead of returning to the battlefield after the first cavalry charge had pursued fleeing Roundheads behind enemy lines to the village of Kineton. There he and his troops discovered the Earl of Essex's baggage trains and opted for plundering rather than going back into battle. Bulstrode recalls how it was only by encountering a troop led by John Hampden, the Buckinghamshire landowner who had fought the original ship money case, that they were forced to return:

And we of the Prince of Wales's Regiment, (who were all scattered) pursued also, till we met with two Foot Regiments of Hampden and Hollis, and with a Regiment of Horse coming from Warwick to their Army, which made us hasten as fast back as we had pursued. In this Pursuit I was wounded in the Head by a Person who turned upon me, and struck me with his Pole-axe, and was seconding his Blow, when Sir Thomas Byron being near, he shot him dead with his Pistol, by which Means I came back. In fine, by meeting these three Regiments, we were obliged to return back to our Army, and then found our great Error, in leaving our Foot naked who were rudely handled by the Enemy's Horse and Foot together, in our Absence, who fell principally upon the King's Royal Regiment of Foot Guards, who lost Eleven of Thirteen Colours,

It was, according to Warwick, a costly mistake:

This was our first and great military misadventure; for Essex by his reserves of Horse falling on the King's Foot, pressed on them so hard, that had not some of our Horse returned in some season unto the relief of our foot, we had certainly lost the day, which all circumstances considered, we as certainly won.

Victorian depiction of Charles I going to his execution, by Ernest Crofts (BAL, Towneley Hall Art Gallery, Burnley)

Astley along with his fellow infantry commander the Earl of Lindsey, was certainly having a rough time of it. Essex had cleverly kept cavalry in reserve which now charged into the startled royalist infantry who began to give ground. In the melee, Lindsey was shot in the thigh and fell to the ground. The official royalist chronicler, Sir William Dugdale, describes how Lindsey's son Lord Willoughby,

> Hastened from the head of the Guards to his assistance, and found him lying in front of his own regiment with one leg broken by a musket-shot; Now this happening at that point of time when they received the charge of the Enemy's horse, so that it was impossible to carry him off, he stood undauntedly with his pike in his hand bestriding his father, and in that posture wounded one of their Captains in the face, and almost pushed him off his horse; but his own men at the same time giving back, he was left engaged in the midst of the Enemies, choosing rather to be taken with his father, that so he might be in a condition of rendering him what service was in his power, than to save himself by leaving him in that distress.

Another who fell in the skirmish was Sir Edmund Verney – and with him passed the royal standard into enemy hands. The Roundheads' capture of the standard was a devastating psychological blow which needed to be reversed. Edmund Ludlow describes how it was delivered by Colonel Middleton to Essex and then quickly retaken:

> having brought it to the Earl of Essex, he delivered it to the custody of one Mr. Chambers, his secretary, from whom it was taken by one captain Smith, who, with two more, disguising themselves with orange coloured scarves, (the Earl of Essex's colour) and pretending it unfit that a penman should have the honour to carry the standard, took it from him, and rode it to the King, for which action he was knighted.

The body of Sir Edmund, the reluctant yet loyal warrior, was not retaken and instead lay lost beneath the mud and gore of the Oxfordshire battlefield. By the time Prince Rupert returned from Kineton, the Cavalier advantage had been jettisoned and the battle was descending into stalemate. There was, in the mind of Bulstrode, not a little regret at the missed opportunity of Edgehill:

> Now, when we returned from following the Enemy, the Night came soon upon us, whereas, in all Probability, we had gained the Victory, and made an End of the War, if we had only kept our Ground, after we had beaten the Enemy, and not left our Foot naked to their Horse and Foot:

Night fell and after a few brief skirmishes the following day, the Earl of Essex retreated to Warwick Castle while the King set up camp nearby the battlefield. Soldiers and families now began to count the cost of war and mourn their dead. Edgehill had seen some 1,500 lives lost among whom was Sir Edmund Verney. His parliamentarian son Ralph received a letter from the royalist officer and family friend Sir Edward Sydenham. Tellingly it revealed that Sir Edmund had gone into battle without the least precautions – as if inviting death itself:

> For all our great victory I have had the greatest loss by the death of your noble father that ever any friend did…he himself killed two with his own hands whereof one of them had killed poor Jason, and broke the point of his standard at push of pike before he fell, which was the last account I could receive of any of our own side of him. The next day the king sent a herald to offer mercy to all that would lay down arms, and to enquire for my Lord of Lynsee, my Lord Willoughby and him; he brought word that my Lord Lynsee was hurt, your father dead, and my Lord Willoughby only prisoner; he would neither put on arms or buff coat the day of battle, the reason I know not;

On receiving the news, Ralph wrote to Lady Sussex:

> Madam, I never loved to be the messenger of ill news: therefore I forbore to send you this; which is the saddest and deepest affliction that ever befell any poor distressed man; I will not add to your grief by relating my own deplorable condition, neither can my pen express the miseries I am in; God's will be done, and give me patience, to support me in this extremity. There is no absolute certainty of his Death, that I can

yet learn, but sure it is too true. I have sent three messengers to both armies to be informed. On Saturday I expect one of them back, in the meantime I am forced to make diligent enquiries after that which (if it prove true) will make me most unhappy.

Lady Sussex, who had striven so hard to bring son back into favour with father, was all sympathy:

The most heavy news of your worthy good father's death is come to me, for which I have the saddest heart and deepest wounded soul that ever creature had; he being I confess to you the greatest comfort of my life; I pray God fit me for another; for I am sure I shall never have no more ioy in this. Your loss, I am very sensible is infinite too: I pray God give us both patience.

Ralph replies:

Madam, Last night I had a servant from my Lord of Essex Army, that tells me there is no possibility of finding my Dear father's Body, for my Lord General, my Lord Brooke, my Lord Grey, Sir James Luke and twenty others of my acquaintance assured him he was never taken prisoner, neither were any of them ever possessed of his Body; but that he was slain by an ordinary Trooper. Upon this my man went to all the ministers of several parishes, that buried the dead that were slain in the battle, and none of them can give him any information of the body. One of them told him my Lord Aubigney was like to have been buried in the fields, but that one came by chance that knew him and took him into a church, and there laid him in the ground without so much as a sheet about him, and so divers others of good quality were buried: the ministers kept Tallies of all that were buried, and they amount to near 4,000. Madam you see I am every way unhappy.

In fact, only the hand of Sir Edmund was ever recovered for burial. It was identified by a ring containing the King's miniature which Charles had given to his ill-fated standard bearer. It seemed that the trial of civil war, complete with the unnatural estrangement from his own son, was not something Sir Edmund wanted to endure. He went into battle not hoping to return.

London and Oxford

Technically, the battle of Edgehill was a military draw but by withdrawing to Warwick Essex had left the road open for Charles to march on London. If the King had acted quickly on Rupert's advice and charged the capital he might well have crushed Parliament. Instead, he wasted time capturing Banbury, Oxford and Reading. He was also seduced by friendly petitions from Parliament into believing a negotiated truce was in the offing. By the time the Cavalier army reached the outskirts of London in mid-November, the initiative had indeed been squandered. Yet Londoners didn't know that. Fed by gruesome tales of royalist atrocities at Edgehill and fearing an attack any moment, pandemonium gripped the city. Shops and houses were boarded up, chains went across the streets, and the London militia or 'Trained Bands' began to muster on Chelsea fields. After some bitter skirmishes around Brentford, the Cavaliers advanced towards Turnham Green; today a nondescript residential area in west London, but in the 1640s a vital gateway into the capital. To guard against the King's invasion, London had mobilised a 24,000-strong militia. Among those defending the city was Bulstrode Whitelocke who had joined John Hampden's regiment. He was one of a number of Parliamentarians now manning the barricades:

> Beyond Hammersmith, in a lane, were placed the great guns, ready to be drawn up as there should be occasion, and a little beyond that were the carriages, in a field close to the highway, placed with great guards about them for their defence. The whole army was drawn up in battalia in a common called Turnham Green, about a mile from Brentford…The other regiments of horse were placed on both wings, the foot of the army were in good plight, and well armed; and were placed in the body one regiment of them, and another of the city band, one by another, and some were left for reserves.
>
> The order and marshalling of them was chiefly by the earl of Holland, who took great pains, and showed good skill in martial affairs. With him were the Earl of Northumberland and most of the Lords who continued with the parliament, and divers members of the House of Commons, and all were armed.

One of the problems the Roundhead troops faced was sightseers coming down from the city to watch the engagement:

> Wheresoever either of them [the two sides] advanced towards the other, or that the soldiers shouted, then two or three hundred horsemen, who came from London to be spectators, would gallop away towards London as fast as thy could ride, to the discouragement of the Parliament's army, and divers of the soldiers would steal from their colours towards their home, the city.
>
> It was then consulted whether the Parliament army should advance, and fall upon the King's forces, which was the opinion of most of the Parliament-men, and gentlemen, who were officers; but the soldiers of fortune were altogether against it; and while we were consulting, the King had drawn of his carriages and ordinance;

With his 'harassed, weatherbeaten and half-starved troops', King Charles thought better of taking on the Trained Bands. Instead, with the moment lost he retreated from London to Oxford which now became home to the royalist court.

Divisions in Oxford reflected the old town–gown hostility with the university supporting the King and the townspeople broadly on the side of Parliament. However, with the entire Cavalier high command requisitioning the city for the winter of 1642–3 there was little room for opposition. King Charles based himself at Christchurch, where the main quad was used as a cattle-pen; a new mint was created at New Inn Hall; All Souls and New College were turned into weapons arsenals; while the High Street and New Parks were used for drilling and training exercises. The wealthy and connected fled Puritan London and settled in Oxford. It was here that the cult of the Cavalier blossomed with Prince Rupert as the toast of the social scene. He was almost as famous as his dog, 'Boy'. The enormous poodle excited particular opprobrium among the Roundheads who attributed to it supernatural powers. This contemporary ballad was typical of the time:

The dog's mother was a witch who, with the aid of her familiar, cast a spell…

> *No sooner had she spake, but a blacke clowde*
> *With elastic curtains did them both enshrowde,*
> *Where was begotten this Malignant Curr,*
> *Who in this llande hath made all this stirre…*
> *Women stand off and come not neer it,*
> *The Devill, if he saw it, sure would fear it,*
> *For by it's shape, for ought that I can gather,*
> *The childe is able to afright the Father:*
> *'Twas like a dog, yet there was none did know*
> *Whether it Devill was, or Dog, or no.*
> *Scarce twice two years past o're, but quickly hee*
> *Excell'd his Mother in her Witcherie,*
> *And in black and gloomy arts so skill'd,*
> *That he even Hell in his subjugation held;*
> *Hee could command the spirits up from below,*
> *And binde them strongly, till they let him know*
> *All the dread secrets that belonged them to,*
> *And what those did, with whom they had to doe.*

The censorious journal of a local Roundhead commander, Sir Samuel Luke, gives an impression of what the Puritans thought of this Oxonian Sodom and Gomorrah:

Samuel Brayne returned this day from Oxford and informed that he quartered for two nights last past at the White Swan at Oxford and that he saw Prince Rupert gathering his body of horses and dragoons together intending to march to Henley…That at court two gentlemen fell out and fought for a horse that was given between them, and one of them ran the horse through, and that Prince Rupert came forth with a poleaxe and parted them. That he went into the mint, where there were about 30 men at work, and that as he conjectures, there was not above 200 weight of plate to be coined. And further said that he saw Prince Rupert and a lady in a coach together who went into the court with him, and that she had a round black velvet cap on, and a long white feather with a velvet tip at the end of it. And that she went in with her arm akimbo, like a commander.

'William the Conqueror': Sir William Waller, Commander of the Parliamentary Forces in the West (NPG)

Sᵗ Wᵐ Waller.

War in the West

After a bitterly cold winter, and a series of failed peace negotiations, war began again in spring 1643. Though there were plenty of skirmishes around Oxford and the Midlands, the most active theatre of war was in the West Country. And the conflict was conducted by two old friends set against each other by the cruel necessities of civil war.

Sir William Waller and Sir Ralph Hopton had struck up a firm friendship in the early 1620s when both had fought Catholic forces on the Continent during the Thirty Years War. After two decades of companionship they now found themselves on opposing sides, with Sir William driven to support parliament because of his Puritan beliefs and Sir Ralph obeying his traditional fealty to the monarch. In a very English, understated way they were determined this little matter of war was not going to interfere in their friendship:

To my noble friend Sir Ralph Hopton at Wells,

Sir,

   The experience I have had of your worth and the happiness I have enjoyed in your friendship are wounding considerations when I look upon this present distance between us. Certainly my affections to you are so unchangeable that hostility itself cannot violate my friendship to your person, but I must be true to the cause wherein I serve…I should most gladly wait on you according to your desire, but that I look upon you as you are engaged in that party beyond a possibility of retreat and consequently incapable of being wrought upon by any persuasion. And I know the conference could never be so close between us, but that it would take wind and receive a construction to my dishonour. That great God which is the searcher of my heart, knows with what a sad sense I go upon this service and with what a perfect hatred I detest this war without an enemy, but I look upon it as *opus domini*, which is enough to silence all passion in me. The god of peace in his good time send us peace and in the meantime fit us to receive it. We are both upon the stage and must act those parts that are assigned us in this tragedy. Let us do it in a way of honour and without personal animosities. Whatsoever the issue be, I shall never willingly relinquish the dear title of your most affectionate friend and faithful servant,

> William Waller.

The two friends met at Lansdown Hill outside Bath on 5 July 1643. Waller's troop of Roundheads had arrived first and taken up defensive positions at the top of the steep hill. Beneath their cannon and lines of muskets stood Hopton. When he realised the strength of Waller's position he started to retreat. Seeing this, the Roundhead cavalry led by Sir Arthur Haselrig charged down the embankment into the disordered Cavaliers. While Hopton's cavalry fled in despair, a regiment of sturdy Cornish pikemen led by Sir Bevil Grenville stood their ground and managed to repulse the attack. Then, in an act of extraordinary bravery, the Cornishmen advanced up the hill to capture Waller's cannon. A royalist captain, Richard Atkyns, takes up the story:

> As I went up the hill, which was very steep and hollow, I met several dead and wounded officers brought off, besides several running away, that I had much ado to get up by them. When I came to the top of the hill I saw Sir Bevil Grenville's stand of pikes, which certainly preserved our army from a total rout with the loss of his most precious life. They stood as upon the eaves of a house for steepness, but as unmoveable as a rock. On which side of this stand of pikes our horse were, I could not discover, for the air was so darkened by the smoke of the powder that for a quarter of an hour together (I dare say) there was no light seen, but when the fire of the volleys of shot gave; and 'twas the greatest storm that I ever saw, in which thought I knew not whither to go, nor what to do, my horse had two or three musket bullets in him immediately, which made him tremble under me at a rate, and I could hardly with spurs keep him from lying down, but he did me the service to carry me off to a led horse and then die.

It was a bloody victory, costing the death of Sir Bevil and many of his brave pike-men, but Hopton and the Cavaliers had won the high ground of Lansdown Hill. Haplessly the victory was then squandered and Waller's force managed to regroup without much difficulty. Little more than a week later, the two armies met again at Roundway Down outside the town of Devizes. This time there was no escape for Waller. With substantial cavalry reinforcements, the Cavaliers were able to fin-ish off the Roundheads in a brutal pincer move. In the field again was Richard Atkyns who transcribed a fascinating record of the violent but often tragicomic experience of war:

> 'Twas my fortune in a direct line to charge their general of horse [Sir Arthur Haselrig], which I supposed to be so by his place; he discharged his carbine first, but at a distance not to hurt us, and afterwards one of his pistols, before I came up to him, and missed with both: I then immediately struck into him, and touched him before I discharged mine; and I'm sure I hit him, for he staggered, and presently wheeled off from his party and ran...in six score yards I came up to him, and discharged the other pistol at him, and I'm sure I hit his head, for I touched it before I gave fire, and it amazed him at that present, but he was too well armed all over for a pistol bullet to do him any hurt; but in this attempt he cut my horse's nose, that you might put your finger in the wound, and gave me such a blow on the inside of my arm, amongst the veins that I could hardly hold my sword; he went on as before, and I slackened my pace again, and found my horse drop blood, and not so bold as before; but about eight score more I got up to him again, thinking to have pulled him off his horse; but he having now found the way, struck my horse upon the cheek, and cut off half the headstall of my bridal, but falling off from him, I ran his horse into the body and resolved to attempt nothing further than to kill his horse; all this time we were together hand and fist.
>
> In this nick of time came up Mr. Holmes to my assistance, and went up to him with great resolution, and felt him before he discharged his pistol, and though I saw him hit him, 'twas but a flea-biting to him; while he charged him, I employed myself in killing his horse, ...then came in Captain Buck and discharged his pistol upon him also, but with the same success as before, and being a very strong man, and charging with a mighty hangar, stormed him and amazed him, but fell off again; by this time his horse began to be faint with bleeding, and fell off from his rate, at which said Sir Arthur, 'What good will it do to you to kill a poor man?'

With such a string of successes, Prince Rupert hurried down from Oxford to help the Cavaliers capture the strategic jewel of the West Country: Bristol. On 24 July 1643 Rupert summoned the city to surrender. The parliamentarian governor, Nathaniel Fiennes refused, and two days later with the Cavaliers adorned in green for easy identification they began the assault. Richard Atkyns was there for this final stage of the western push and once again it was the unparalleled bravery of the Cornish foot that proved crucial:

> When we came to Bristol, Prince Rupert (whose very name was half a conquest) with the Oxford Army lay before it on the West side, and Prince Maurice [Prince

Rupert's brother] with the Western army on the East: both armies not being half enough to besiege it; our Cornish foot were to fall on first, which they performed with a great deal of gallantry and resolution; but it proving the stronger part of the town, they were beaten off, with a great deal of loss; when they found it inaccessible, they got carts laden with faggots, to fill up the 'graft'; but it being so deep, and full of water they could do no good upon it; but as gallant men as ever drew sword (pardon the comparison) lay upon the ground like rotten sheep… howsoever this loss of ours drew the town forces that way, which might be some advantage to Prince Rupert's forces, who stormed that part of town with such irresistible courage, that forced them from their works, and gave admission to the horse.

Rupert seized the moment and piled into the city with abandon. Clarendon records the moment:

The enemy, as soon as they saw their line entered in one place, either out of fear, or on command of their officers, quit their posts; so that the Prince entered with his foot and horse into the suburbs, sending for one thousand of the Cornish foot… marched up to Froomgate, losing many men and some very good officers by shot from the walls and windows. All men were much cast down to see so little gotten with so great a loss; for they faced a more difficult entrance into the town than they had yet passed, and one where the horse could be no use to them. Then, to the exceeding comfort of generals and soldiers, the city beat a parley.

Fiennes surrendered and was given an assurance of safe exit. But after the bitter fighting and high casualties involved in storming the city, the Cavaliers were in no mood for forgiveness. In typically overblown language, the Puritan turner Nehemiah Wallington describes how the defeated Roundheads were harassed as they fled Bristol:

The Cavaliers fell upon us in a most furious and barbarous manner, plundering and rifling all sorts of persons sparing neither age nor sex, but took away our horses, cloaks, bags, monies, and stripped divers of their clothes, throwing men, women, and children off their horses that rode double, searching the women in an uncivil manner for money, presenting their swords and pistols at such as did in any sort deny them, and when we alleged the terms of agreement, they would not acknowledge any at all, besides other villainies. When they had thus pillaged and rifled us, we were brought without the works, about eight horse and foot. Then we were committed to a convoy of about five troops of horse, and so brought through their army, who fell a raving and reviling at us, and blaspheming God in a most fearful manner, saying it grieved them that they could not butcher us, and bereave us of our lives and asking, 'Where is now your God? Where are your fastings, your prayers and profession, where is your King JESUS?' and said, 'King Charles shall be King, for all King JESUS,' and that God was now turned Cavalier.

After the capture of Bristol, the West fell into Cavalier hands with Poole, Dorchester, Portland and Weymouth surrendering. In the North of England, the King's commander the Earl of Newcastle was enjoying similar successes. The triumphant Charles pressed back towards London, but in the process foolishly decided to lay siege to Gloucester. Hoping for the same swift victory he had gained at Bristol, Charles did not count on the resilience of the 23-year-old governor Edward Massey nor the utter determination of Parliament not to lose Gloucester as it had Bristol. After a tortuous month's siege, with royalist miners making frequent attempts on the walls, the Earl of Essex came to the city's relief. Prince Rupert was furious at the loss and now sought to impede Essex's return to London. On 20 September 1642, just outside Newbury, Rupert and Essex tore into each other just as they had at Edgehill. And just as at Edgehill, there was no decisive victory. But in this case, it was the Cavaliers who left the road open for Essex to return to London where he was garlanded as the saviour of Gloucester and 'victor' of Newbury.

The Return of the Three Kingdoms

Watching the war unfold from the safety of Westminster was the King's original and still committed opponent, John Pym. After the military fiasco of Roundway Down, he knew the Roundheads needed outside reinforcements if they were ever going to vanquish the Cavaliers. So Pym, though wracked with cancer of the bowel, entered negotiations with Parliament's allies in Scotland, the Covenanters. Both shared a broadly Puritan religious outlook and neither trusted King Charles in matters of church or constitution. They had already worked together behind the scenes during the Second Bishops' War and orchestrating of the Long Parliament. On 25 September 1643, the two rebel parties formally signed up to the Solemn League or Covenant. As ever, all they professed to want was 'the happiness of his King's Majesty':

> having before our eyes the glory of God and the advancement of the Kingdom of Our Lord and Saviour Jesus Christ, the honour and happiness of the King's Majesty and his posterity, and the true public liberty, safety and peace of the Kingdom, wherein everyone's private condition is included; and calling to mind the treacherous and bloody plots, conspiracies, attempts and practices of the enemies of God against the true religion and professors thereof in all places, especially in these three kingdoms, ever since the reformation of religion; and how much their rage, power and presumption are of late at this time increased and exercised, whereof the deplorable estate of the Church and Kingdom of Ireland, the distressed estate of the Church and Kingdom of England, and the dangerous estate of the church and Kingdom of Scotland, are present and public testimonies: we have now at last, after other means of supplication, remonstrance, protestation and sufferings, for the preservation of ourselves and our religion from utter ruin and destruction, according to the commendable practice of these kingdoms in former times, and the example of God's people in other nations, after a mature deliberation resolved and determined to enter into a mutual and solemn league and covenant

Contemporary engraving depicting Roundhead iconoclasm and the alliance of the Parliamentary and Covenanter Armies (BAL, BL)

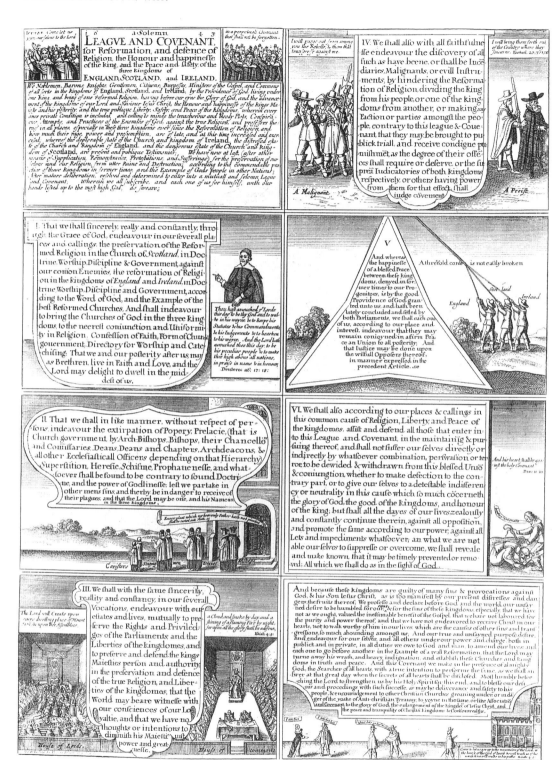

The Solemn League and Covenant of 1643, contemporary engraving (BAL)

The new allies agreed to extirpate papacy, preserve the rights and privileges of Parliament and, above all, reform religion 'according to the word of God and the best reformed churches'. This was a phrase which would return to haunt the Covenanters in coming years. But in September 1643, the Covenanters believed they had a clear commitment from Parliament to reform the Church of England along Presbyterian lines and in exchange they began mustering an army to help in the struggle against the King. Three months after the Covenant was agreed, Pym succumbed to the cancer which had been rotting his insides. The strategic mastermind of Parliament's cause was gone, but he left in the Covenant a bequest which was vital to the Roundhead's future success. While he was generously mourned on Parliament's side, Clarendon had little doubt about the blood on Pym's hands:

> No man had more to answer for the miseries of the kingdom, or had his hand or head deeper in their contrivance; and yet I believe they grew much higher even in his life than he designed.

Yet Pym had not been the only one seeking outside assistance. Clarendon explains that while Parliament looked to Scotland, the King found new hope in Ireland:

> The King was not all this while without a due sense of the dangers that threatened him in the growth and improvement of the power and strength of the enemy, and how impossible it would be for him without some more extraordinary assistance to resist that torrent which he foresaw by the next spring would be ready to overwhelm him, if he made not provision accordingly. When he saw therefore that it was not in his power to compose the distractions of England, or to prevent those in Scotland, and abhorring the thought of introducing a foreign nation to subdue his own subjects, he began to think of any expedients which might allay the distempers in Ireland; that so, having one of his kingdoms in peace, he might apply the power of that towards the procuring it in his other dominions.

Charles was not simply interested in peace in Ireland, he also wanted to retrieve some of the royalist army based there fighting the Catholic rebels (now known as the Confederates). By the close of 1643, his Lord Lieutenant in Ireland, James Butler, Earl of Ormond, had secured a cessation of conflict with the Confederates so freeing up Cavalier reinforcements. In London, Nehemiah Wallington could barely contain himself at the news of Charles's deal with the same seditious Papists who had slaughtered innocent Protestants during the rebellion of 1641. It merely confirmed his already bleak view of the King:

> those Rebels of *Ireland* that have been the death of an hundred thousand souls, for no other cause but that they were Protestants, have found at Court, not only by the Agreement of the said Cessation of Arms, but throughout all the Articles of the said Cessation, to be styled by his Majesty 'Our Roman Catholic Subjects,' (not the least mention of Rebels or Traitors), whereas the Parliament, and well affected party of this kingdom, taking up arms for the just defence of his Majesty's person, Religion, laws,

and liberty of the subject, have been by a hundred proclamations, one after another, declared Rebels and Traitors.

All three of Charles's kingdoms were now sucked into the civil war. But it was Parliament who gained the first fruits of diplomacy. On 19 January 1644, Alexander Leslie, Earl of Leven, veteran of the Bishops' Wars, crossed the River Tweed with a 20,000 strong force of Scottish Covenanters. They were marching south to join the Roundheads. Together, the two armies would soon be engaged in the largest battle ever fought on British soil.

VI

A Brave,
Bad Man

1644 *January*	A Scottish Covenanter army invades England on behalf of Parliament
1644 *July*	Roundhead-Covenanter victory at the Battle of Marston Moor, partly due to Oliver Cromwell's skill as a cavalry commander
1644 *August*	Royalist victories at Battles of Beacon Hill and Castle Dore in Lostwithiel, Cornwall
1644 *September*	Royalist victory led by the Earl of Montrose at the Battle of Tippermuir in Scotland
1644 *October*	The Second Battle of Newbury proves indecisive
1644 *November*	Cavaliers relieve the Siege of Donnington Castle under the nose of the Roundheads. Debacle leads to infighting between Manchester and Cromwell over direction of war.

Previous page: *Cromwell by R. Hutchinson after S. Cooper (NPG)*

WHEN WAR RESUMED IN SPRING 1644 THE COUNTRY LAY EVENLY DIVIDED BETWEEN ROUNDHEADS AND CAVALIERS. Wales, the West Country and northern England remained in royalist hands while southern and central England were under parliamentary control. Yet with the help of their new Scottish allies, the Roundheads were beginning to put pressure on the King's forces in the north. With Alexander Leslie and his Covenanter army marching south and the father-son partnership of Lord and Sir Thomas Fairfax pushing north, the King's commander in the north, the Earl of Newcastle, was forced to seek refuge in York. The Roundheads had him trapped. On 22 April 1644, a combined Roundhead and Covenanter force of some 28,000 soldiers gathered around the thick city walls to lay siege to this solitary royalist outpost.

King Charles was desperate not to lose York. The city was crucial if he wanted to maintain a strategic presence in the north. He sent an urgent letter to his nephew, Prince Rupert, who was then conducting a highly successful campaign in the north-west.

> NEPHEW,
> ...I must give you the true state of my affairs, which, if their condition be such as enforces me to give you more peremptory commands than I would willingly do, you must not take it ill. If York be lost, I shall esteem my crown less, unless supported by your sudden march to me, and a miraculous conquest in the South, before the effects of the northern power can be found here; but if York be relieved, and you beat the rebel armies of both kingdoms which are before it, then, but otherwise not, I may possibly make a shift (upon the defensive) to spin out time, until you come to assist me: wherefore I command and conjure you; by the duty and affection which I know you bear me, that (all the new enterprises laid aside) you immediately march with all your force to the relief of York; but if that be either lost, or have freed themselves from besiegers, or that for want of powder you cannot undertake that work, you immediately march your whole strength to Worcester, to assist me and my army; without which, or your having relieved York by beating the Scots, all the successes you can afterwards have most infallibly will be useless to me. You may believe nothing but an extreme necessity could make me write thus to you; wherefore, in this case, I can noways doubt of your punctual compliance with
>
> > Your loving uncle and faithful friend,
> > CHARLES R.

Despite the studied ambiguity of the letter (was he being ordered to York or to rush back to fight with Charles at Worcester?), Rupert abandoned his conquering of Lancashire and headed east to relieve the embattled Earl of Newcastle. He took with him the notoriously brutal royalist commander, Lord Goring.

William Cavendish, Earl of Newcastle, the King's commander in the North. Panel by William Larkin (BAL)

By mid-June Newcastle's Cavalier army had been under siege for two fretful months. Their daily ration of a pint of beans, ounce of butter and penny loaf had been dwindling slowly. There was also the constant fear of an enemy incursion. On 16 June, the Roundheads almost broke through after detonating a series of mines under the city walls. For the trapped Cavaliers, Prince Rupert's reinforcements could not arrive too soon. On 30 June it was reported that they had reached Knaresborough. The following day, the Roundhead–Covenanter army marched out to Long Marston, a small village five miles west of York, hoping to confront the Cavalier army head-on, but Rupert was too clever for them. He used a small decoy of royalist cavalry to trick the enemy into lining up for battle – then quickly sprinted north, crossed the tributaries of the River Ouse, and circled behind the Roundheads to relieve York.

Mindful of the King's impatience for his speedy return, Rupert decided to cement his advantage and finish off the Roundhead–Covenanter army the following day. He spent the night outside York's city walls, sending Goring in to tell Newcastle that he expected his troops ready for battle the following morning. After two months of siege warfare and selflessly defending the King's interests in the north, Newcastle was indignant at such peremptory demands from this precocious general. He had no intention of jumping to Rupert's orders.

With only 18,000 men at his disposal, some 10,000 less than the enemy, Rupert's only hope of victory lay in speed and surprise. He rose at 4 a.m. on 2 July and marched his men out to Long Marston. The Roundheads had assumed Rupert would attempt to retreat after his relief of York and had begun to march to Tadcaster in the hope of cutting him off. When their rear-guard scouts saw the Cavalier army draw up at Long Marston, the vast army had to perform a desperate about-turn. In this disarrayed state, it was essential that Rupert charged them then and there, but maddeningly, he had not been joined by the Earl of Newcastle's men. The siege-weary troops had spent the day plundering the discarded Roundhead camp, drinking liberally and arguing over wage arrears. When they finally appeared at 4 p.m., Rupert greeted Newcastle coolly: 'My Lord, I wish you had come sooner with your forces. But I hope we shall have a glorious day.' Yet still the Cavaliers didn't attack the disorganised Roundheads and instead fell to squabbling over tactics. Apart from a little cannonfire, the two armies merely glared at each other across the moor in a day-long stand-off. A Roundhead scout master, Lion Watson, describes the scene:

> About two of the clock, the great Ordnance of both sides began to play, but with small success to either; about five of the clock we had a general silence on both sides, each expecting we should begin the charge, there being a small ditch and a bank betwixt us and the Moor, through which we must pass if we would charge them upon the Moor, or they pass it, if they would charge us in the great corn field, and closes; so that it was a great disadvantage to him that would begin the charge, feeling the ditch must somewhat disturb their order, and the other would be ready in good ground and order, to charge them before they could recover it.
>
> In this posture we stood till seven of the clock, so that it was concluded on our sides, that there would be no engagement that night, neither of the two Armies agreeing to begin the charge.

By 7 p.m., Rupert decided it was too late to fight and announced he was off for supper. The Earl of Newcastle's wife recalls her husband's reaction:

> My lord asked his Highness [Prince Rupert] what service he would be pleased command him; who returned his answer that he would begin no action upon the enemy till early in the morning; desiring my lord to repose himself until then. Which my lord did, and went to rest in his own coach…Not long had my lord been there, but he heard a great noise and thunder of shooting, which gave him notice of the armies being engaged.

On the other side of the moor, the Roundhead and Scottish commanders had no intention of retiring for the evening. After a day of endless troop marshalling, their army was now fully in place. On the left wing stood a brilliant young cavalry commander from East Anglia, Oliver Cromwell; on the right wing the leader of Roundhead troops in the North, Sir Thomas Fairfax; and in the middle the mass of infantry led by the Major-General Crawford and Lieutenant-General Baillie.

The Battle of Marston Moor, 2 July 1644, nineteenth-century painting (BAL, Harris Museum and Art Gallery, Preston)

Through their 'perspective glasses' they saw the smoke rising from the Cavalier cooking fires and decided this was their moment. As the sky darkened and a summer hailstorm broke, the Roundheads lit their cannons and under a mist of cannonsmoke the infantry charged through the thick rye fields. Lion Watson was in the first wave:

> About half an hour after seven o'clock at night, we seeing the enemy would not charge us, we resolved by the help of God, to charge them, and so the sign being given, …We came down the Hill in the bravest order, and with the greatest resolution that was ever seen: I mean the left Wing of our Horse lead by *Cromwell*, which was to charge their right Wing, led by Rupert, in which was all their gallant men: they being resolved, if they could scatter Cromwell, all were their own.

Cromwell's cavalry, labelled the 'Ironsides' after Rupert's generous nickname for Cromwell, smashed into the Cavalier right wing and sent them scurrying back.

'Truly England and the Church of God hath had a great favour from the Lord, in this great victory given unto us.' Cromwell after the battle of Marston Moor, by Ernest Crofts (BAL, Towneley Hall Art Gallery and Museum, Burnley)

When Rupert realised what had happened, he threw down his supper, mounted his steed and shouted at his fleeing troops: 'Swounds! Do you run? Follow me.' And in he went with what Watson recalls as a fearsome counter-attack:

> Cromwell's own division had a hard pull of it: for they were charged by Rupert's bravest men, both in Front and Flank: they stood at the swords point a pretty while, hacking one another: but at last (it so pleased God) he brake through them, scattering before them like a little dust…

It was the bravery of the Scottish infantry supporting the Roundhead cavalry that crucially halted the Cavalier attack. In the melee, Cromwell was injured in the neck and briefly retired from the field. Rupert too was forced to retreat after his horse was killed from under him. He ignominiously hid in a nearby bean-field. While the Cavaliers fled the field, Cromwell's Ironsides displayed their superior discipline by remaining on the battlefield to support the infantry rather than pursuing the retreating enemy or plundering baggage trains.

On the Roundhead right wing, the situation was nowhere near as rosy. Sir Thomas Fairfax's cavalry charge had been brought to a grinding halt by a volley of musketshot, and now a royalist cavalry counter-attack led by Lord Goring and supported by the Earl of Newcastle's troop of Whitecoats (so-called because of their undyed woollen cloth outfits) sliced through the Roundhead troops. Fearing the battle was lost, many Scots and Roundheads simply deserted the battle. Arthur Trevor, a royalist messenger searching for Prince Rupert, was overwhelmed by the number of deserters he met:

> The runaways on both sides were so many, so breathless, so speechless, and so full of fears, that I should not have taken them for men, but by their motion which still served them very well; not a man of them being able to give me the least hope where the Prince was to be found; both armies being mingled, both horse and foot; no side keeping their own posts.
>
> In this horrible abstraction did I coast the country; here meeting with a shoal of Scots crying out *Weys us, we are all undone;* and so full of lamentation and mourning, as if their day of doom had overtaken them, and from which they knew not whither to fly: and anon I met with a ragged troop reduced to four and a Cornet; by and by with a little foot officer without hat, band, sword, or indeed anything but feet and so much tongue as would enquire the way to the next garrisons, which (to say the truth) were well filled with the stragglers on both sides within a few hours, though they lay distant from the place of fight 20 or 30 miles.

Contemporary woodcut of Prince Rupert hiding in the bean field after the Battle of Marston Moor. Note Prince Rupert's mutilated dog, Boy. (WA)

Seeing his fellow Roundheads in trouble on the right wing, Oliver Cromwell led his Ironsides along with a troop of Covenanter cavalry across the field of battle to take on the victorious Goring. Under the glimmering light of a harvest moon, Cromwell's men slammed into the Cavaliers. Lion Watson recounts the vital moment:

> Just then came our Horse and Foot...seeing the business not well in our right, came in a very good order to a second charge with all the enemies Horse and Foot that had disordered our right wing and main battle. And here came the business of the day (nay almost of the kingdom) to be disputed upon the second charge....The enemy seeing us to come in such a gallant posture to charge them, left all thoughts of pursuit, and began to think that they must fight again for that victory which they thought had been already got. They marching down the hill upon us, from our Carriages, so that they fought upon the same ground, and with the same front that our right wing had before stood to receive their charge...our Foot and Horse seconding each other with such valour, made them fly before us, that it was hard to say which did the better out of Horse and Foot....To conclude, about nine of the clock we had cleared the Field of all enemies recovered our Ordnance and Carriages, took all the enemies Ordnance and Ammunition, and followed that chase of them within a mile of York, cutting them down so that their dead bodies lay three miles in length.

In the wake of this Roundhead onslaught, only Newcastle's Whitecoats stood firm. Despite sustained musket fire, they would:

> Take no quarter, but by mere valour for one whole hour kept the troops of Horse from entering amongst them at near push of pike; when the Horse did enter they would have no quarter, but fought it out till there was not thirty of them living; whose hap [fate] it was to be beaten down upon the ground, as the troopers came near them, though they could not rise for their wounds, yet were desperate as to get either pike or sword or a piece of them, and to gore the troopers' horses as they came over them or passed them by...every man fell in the same order and rank wherein he had fought.

As Cromwell wiped up the remnants of Goring's cavalry, the rest of the Cavalier army retreated to York. There Rupert and the Earl of Newcastle had a full and frank exchange of views concerning the conduct of the battle, after which the Prince headed north to Richmond while Newcastle fled to Scarborough and then abroad to Holland. He could not bear to endure 'the laughter of the court'. With some 4,500 dead (as well as Prince Rupert's infamous dog, Boy) and 1,500 taken prisoner, Marston Moor was a calamity for the royalist cause. The commander who had done so much to crush the Cavaliers offered up his thanks to God. In the wake of the battle, Oliver Cromwell wrote a letter to one Colonel Valentine:

> DEAR SIR,
> It's our duty to sympathise in all mercies; that we may praise the Lord together in chastisements or trials, that so we may sorrow together.

Truly England and the Church of God hath had a great favour from the Lord, in this great victory given unto us, such as the like never was since the war began. It had all the evidences of an absolute victory obtained by the Lord's blessing upon the godly party principally. We never charged but we routed the enemy. The left wing, which I commanded, being our own horse, saving a few Scots in our rear, beat all the Prince's horse. God made them as stubble to our swords, we charged their regiments of foot with our horse, routed all we charged. The particulars I cannot relate now, but I believe, of twenty-thousand the prince hath not four-thousand left. Give glory, all the glory, to God.

Sir, god hath taken away your eldest son by a cannon-shot. It broke his leg. We were necessitated to have it cut off, whereof he died.

Sir, you know my trials this way; but the lord supported me with this: that the Lord took him into the happiness we all pant after and live for. There is your precious child full of glory, to know sin nor sorrow any more. He was a gallant young man, exceeding gracious. God give you His comfort.

...few knew him, for he was a precious young man, fit for God. You have cause to bless the Lord. He is a glorious saint in heaven, wherein you ought exceedingly to rejoice. Let this drink up your sorrow; seeing these are not feigned words to comfort you, but the thing is so real and undoubted a truth. You may do all things by the strength of Christ. Seek that, and you shall easily bear your trial. Let this public mercy to the church of God make you to forget your private sorrow. The Lord be your strength; so prays

Your truly faithful and loving brother,
Oliver Cromwell

Battlefield Memorial at Marston Moor (AA)

Oliver Cromwell

Who was this messianic soldier for God? Since his own time, opinions on Oliver Cromwell have remained divided. According to the ever-prescient Richard Baxter, who would soon take up a post as preacher in Cromwell's army:

> Never man was higher extolled, and never man was baselier reported of and vilified than this man. No (mere) man was *better* and *worse* spoken of than he, according as men's interests led their judgements.

While Clarendon loathed the man he too could not but admire Cromwell's sheer force of character:

> Without doubt, no man with more wickedness ever attempted anything or brought to pass what he desired more wickedly, more in the face and contempt of religion, and moral honesty; yet wickedness as great as his could never have accomplished those trophies, without the assistance of a great spirit, an admirable circumspection and sagacity, and a most magnanimous resolution....In a word, as he had all the wickedness against which damnation is denounced, and for which hell-fire is prepared, so he had some virtues which have caused the memory of some men in all ages to be celebrated; and he will be looked upon by posterity as a brave bad man.

Born in 1599 (one year before King Charles), Cromwell described himself as 'by birth a gentleman, living neither in any considerable height, nor yet in obscurity'. As the eldest son of the younger son of a knight, Cromwell's social and economic situation started precariously. He spent the early 1630s as a struggling yeoman farmer tilling the land around St Ives in East Anglia. Thanks largely to a bequest from an uncle, his status grew during the decade such that he became a substantial landowner around Ely, living in a former vicarage under the shadow of the town's sumptuous cathedral.

As he rose in status, Cromwell became more involved in politics. Although he dutifully paid his ship money, he was noted for his opposition to royal plans for draining the East Anglian fens. Above all, he opposed Laudian reforms to the Church of England. For Cromwell was never a social or political revolutionary. As a gentleman of large estate, he always retained a strong belief in social hierarchy and private property. But he was a religious revolutionary. Some time during the mid-1630s, he underwent a spiritual conversion which he later recounted in a letter: 'Oh, I lived and loved in darkness and hated the light. I was a chief, the chief of sinners...Oh the riches of his mercy.' From that moment he became a committed Puritan. Like many of his fellow-brethren, Cromwell believed King Charles was imperilling England's unique Protestant heritage. Cromwell revered the England of Elizabeth I and saw the Catholic court of Charles I as a shameful stain on the country's status as God's chosen land. His mother, his wife and his favourite daughter (one child of eight) were all called Elizabeth.

Emboldened by his religious convictions and assisted by his circle of Puritan cousins, Cromwell raised his voice against the King and the Laudian Church. Having briefly represented Huntingdon in the ill-fated Parliament of 1628, he was returned in 1640 as MP for Cambridge during the Short and Long Parliaments. It is there that the suave, royal courtier Sir Philip Warwick first set eyes on the uncouth farmer from East Anglia:

> I came into the House well clad and perceived a gentleman speaking (whom I knew not) very ordinary apparelled, for it was a plain cloth-suit, which seemed to have bin made by an ill country tailor; his linen was plain, and not very clean; and I remember a speck or two of blood upon this little band, which was not much larger than his collar; his hat was without a hatband, his stature was of a good size, his sword stuck close to his side, his countenance swollen and reddish, his voice sharp and untunable, and his eloquence full of fervour; for the subject matter could not bear much of reason; it being in behalf of a servant of Mr. Prynn's who had dispersed libels against the Queen for her dancing and such like innocent and courtly sports; and he aggravated the imprisonment of this man by the Council Table unto the height, that one would have believed the very Government itself had been in great danger by it. I sincerely profess it lessened much my reverence unto that great council; for was very much harkened unto.

Yet as Clarendon later remarked, his parliamentary demeanour hid a deeper reserve:

> When he appeared first in the parliament, he seemed to have a person in no degree gracious, no ornament of discourse, none of those talents which use to reconcile the affections of the stander by: yet as he grew into place and authority, his parts seemed to be raised, as if he had had concealed faculties, till he had occasion to use them; and when he was to act the part of a great man, he did it without any indecency, notwithstanding the want of custom.

When war broke out in 1642, Cromwell became a Captain of Horse in Parliament's Eastern Association army under the command of the Earl of Manchester. He also served briefly under Sir William Waller, the commander in the West Country, who here gives a retrospective account of the 'cunning' Cromwell of future infamy:

> And here I cannot but mention the wonder which I have oft times had to see this eagle in his eyrie. He at this time had never shown extraordinary parts, nor do I think that he did himself believe that he had them. For although he was blunt, he did not bear himself with pride or disdain. As an officer he was obedient and did never dispute my orders nor argue upon them. He did, indeed, seem to have great cunning, and whilst he was cautious of his own words, not putting forth too many lest they should betray his thoughts, he made others talk, until he had as it were sifted them, and known their inmost designs.

From his earliest operations in the military, Cromwell believed in meritocracy and religiosity. He wanted soldiers who were good at their jobs and committed believers. Baxter explains Cromwell's thinking:

> At his first entrance into the wars, being but a captain of horse, he had a special care to get religious men into his troop. These men were of greater understanding than common soldiers, and therefore were more apprehensive of the importance and consequence of the war, and making not money but that which they took for the public felicity to be their end, they were the more engaged to be valiant; for he that makes money his end does esteem his life above his pay, and therefore is like enough to save it by flight when danger comes, if possibly he can; but he that makes the felicity of Church and State his end esteems it above his life, and therefore will the sooner lay down his life for it. And men of parts and understanding know how to manage their business, and know that flying is the surest way to death, and that standing to it is the likeliest way to escape, there being many usually that fall in flight for one that falls in valiant fight. These things it's probable Cromwell understood, and that none would be such engaged valiant men as the religious.

'Ironside': Cromwell, contemporary oil painting (BAL, Leeds Museums and Art Galleries, City Art Gallery)

Oliver Cromwell's watch (BAL, Ashmolean Museum, Oxford)

In a famous letter to his fellow officers in the Eastern Association, he set out his prerequisites for fighting men:

Gentlemen,

I have been now two days at Cambridge, in expectation to hear the fruit of your endeavours in Suffolk towards the public assistance. Believe it, you will hear of a storm in few days. I beseech you be careful what captains of horse you choose, what men be mounted; a few honest men are better than numbers. If you choose godly honest men to be captains of horse, honest men will follow them, and they will be careful to mount such.

The King is exceeding strong in the West. If you be able to foil a force at the first coming of it, you will have reputation; and that is of great advantage in our affairs. God hath given it to our handful; let us endeavour to keep it. I had rather have a plain russet-coated captain what knows what he fights for, and loves what he knows, than that which you call a gentleman and is nothing else. I honour a gentleman that is so indeed.

[Cambridge August 29th, 1643.]

Your faithful servant,

OLIVER CROMWELL.

In a later letter, he defended a soldier accused of being an Anabaptist (extreme

Oliver Cromwell's hat
(Cromwell Museum,
Huntingdon; WA)

Puritan) from punishment at the hands of the strict Presbyterian Major General Crawford:

> Ay, but the man is an Anabaptist. Are you sure of that? Admit he be, shall that render him incapable to serve the public. He is indiscreet. It may be so, in some things, we have all human infirmities…
>
>   Sir, the State, in choosing men to serve them, takes no notice of their opinions, if they be willing faithfully to serve them, that satisfies. I advised you formerly to bear with men of different minds from yourself; if you had done it when I advised you to it, I think you would not have had so many stumbling blocks in your way. It may be you judge otherwise, but I tell you my mind. I desire you would receive this man into your favour and good opinion. I believe, if he follow my counsel, he will deserve no other but respect from you. Take heed of being sharp, or too easily sharpened by others, against those to whom you can object little but that they square not with you in every opinion concerning matters of religion. If there be any other offence to be charged upon him, that must in a judicial [way] receive a determination. I know you will not think it fit my Lord should discharge an officer of the Field but in a regulate way. I question whether either you or I have any precedent for that.
>
>   I have not further to trouble you, but rest,
> [Cambridge, March 10th]
>   Your humble servant,
>   OLIVER CROMWELL.

From his obscure post as Captain of Horse, Cromwell rose steadily through the Roundhead army thanks to his own skills as a horseman, but above all thanks to the professionalism and discipline of his 'Ironside' cavalry. At the Battle of Winceby in October 1643, he affirmed his credentials as a cavalry commander by helping to crush the royalist horse. While other Roundheads lost battles during 1643, Cromwell seemed to keep winning. As John Morrill points out, Cromwell saw in these victories a divine plan for England in which he was to play a leading role. By the time he rode onto Marston Moor in July 1644, Cromwell was very much the coming man.

Scotland, Newbury and Donnington

The English Civil War was never an entirely English affair. After the debacle of Marston Moor events in Charles's second kingdom, Scotland, gave the King new hope. With the Scottish Covenanters absent in England fighting for Parliament, the Royalists seized the opportunity for a counter-attack under the inspired leadership of James Graham, Earl of Montrose. His views on kingship and the baleful consequence of rebellion were fairly clear-cut:

> And you, ye meaner people of Scotland...Do ye not know, when the monarchical government is shaken, the great ones strive for the garland with your blood and your fortunes? Whereby you gain nothing; but, instead of a race of kings who have governed you two thousand years with peace and justice, and have preserved your liberties against all domineering nations, shall purchase to yourselves vultures and tyrants to reign over your posterity.

Charles I's ally in Scotland, James Graham, Earl of Montrose (BAL, The Royal Cornwall Museum, Truro)

Montrose rallied together a disparate force of clansmen, Royalists and Catholics. At the core of his army was a Celtic contingent of Irish MacDonnells and Scottish MacDonalds keen to renew their ancient feud with the Campbells. Happily, the leader of the Covenanters and clan leader of the Campbells coincided in the figure of the Earl of Argyll.

Coming together at Blair Atholl in the Highlands in August 1644, Montrose's haphazard force embarked on a year-long campaign against Argyll, the Campbells and the Covenanters. The hope was to secure Scotland for the King and then invade England on his behalf. At the very least it had the effect of tying up any remaining Covenanter troops from joining the Roundheads. During Montrose's so-called 'Year of Miracles' he stormed Perth, sacked Aberdeen, and crushed Argyll at the battle of Tippermuir in September 1644 and again more brutally at Inverlochy in February 1645. It was a staggeringly successful campaign which gave Charles fresh resolution. With the wind in his sails, Montrose thought it helpful to give the King some advice:

> The more your Majesty grants, the more will be asked; and I have too much reason to know that they will not rest satisfied with less than making your Majesty a King of straw…it is unworthy of a King to treat with rebel subjects, while they have the sword in their hands.

Yet despite the setback of Marston Moor, Charles wasn't doing too badly on his own. At a series of battles surrounding Lostwithiel in southern Cornwall, he decimated the increasingly hapless Earl of Essex's parliamentary army. Yet the King got lazy and during his march back to Oxford in October 1644 was surprised by forces led by the Earl of Manchester, Oliver Cromwell and William Waller. The second battle of Newbury was a parliamentary victory with the King forced to retreat to Bath, but it was not the emphatic win it so easily should have been. When Manchester was urged by Sir Arthur Haselrig to pursue the King to Bath, he replied disdainfully: 'Thou art a bloody fellow! God send us peace, for God doth never prosper us in our victories to make them clear victories.' The fiasco was worsened when Cavalier troops returned to Donnington Castle outside Newbury and recaptured all their weapons and ammunition lost in the battle. The King then sauntered through to Oxford for his winter retirement. The English Civil War showed no sign of abating.

The Horror of War

For the country at large this stalemate was the worst of all worlds. As the fighting ground on, so the plunder, the destruction, the murder and misery continued. Across every county at war, crops were lost, houses burnt, and loved ones butchered. For the millions of agricultural workers who survived on a precarious economic base, the loss of a horse, or one year's harvest, or a working son could be disastrous. In 1643, the moderate parliamentarian Bulstrode Whitelocke voiced his concern at the self-inflicted futility of civil war:

> The land is weary of our discords, being thereby polluted with our blood.
>
> God hath given you great successes in many places against our enemies, and sometimes he is pleased to give our enemies successes against us; in all of them, whether of the one or the other party, the poor English are still sufferers.
>
> Whose goods, I pray sir, are plundered? Whose houses are burnt? Whose limbs are cut or shot off? Whose persons are thrown into loathsome dungeons? Whose blood stains the walls of our towns and defiles our land?
>
> Is it not all English? And is it not then time for us, who are all Englishmen, to be weary of these discords, and to use our utmost endeavours to put an end to them?
>
> I know, sir, you are all here of the same opinion with me in this point; and that it was an unhappy mistake of those who told us in the beginning of our warfare, that it would be only to show ourselves in the field with a few forces, and then all would be presently ended.
>
> We have found it otherwise: let us now again seek to recover these blessings of peace, whereof we are told, that *nihil tam populare quam pax,* that nothing is than peace more gracious to be heard of, more pleasing to be desired, and more profitable to be enjoyed.

Since hostilities began in 1642, numerous towns and counties had suffered at the hands of marauding soldiers. The Puritan turner and skilled propagandist Nehemiah Wallington describes the scene in Marlborough as Cavaliers stormed in:

> For when these rebels had got into the town, they ran through the streets with their drawn swords, cutting and slashing those men they met with, whether soldiers or not. They set their houses on fire; they had four great fires at one time flaming in four several places. A very sad thing to behold, and at the same time their soldiers breaking up of shops and houses, and taking away all sorts of goods, breaking of trunks, chests, boxes, cabinets, bedsteads, cupboards, presses, coffers, and many that were not locked, but yet they would break and dash them all to pieces; and thence rifled and carried away all kinds of wearing apparel, all money or plate they met with, all sorts of shoes and boots, stockings, hats, and woollen and linen cloth of all sorts, sheets, beds, bolster cases, cutting up the cases and scattering the feathers in the streets to be trampled on by horses and men; also searching men's and women's pockets for money, and threatening them with pistols and swords to shoot, or run them through, if that they would not give them money, by which means compelling many men to lead them to the places where they had hid their money.

According to an equally biased parliamentary tract, the solidly Puritan town of Birmingham suffered just as harshly at Prince Rupert's hands:

> Having thus possessed themselves of the town they ran into every house cursing and damning, threatening and terrifying the poor women most terribly, setting naked swords and pistols to their breasts, they fell to plundering the town before them

Royalist depictions of The Rape of England, contemporary engraving (WA, British Library)

....They beastly assaulted many women's chastity, and impudently made their brags of it afterwards, how many they had ravished; glorying in the shame. Especially the French among them were outrageously lascivious and lecherous....That night few or none went to bed, but sat up revelling, robbing and tyrannising over the poor affrighted women and prisoners, drinking drunk healthing upon their knees, yea, drinking drunk healths to Prince Rupert's dog....Nor did their rage here cease, but when on the next day they were to march forth of the town, they used all possible diligence in every street to kindle fire in the town with gunpowder, match, wisps of straw, and besomes, burning coals of fire, etc., flung into straw, hay, kid piles, coffers, any other places where it was likely to catch hold.

With her husband Colonel Hutchinson now the Roundhead Governor of Nottingham Castle, Lucy Hutchinson recalls how the less protected town was the subject of a terrifying Cavalier assault:

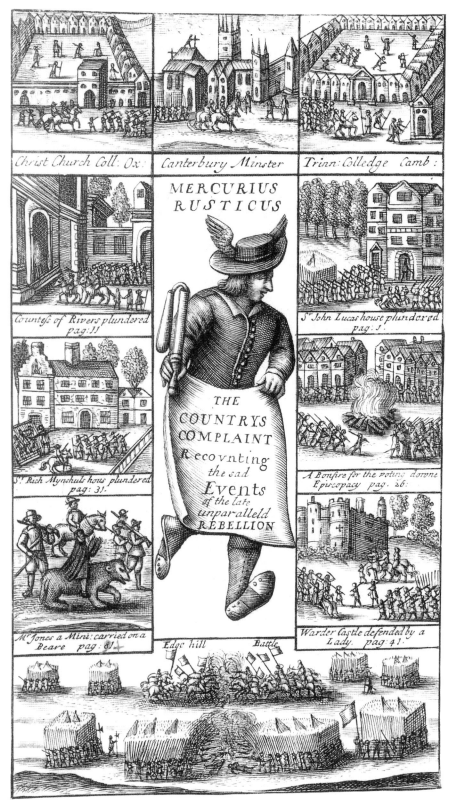

Christ Church Coll: Ox:

Canterbury Minster

Trinn: Colledge Camb:

MERCURIUS RUSTICUS

Countess of Rivers plundered pag: 11

Sr. John Lucas house plundered pag: 5

THE COUNTRYS COMPLAINT Recovnting the sad Events of the late unparalleld REBELLION

Sr. Rich Mynshuls hous plundered pag: 31.

A Bonfire for the voting downe Episcopacy pag: 26.

Mr Jones a Mini: carried on a Beare pag: 61.

Warder castle defended by a Lady. pag: 41.

Edge hill Battle

Late Stuart propaganda warning of the dangers of civil war: engraved title page of Mercurius Rusticus, the Royalist newspaper, 1685 (BAL)

The Governor's men chased them from street to street, till they had cleared the town of them, who ran away confusedly. The first that went out shot their pistols into the thatched houses to have fired them, but by the mercy of God neither that, nor other endeavours they showed to have fired the town, as they were commanded, took effect. Between thirty and forty of them were killed in the streets, fourscore were taken prisoners, and abundance of arms were gathered up, which the men flung away in haste, as they run; but they put some fire into a hay barn and hay mows, and to all other combustibles things they could discern in their haste, but by God's mercy, the town, notwithstanding, was preserved from burning....Many of them died in their return, and were found dead in the woods and in the towns they past through. Many of them, discouraged with this service, ran away, and many of their horses were quite spoiled: for two miles they left a great track of blood, which froze as it fell upon the snow, for it was such bitter weather that the foot had waded almost to the middle in snow as they came, and were so numbed with cold when they came into the town, that they were fain to be rubbed to get life in them, and in that conditions, were more eager of fires and warm meat than of plunder, which saved many men's goods.

War-time atrocities were also prevalent on the battlefield. Summary executions and punishment attacks increased as Irish and Scottish forces became more involved in the conflict. Sir Edmund Ludlow recalls a particularly nasty incident:

In the mean time Sir Francis Doddington had caused the two men that he had taken at Warder to be hanged, upon pretence that they ran away from him; and having brought some pieces of cannon before Woodhouse, made a breach so considerable in the wall, that the besieged were necessitated to surrender at mercy, but they found very little, for they were presently stripped of all that was good about them: and Sir Francis Doddington being informed by one Bacon, who was parson of the parish, that one of the prisoners had threatened to stick in his skirts, as he called it, for reading the Common-Prayer, struck the man so many blows upon the head, and with such force, that he broke his skull, and caused him to fall into a swound; from which he was no sooner recovered, but he was picked out to be one of the twelve which Sir Francis had granted to Sir William St. Leger to be hanged, in lieu of six Irish rebels who had been executed at Warum by Col. Sydenham, in pursuance of an order from the Parliament to give them no quarter. These twelve being most of them clothiers, were hanged upon the same tree; but one of them breaking his halter, desired that what he had suffered might be accepted, or else that he might fight against any two for his life...

There was also the more mundane but dispiriting costs of war as troops were billeted and houses invaded. In his third-person diary, Bulstrode Whitelocke describes the moment when Cavalier troops raided his estate at Fawley Court:

The King resolved to march to London, his Army advanced to Reading, Henley, and those parts, and a Regiment under Sir John Byron quartered at Whitelocke's house at Fawley Court, wherof his tenant William Cooke and his servants having some notice, they threw into the moat there pewter, brass, and iron things, and removed to some of his tenants houses, and into the woods, some of his books, linen and household stuff, as much as the short warning would permit. Sir John Byron and his brothers com-

Parliamentarian and lawyer,
Bulstrode Whitelocke,
seventeenth century (NPG)

manded the horse quartered there to commit no insolence, nor to plunder Whitelocke's goods, but 1000 of them being in and about his house, there was no insolence or outrage which such guests use to commit upon an Enemy but these brutish common soldiers did at Fawley Court.

There they had their whores, they spent and consumed in one night 100 load of corn and hay, littered their horses with good wheat sheafs, gave them all sorts of corn in the straw, made great fires in the closes, and William Cooke telling them that there were billets and fagots nearer to them then the plough timber which they burned, they threatened to burn him, divers books, and writings of Consequence which were left in his study, they tore and burnt, and lighted Tobacco with them, and some they carried away to Whitelocke's extreme loss and prejudice, in his Estate, and in his profession loosing many excellent manuscripts of his fathers and others, and some of his own Labours. They broke down his Park Pale, killed most of his deer though rascals and carrions, and let out the rest, only a Tame Hind and his hounds they presented to Prince Rupert.

They ate and drank up all that the house could afford, broke up all trunks, chests and places, any goods, linen, or household stuff that they could find, they carried away, cut the beds, let out the feathers, and took away the tykes, the curtains, covers of chairs and stools, his coach and four good coach horses, and all his saddle horses, and whatsoever they could lay their hands on, they carried away or spoiled, and did all that malice and rapine could provoke barbarous mercenaries to commit, and so they left William Cooke and his company in the highest affright and detestation of them, that lewdness, and damage could persuade him unto.

In Oxfordshire, the far less wealthy Thomas Tasker petitioned a parliamentary committee of accounts for the return of his goods following his persecution by the Roundhead commander Major Purefoy:

> Your petitioner, being a poor man and aged, in December 1644, in the middle of the night, a party of Major Purefoy's soldiers...came into his house and violently took away the most part of his household goods, to the value of £10 or upwards and also took away your petitioner to Compton where he was unjustly imprisoned by the space of five or six days, and nothing being alleged against him, the Major came to him and used many harsh speeches and so gave order to the Marshal for to release him, but never examined him of anything at all, neither would he give him leave to speak for himself to desire any of his goods again.
>
> His humble request unto your worships is that you will be pleased for to take into your considerations that he may be satisfied for his goods in regard he and his wife are aged, and the sudden fight hath made them both so sickly and weak that they are altogether unable to get their living....
>
> They [the soldiers] had in money 10s, 7 pairs of sheets, 3 brass kettles, 2 brass pots, 5 pewter dishes and other small pewter, 4 shirts, 4 smocks, other small linens, 2 coats, 1 cloak, 1 waistcoat, 7 dozen of candles, 1 frying pan, 1 spit, 2 pairs of pot hooks, 1 peck of wheat, 4 bags, some oatmeal, some salt...a basket full of eggs...pins, bowls, dishes, spoons, ladles, drinking pots and whatsoever else they could lay their hands on.

By 1644, Parliament was also using more 'legal' methods to extract resources. The sequestration of royalist estates cleverly demoralised the Cavalier opposition and raised much needed funds for the Roundhead force. One Royalist to suffer from Parliament's unwelcome attention was the Norfolk baronet Sir Thomas Knyvett. Here he writes to his wife in the most pathetic terms:

> My deer   *May 30th 1644*
> Heart, I must be brief with thee, I am so full of troubled business in my head. I fear I shall doe little in my business a great while, for now I am advised that I must petition the House [of Commons] first and get my case referred to the Committee before that will meddle with it, And when I shall get a motion there, God knows. I wish thou were here with all my hart, for your solicitation would doe more in a week then I am like to do in a Quarter...
>
> Sr W: P: is got his sequestration discharged. Sr Robt. Kempe the like, with a wart from the Committee to take his goods that have been plundered that are unsold where ever he can find them. I hope I shall not be made the only object of pity and scorn in the country.
>
> I am under the lash and must endure the scourge with patience.
>
> I fear the late new officer will be fierce in his execution. You may tell him, if he comes, that I have propounded terms of composition to Mr Cort for my goods, which

he likes well, and a sum is partly agreed on, if I may have security for the future. I am most troubled for my farmers that have paid their rents, least their cattle should be driven. Truly sweet heart these things were able to distract a well resolved patience, if there were not a good God to trust in, and a heavenly Kingdom to expect. I pray satisfy my best tenants that they shall be no losers if I be master of my own....I know not what to do for money to go through with my business. My stock is very low. If I get not off this sequestration we are all undone.

The misery of war was further exacerbated by the absence of any sign of peace. It seemed the theft, the pillage, the death would go on without end. There were many in the Roundhead camp just as frustrated as Sir Thomas Knyvett at the length and cost of war, but unlike Knyvett and his dispirited fellow Royalists, they had the vision and determination to bring the conflict to a brutal conclusion.

'And When Did You Last See Your Father?', by William Frederick Yeames. The painting displays Victorian sympathy for the Royalist cause. (BAL, Walker Art Gallery, Liverpool)

VII
Saturn's Children

| 1644 November | The Parliamentarian Council of War at Shaw Field exposes differences between war and peace parties | 1645 October | Basing House falls to Roundhead besiegers in a bloody rout |

| 1645 February | Royalist victory at the Battle of Inverlochy | 1646 May | Charles surrenders himself to the Scottish Covenanters at Newark |

| 1645 April | Self-Denying Ordinance passed excluding Parliamentarians from positions of command in the army. New Model Army created as a more unified and aggressive fighting force. | 1647 January | The Scots hand Charles over to Parliament despite tensions over religious policy |

| | | 1647 June | The Army strengthens its position by seizing Charles at Holmby House and rallying on Newmarket and Triploe Heaths |

| 1645 June | Roundhead victory at the Battle of Naseby finishes off the Cavaliers as a fighting force | | |

| 1645 September | Cavaliers surrender Bristol. Royalists in Scotland are defeated at the Battle of Philiphaugh | 1647 October | Army Grandees consider Leveller demands and broader philosophical issues at the Putney Debate |

THE FIASCO OF NEWBURY AND DONNINGTON REVERBERATED THROUGH PARLIAMENT. Not only had the Roundheads failed to finish off the Cavaliers in battle, but had actually allowed them to steal back into Donnington Castle and retrieve their arms and ammunition. Cromwell for one was furious and in a brutal internal enquiry turned upon the louche officer in charge at Newbury, the Earl of Manchester. Manchester was the commander of the Eastern Association, one of the many regional associations that collectively formed the Roundhead army, and Cromwell was his subordinate as Lieutenant-General of Horse, but it did not stop the latter's coruscating tongue. He accused Manchester of laziness, incompetence and, most worryingly of all, a fear of victory:

> his Lordship's miscarriage in these particulars were neither through accidents (which could not be helped) nor through his improvidence only, but through his backwardness to all action, and [I] had some reason to conceive that that backwardness was not (merely) from dullness or indisposedness to engagement, but (withall) from some principle of unwillingness in his Lordship to have this war prosecuted unto a full victory, and a design or desire to have it ended by accommodation (and that) on some such terms to which it might be disadvantageous to bring the King too low. To the end therefore that (if it were so) the state might not be further deceived in their expectations from their Army, I did (in the faithful discharge of my duty to the Parliament and kingdom) freely discover those my apprehensions, and what grounds I had for them.

At a fraught Council of War on the Newbury battlefield, Manchester had already criticised what he regarded as Cromwell's reckless bellicosity: 'The King need not care how oft he fights, but it concerns us to be wary, for in fighting we venture all to nothing. If we fight a hundred times and beat him ninety-nine times, he will be King still. But if he beat us once, or the last time, we shall be hanged, we shall lose our estates, and our posterities be undone.' To which a contemptuous Cromwell replied: 'My Lord, if this be so why did we take up arms at first? This is against fighting hereafter; if so let us make peace, be it never so base.' But Manchester suspected Cromwell of having a more sinister egalitarian agenda. During the parliamentary enquiry into the events at Donnington, he accused Cromwell of hoping to 'live to see never a nobleman in England.' His ally the Earl of Essex plaintively asked: 'Is this the liberty which we claim to vindicate by shedding our blood? Posterity will say that to deliver them from the yoke of the King we have subjugated them to that of the common people.'

As Roundheads scented the possibility of victory, they became divided. Many of the original combatants were fearful of the radical forces war had unleashed. There now emerged a more conciliatory 'Peace Party' led by Manchester, Essex and Sir

William Waller hoping for a negotiated settlement with the King. However, Cromwell and his followers pressed for a continuation of the conflict in the quest for total victory. The Wiltshire commander Edmund Ludlow certainly knew which side he was on:

> by this time it was clearly manifest that the nobility had no further quarrel with the King, that till they could make their terms with him, having, for the most part, grounded their dissatisfactions upon some particular affront, or the prevalence of a faction about him…yet if a war of this nature must be determined by treaty, and the King left in the exercise of the royal authority after the utmost violation of the laws, and the greatest calamities brought upon the people, it does not appear to me what security can be given them for the future enjoyment of their rights and privileges; nor with what prudence wise men can engage with the Parliament, who being, by practice at least, liable to be dissolved at pleasure, are thereby rendered unable to protect themselves if after infinite hardships and hazards of their lives and estates, they must fall under the power of a provoked enemy, who being once re-established in his former authority, will never want means to revenge himself upon all those who, in defence of the rights and liberties of the nation, adventured to resist him in his illegal and arbitrary proceedings.

The split was also religious. Manchester and the majority of MPs in Parliament veered towards Presbyterianism, but Cromwell, Ludlow and many in the army rank and file followed a more libertarian brand of Puritanism known as 'Independency'. They viewed Presbyterianism as just as tyrannical and impure as the old Church of England. They wanted near total freedom of religion. In his evidence to the Donnington enquiry, Manchester criticised Cromwell's promotion of such dangerous religious radicals:

> Coll. Cromwell raising of his regiment makes choice of his officers, not such as were soldiers or men of estate, but such as were common men, poor and of mean parentage, only he would give them the title of godly precious men; yet his common practise was to cashier honest gentlemen and soldiers that were stout in the cause as I conceive, witness those that did suffer in that case.
>
> I have heard him oftentimes say that it must not be soldiers nor [the] Scots that must do this work, but it must be the godly to this purpose….If you look upon his own regiment of horse see what a swarm there is of those that call themselves the godly; some of them profess they have seen visions and had revelations.

The New Model Army

Despite their differences, all sides agreed that Donnington showed the army needed restructuring. With its competing regional associations and uncoordinated command structure it was failing to prosecute the war effectively. Cromwell manipulated this frustration to carve out the Roundhead old guard from positions of authority within the army. By removing Manchester, Essex and Waller from any command, Cromwell believed the army would have a far better chance of finishing off the Cavaliers. His tool was a Self-Denying Ordinance which precluded members of Parliaments, peers and MPs, from holding military command. Cromwell and his allies argued that religious and political disagreements between politicians were preventing a successful pursuit of the war. The army needed to be allowed to do its job free of political egos. The Ordinance's real purpose was to allow Cromwell and his Independent cohorts assume full control of Parliament's military operations. On 9 December 1644, Cromwell, still the MP for Cambridge, rose in Parliament to eliminate the 'Peace Party' from the conduct of war:

> It is now the time to speak, or forever hold the tongue. The important occasion now is no less than to save a nation out of a bleeding, nay almost dying, condition...casting off all lingering proceedings, like those of soldiers of fortune beyond the sea, to spin out a war...The Members of both Houses have got great places and commands, and the sword into their hands; and, will perpetually continue themselves in grandeur, and not permit the War speedily to end, lest their own power should end with it...I know the worth of those commanders, Members of both Houses, who are still in power. But, if I may speak my conscience without reflection upon any, I do conceive if the Army be not put into another method, and the War more vigorously prosecuted, the people can bear the War no longer, and they will enforce you to a dishonourable peace.

With Cromwell giving the lead, Parliament passed the Ordinance which came into effect in April 1645:

> Be it ordained by the Lords and Commons assembled in Parliament, that all and every of the members of either House of Parliament shall be, and by authority of this Ordinance are discharged at the end of forty days after the passing of this Ordinance, of and from all and every office or command military or civil, granted or conferred by both or either of the said Houses of this present Parliament, or by any authority derived from both or either of them since the 20th day of November, 1640.

With that Essex and Manchester resigned their commissions. Yet this was only the start. Cromwell's vision was to 'new model' the Roundhead army from top to bottom. In place of regional forces, he introduced a unified command structure free from the localism of the old parliamentary barons. Henceforth, soldiers were (in theory at least) paid regularly and promoted on merit. At its head was the Marston Moor hero Sir Thomas Fairfax, whose commission tellingly no longer included a clause for the preservation of the King's person. But the army preacher Richard Baxter suspected the real power did not lie with Fairfax:

> This man was chosen because they [Cromwell and his Puritan fixer in Parliament Henry Vane] supposed to find him a man of no quickness of parts, of no elocution, of no suspicious plotting wit, and therefore one that Cromwell could make use of at his pleasure. And he was acceptable to sober men, because he was religious, faithful,

valiant and of a grave, sober, resolved disposition, very fit for execution and neither too great nor too cunning to be commanded by the parliament.

For Cromwell managed to avoid the Self-Denying Ordinance. Fairfax told Parliament that Cromwell's military skills were essential in the West Country and he was given special exemption from the Ordinance. Cromwell now positioned himself at the heart of the New Model Army. By assiduously promoting Independents and other Puritan acolytes, he shaped a force in his own spiritual image. Baxter, who proudly counted himself among the godly, was taken aback by the New Model Army's fervent religiosity:

> And when the court news-book told the world of the swarms of Anabaptists in our armies, we thought it had been a mere lie, because it was not so with us nor in any of the garrison or country forces about us. But when I came to the army among Cromwell's soldiers I found a new face of things which I never dreamt of. I heard the plotting heads very hot upon that which intimated their intention to subvert both Church and State...
>
> Abundance of common troopers and many of the officers I found to be honest, sober, orthodox men, and others tractable, ready to hear the truth and of upright intentions. But a few proud, self-conceited, hot-headed sectaries had got into the highest places and were Cromwell's chief favourites, and by their very heart and activity bore down the rest or carried them along with them, and were the soul of the army, though much fewer in number than the rest...I perceived that they took the King for a tyrant and an enemy, and really intended absolutely to master him or to ruin him; and that they thought if they might fight against him they might kill or conquer him.

Opponents of the New Model Army were even less kind. Among the most sustained of its critics was Thomas Edwards whose *Gangraena: or A Catalogue and Discovery of Many of the Errours, Heresies, Blasphemies and Pernicious Practices of the Sectaries of this Time* clinically analysed the army's religious constitution:

> The Army that is so much spoken of upon all occasions in the news books, pulpits, conferences, to be Independent (though I conceive upon good information, that upon a true muster of the whole, commanders and common soldiers, there would not be found above one in six of that way) yet of that Army, called by the sectaries Independent, and of that part of it which truly is so, I do not think that there are 50 pure Independents, but higher flown, seraphical (as a Chaplain, who knows well the state of that Army, expressed it) made up and compounded of Anabaptism, Antinomianism, Enthusiasm, Arminianism, Familism, all these errors and more too sometimes meeting in the same persons, strange monsters, having heads of Enthusiasm, their bodies of Antinomianism, their thighs of Familism, their legs and feet of Anabaptism, their hands of Arminianism, and Libertinism, as the great vein going through the whole; in one word, Religion of that sort of men in the Army, is liberty of conscience, and liberty of preaching.

Sir Thomas Fairfax, Lord General of the New Model Army, contemporary engraving after Edward Bowers (WA, BL)

Edwards also records how the Puritan soldiers even baptised a horse in mockery of the sacrament:

> July the third 1646, Two citizens, honest men related to me this story in the hearing of another minister, and that with a great deal of confidence (one of them having lain in the town where the fact was committed...) that summer was a two years [since] Captain Beaumant and his company being quartered at Yakesly in Huntingdonshire, there being a child in the town to be baptised, some of the soldiers would not suffer the child to be carried to church to be baptised, and the lieutenant of the troop drew out part of the troop to hinder it, guarding the church that they should not bring the child to be baptised, and instead of the child being baptised, in contempt of Baptism, some of the soldiers got into the church, pissed in the font, and went to a gentleman's stable in the town, and took out a horse, and brought it into the church, and there baptised it, and after they had done so, such of the townsmen as spoke against them before they went away they did them mischief...in the church at the font [they] did sprinkle it on the horse, and call him Ball Esau (because he was hairy) and crossed him in the forehead. They had soldiers Godfathers, and one Widow Shropshire, a soldier so nicknamed, was the Godmother.

Certainly the catechism that was drilled into the army recruits instilled a sense of divine mission:

> *Q. What is it that you chiefly aim at in this war?*
> At the pulling down of Babylon, and rewarding her as she hath served us, *Psalms* I
>   37.8
> At the suppression of an Antichristian Prelacy consisting of Archbishops, Bishops etc.
> At the Reformation of a most corrupt, lazy, infamous, superstitious, soul-murdering
>   Clergie.
> At the advancement of Christ's Kingdom and the purity of his Ordinances.
> At the bringing to Justice the enemies of our Church and State.
> At the upholding of our Parliaments, which are the Subjects best inheritance, and the
>   Crowne of our Nation
>
> *Q. What are the principal things required in a Soldier?*
> That he be religious and godly.
> That he be courageous and valiant.
> That he be skilful in the military profession

The birth of the New Model Army was christened with the blood of Archbishop Laud. Their goal was to cleanse the nation of Popery and the first victim was Charles's most committed religious partisan. Imprisoned for over four years, on 4 January 1645 he finally followed the path of his old ally Strafford to the executioner's block. Parliament's mission was now extending far beyond the early attempts to limit royal prerogative powers and curb the more Catholic instincts of some Anglican churchmen. The civil war was beginning to turn into a political and religious revolution.

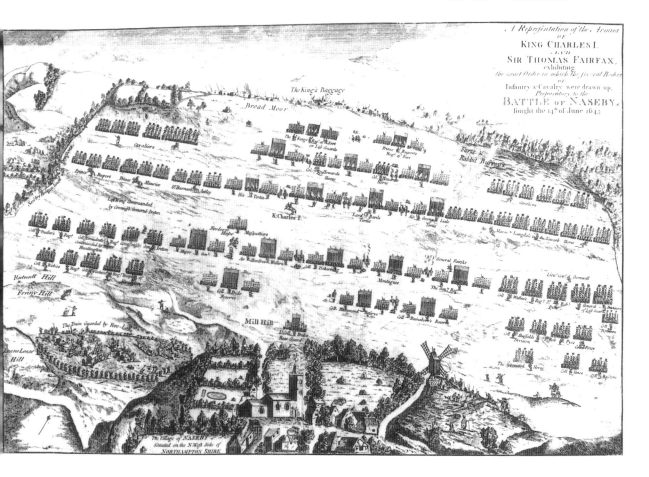

Preparation for the Battle of Naseby, contemporary engraving (BAL)

The Battle of Naseby

By early 1645, the Cavaliers' pyrrhic victory at Donnington was long since forgotten and the strategic barrenness of their position was inescapable. Charles once again searched for support in his other kingdoms, appealing to his Lord Lieutenant in Ireland, the Earl of Ormond. For some four years, Ormond had been fighting the armies of the Catholic confederates who had emerged out of the Irish rebellion of October 1641. Late in 1643 Ormond had managed to secure a cease-fire, but now showing his desperation Charles wanted a full-blown alliance with the Catholic rebels:

ORMOND,

The impossibility of preserving my Protestant subjects in Ireland by a continuation of the war, having moved me to give you those powers and directions, which I have formerly done, for the concluding of a peace there. But besides these considerations, it being now manifest that the English rebels have (as far as in them lies) given the command of Ireland to the Scots; that their aim is a total subversion of religion and regal power; and that nothing less will content them or purchase peace here, I think myself bound in conscience not to let slip the means of settling that kingdom (if it may be) fully under my obedience, nor to lose that assistance, which I may hope from my Irish subjects for such scruples as (in a less pressing condition) might reasonably be stuck at by me for their satisfaction. I do therefore command you to conclude a peace with the Irish, whatever it cost, so that my Protestant subjects there may be secured, and my regal authority preserved. But for all this, you are to make me the best bargain you can…and [if] the present taking away of the penal laws against Papists by a law will do it, I shall not think it a hard bargain, so that freely and vigorously they engage themselves in my assistance against my rebels of England and Scotland, for which no conditions can be too hard, not being against conscience and honour. So I rest

Your most assured, constant friend,

CHARLES R.

It was a forlorn hope and the promised reinforcements never arrived. Instead, Charles thought he would head north from Oxford to try and combine forces with the still-marauding Montrose in Scotland. After a successful assault on Leicester, his progress was brought to a shuddering halt. Two miles south of Market Harborough, among the ridges, streams and small hills which surround the tiny village of Naseby, the Cavaliers faced the New Model Army in what was the force's first major engagement. If Charles retained any hope of winning the civil war, it was essential he destroyed this army in its infancy.

On 14 June 1645 the battle of Naseby started with a charge led by Prince Rupert from the Cavalier right wing. What follows is the official royalist account:

About ten of the Clock the Battle began, the first Charge being given by Prince Rupert with his own and Prince Maurice's Troops; who did so well, and were so well seconded, as that they bore all down before them. Presently our Forces advanced up the Hill, the Rebels only discharging five Pieces at them, but over shot them, and so did their Musketeers. The Foot on either side hardly saw each other until they were within Carabine Shot, and so only made one Volley; ours falling in with Sword and butt end of the Musket did notable Execution; so much as I saw their Colours fall, and their Foot in great Disorder.

While Rupert cut through the Roundheads on the right, Sir Marmaduke Langdale was not having such an easy time against Cromwell on the left:

And had our left Wing but at this time done half so well as either the Foot or right Wing, we had got in few Minutes a glorious Victory. Our Foot and Right Wing being

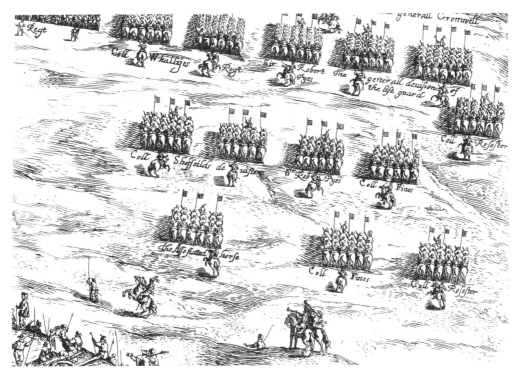

Detail from the Battle of Naseby (WA)

thus engaged, our left Wing advanced, consisting of five Bodies of the Northern and Newark Horse; who were opposed by seven great Bodies drawn to their right Wing by Cromwell who commanded there, and who besides the Advantage of Number had that of the Ground, ours marching up the Hill to encounter them. Yet I must needs say ours did as well as the Place and their Number would admit; but being flanked and pressed back, they at last gave Ground and fled: Four of the Rebels Bodies close and in good Order followed them, the rest charged our Foot.

Doing their best in the terrain wasn't good enough and Cromwell's men made quick work of it. Typically, Rupert's cavalry had also over-charged the enemy, leaving the field to the New Model Army horse. The Roundhead Ironsides destroyed the Cavalier left wing, then turned on the infantry positioned in the middle. As his foot regiments began to flee the field, King Charles decided to lead an assault from the centre. The decision backfired calamitously. Clarendon describes the moment:

The King's reserve of horse – which was his own guards, with himself in the head of them – were even ready to charge the enemy horse who followed those of the left wing, when, on a sudden, such a panic fear seized upon them that they all ran near a quarter of a mile without stopping. This happened upon an extraordinary accident, which hath seldom fallen out, and might well disturb and disorder very resolute troops, as these were the best horse in the army. The King, as was said before, was even upon the point of charging the enemy, in the head of his guards, when the Earl of Carnwath, who rode next to him – on a sudden laid his hand on the bridle of the King's horse, and swearing two or three full-mouthed Scots' oaths said, 'Will you go upon your death in an instant?' and, before his majesty understood what he would have, turned his horse round. Upon this a word ran through the troops that they should march to the right hand; which was away both from charging the enemy, or assisting their own men. Upon this they all turned their horses and rode upon the spur, as if they were every man to shift for himself.

The Cavalier army collapsed in disarray. Even the late re-emergence of Prince Rupert could not help matters:

By this time Prince Rupert was returned with a good body of those horse which had attended him in his prosperous charge on the right wing; but...they could never be brought to rally themselves again in order, or to charge the enemy. And that difference was observed shortly from the beginning of the war, in the discipline of the king's troops and of those which marched under the command of Cromwell – that though the King's troops prevailed in the charge, and routed those they charged, they never rallied themselves again in order, nor could be brought to make a second charge again the same day; which was the reason that they had not an entire victory at Edgehill. Whereas Cromwell's troops, if they prevailed, or though they were beaten and routed, presently rallied again, and stood in good order till they received new orders.

As the Cavaliers ran for their lives, Cromwell's men cut them down on the road to Leicester. According to the distraught royalist account, the final moments at Naseby turned into a bloodbath:

Our Foot had Quarter given them, but were all Prisoners, except some few Officers who escaped, and our Horse made haste, never staying until they came under the Works of Leicester, and some not thinking themselves secure there rode that Night to Newark, the first sixteen, the other at least thirty Miles from the Place of Battle. The Number slain that Day is uncertain, those of Quality slain of the King's Army were Sir Thomas, Dalizon, Sir Richard Cave...and above 100 Officers and Gentlemen out of the Northern and Newark Horse and Prince Rupert's Troops. In the Pursuit the Rebels cruelly killed above 100 Women and Soldiers Wives, and some of them of Quality; and with a Party followed us within two Miles of Leicester; whence in the Evening the King and Prince Rupert with the broken Troops marched to Ashby de la Zouche.

The slaughter of a party of Welsh prostitutes and other Cavalier mistresses, falsely believed to be Irish Catholics, was little short of a war crime. It was a harsh testimony to the increased brutality of the war as well as the religious zeal of the New Model Army.

In the aftermath of victory, Cromwell wrote an ecstatic letter to Parliament. Mingled in amongst its thanks to God and self-congratulation was a clear warning to Parliament that the army would brook no limits to full religious toleration:

Sir,

When I saw the enemy drawn up and march in gallant order towards us, and we a company of poor ignorant men, I could not but smile out to God in praises, in assurance of victory, because God would, by things that are not, bring to naught things that are…and God did it. O that men would therefore praise the Lord, and declare the wonders that He does for the children of men!…this is none other but the hand of God; and to Him alone belongs the glory, wherein none are to share with Him. The General [Fairfax] served you with all faithfulness and honour; and the best commendations I can give him is, that I dare say he attributes all to God, and would rather perish than assume to himself. Which is an honest and thriving way, and yet as much for bravery may be given to him, in this action, as to a man. Honest men served you faithfully in this action. Sir, they are trusty; I beseech you in the name of God, not to discourage them. I wish this action may beget thankfulness and humility in all that are concerned in it. He that ventures his life for the liberty of his country, I wish he trust God for the liberty of his conscience, and you for the liberty he fights for.
[Haverbrowe, 14 June 1645]

Your most humble servant,
OLIVER CROMWELL

Basing House and the Godly Reformation

In the detritus of the battle, the Roundheads had captured copies of the King's secret correspondence with the Irish Catholics. It fired their religious zeal against a king willing to ally himself with the same Papists who had slaughtered good Protestants in 1641. Such was their propaganda value, sympathetic publishers in London later issued a pamphlet, *The Kings Cabinet Opened: Or Certain Packets of Secret Letters and Papers, Written with the King's own Hand*, containing extracts from the King's correspondence:

It were a great sin against the mercies of God, to conceal those evidences of truth, which he so graciously (and almost miraculously) by surprisal of these Papers, has put into our hands; nor dare we smother this light under a Bushell, but freely hold it out to our seduced brethren…that they may see their errors, and return into the right way…Therefore, Reader, to come now to the present business of these Letters, thou art either a friend or enemy to our cause: If thou art well affected to that Cause of Liberty and Religion, which the two Parliaments of England and Scotland now maintain against a combination of all the Papists in Europe almost, especially the bloody Tigers of Ireland, and some of the prelatical and Court Faction in England: thou wilt be abundantly satisfied with these letters here printed…

The New Model Army pressed its post-Naseby advantage and began a search and destroy mission against the few remaining royalist strongholds. Cavalier support in the West Country collapsed as Bridgewater and then Bristol fell to the Roundheads.

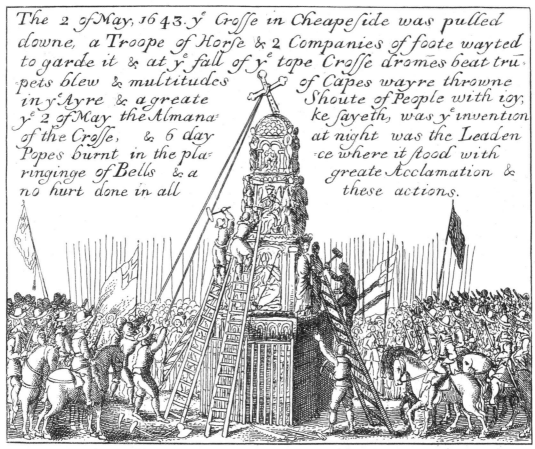

The 2 of May, 1643. y^e Crosse in Cheapeside was pulled downe, a Troope of Horse & 2 Companies of foote wayted to garde it & at y^e fall of y^e tope Crosse dromes beat trūpets blew & multitudes in y^e Ayre & a greate Shoute of People with ioy, y^e 2 of May the Almana ke sayeth, was y^e invention of the Crosse, & 6 day at night was the Leaden Popes burnt in the place where it stood with ringinge of Bells & a greate Acclamation & no hurt done in all these actions.

10 of May the Boocke of Spartes vpon the Lords day was burnt by the Hangman in the place where the Crosse stoode, & at Exhange

Contemporary engraving of Roundhead iconoclasm (BAL)

In Scotland, Montrose's luck finally ran out as the returning Covenanters hammered his guerrilla army at the Battle of Philiphaugh in September 1645. By late 1645, England was almost enveloped under parliamentary control. Only Wales, Devon and Cornwall remained royalist, as well as garrisons such as Oxford, Worcester and Newark. As the New Model Army swept the country, it celebrated its Puritan zeal with iconoclasm and gutted churches. The celebration of Christmas had already been turned from a feast day into a fast day by parliamentary edict:

> Whereas some doubts have been raised whether the next fast shall be celebrated, because it falls on the day which heretofore was usually called the Feast of the Nativity of Our Saviour, the Lords and Commons in Parliament assembled do order and ordain that public notice be given that the fast appointed to be kept on the last Wednesday in every month ought to be observed until it be otherwise ordered by both Houses of Parliament; and that this day in particular is to be kept with the more solemn humiliation, because it may call to remembrance our sins, and the sins of our forefathers, who have turned this feast, pretending the memory of Christ, into an extreme forgetfulness of him, by giving liberty to carnal and sensual delights, being contrary to the life which Christ himself led here upon earth, and to the spiritual life of Christ in our souls, for the sanctifying and saving whereof Christ was pleased both to take a human life, and to lay it down again.

The Marquis of Winchester's Catholic stronghold of Basing House in Hampshire suffered the most atrocious religious assault. While other bastions of royalism had collapsed in the wake of Naseby, Basing House held out from August until October 1645. So when it did fall, the Puritan troops let rip. Hugh Peters, an Independent minister and chaplain to Oliver Cromwell, gave an account of the carnage to Parliament:

> In the several rooms, and about the house, there were slain seventy-four, and only one woman, the daughter of Doctor Griffith, who by her railing provoked our soldiers (then in heat) into a further passion. There lay dead upon the ground, Major Cuffle, (a man of great account amongst them, and a notorious papist,) slain by the hands of Major Harrison (that godly and gallant gentleman) and Robinson the player, who a little before the storm, was known to be mocking and scorning the Parliament and our army. Eight or nine gentlewomen of rank, running forth together, were entertained by the common soldiers somewhat coarsely, yet not uncivilly, considering the action in hand. The plunder of the soldiers continued till Tuesday night. One soldier had 120 pieces in gold for his share, others plate, others jewels. Amongst the rest, one got three bags of silver, which (he being not able to keep his own counsel) grew to be common pillage amongst the rest, and the fellow had but one half crown left for himself at last. Also the soldiers sold the wheat to country people, which they held up at good rates a while, but afterwards the market fell, and there was some abatements for haste. After that they sold the household stuff, whereof there was a good store; and the country loaded away many carts, and continued a great while fetching out all

manner of household stuff, till they had fetched out all the stools, chairs, and other lumber, all which they sold to the country people by piecemeal. In these great houses there was not one iron bar left in all the windows (save only what was in the fire) before night. And the last work of all was the lead, and by Thursday morning they had hardly left one gutter about the house. And what the soldiers left, the fire took hold on…We know not how to give a just account of the number of persons that were within; for we have not three hundred prisoners, and it may be an hundred slain, whose bodies (some being covered with rubbish) came not to our view. Only riding to the house on Tuesday night, we heard divers crying in vaults for quarter, but our men could neither come to them nor they to us. But amongst those that we saw slain, one of their officers lying on the ground, seeming so exceedingly tall, was measured, and from his great toe to his crown was nine foot in length.

Victorian account of the storming of Basing House, by Ernest Crofts (BAL, Leeds City Art Gallery)

Parliament, Army and the Putney Debates

After one of the final throws of Cavalier resistance at Stow-on-the-Wold, the royalist commander and veteran of Edgehill Jacob Astley surrendered to the Roundheads with these words: 'You have done your work boys. You may go play unless you fall out amongst yourselves.' He had spoken too late. The Presbyterian Parliament and Independent Army were already at loggerheads over religion and future strategy. The former was looking for a negotiated peace and the latter for outright victory. Edmund Ludlow, now a committed New Model Army partisan, was scornful of the weak-willed MPs:

> Most of the new elected members were either men of a neutral spirit, and willing to have peace upon any terns, or such, who though they had engaged against the King, yet finding things tending to a composition with him, resolved to have the benefit of it, and his favour, though with the guilt of all the blood that had been shed in the war upon their heads, in not requiring satisfaction for the same, nor endeavouring to prevent the like for the future; designing at the most only to punish some inferior instruments, whilst the capital offender should not only go free, but his authority be still acknowledged and adored.

Ludlow wasn't the only one to notice Parliament's relative lack of enthusiasm. Following the humiliation of Naseby, the Cavaliers were finished as a fighting force. The King realised he no longer had any hope of winning the civil war through military might. Marooned in Oxford, King Charles watched with glee the divisions emerge between Parliament and army. Diplomacy was his only chance. In a letter of March 1646, he revealed his strategy was to split the two factions:

> I am endeavouring to get to London, so that the conditions may be such as a gentleman may own, and that the rebels may acknowledge me as King, being not without hope that I shall be able so to draw either the Presbyterian or Independents to side with me, for extirpating the one or the other, that I shall be really King again.

As his military empire crumbled around him, Parliament, the army and the Scottish Covenanters all waited in anticipation of the King's next move. Among the more regular visitors to his Oxford court was the French ambassador who convinced Charles his wisest choice would be to surrender himself to the Scottish Covenanters. They too were fearful of the New Model Army and were susceptible to returning him to the throne if he promised to protect their Presbyterian religion. Charles realised such a move would greatly assist his strategy of dividing the opposition. In May 1646, the King fled Oxford in disguise and made for the Covenanter camp near Newark. The Covenanters were surprised but delighted at their new guest. They removed him to Newcastle and began a six-month attempt to persuade the King of the merits of Presbyterianism. While Charles enjoyed the debate he refused to abjure his Anglicanism. In January 1647 the frustrated Covenanters handed the king over to the English Parliament (who had been seething at the Scottish abduction of the king) for £400,000. 'Cheap at the price,' Charles quipped.

With the King in their control, the Parliamentarians led by the MP Denzil Holles began negotiations for a Presbyterian settlement to the church and a return of the King to power. The New Model Army smelt a rat. They already had grievances over religious toleration, indemnity for crimes committed during war, and months of back-pay. They now feared Parliament would send them off to fight in Ireland as part of a deal with the King. Lucy Hutchinson describes the mutual distrust:

> And now it grew to a sad wonder that the zealousest promoters of the cause were more spitefully engaged against their own faithful army, by whom God had perfected their victory over their enemies, than against the vanquished foe, whose restitution they henceforth secretly endeavoured, by all the arts of treacherous, dissembling policy, only that they might throw down those who God had exalted in glory and power to resist their tyrannical impositions.....The Presbyterian faction were earnest to have the army disbanded; the army resented their injury and being thereby taught to value their own merit, petitioned the General that they might be satisfied not only in things relating to themselves particularly as an army, but the general concernments and liberties of the good people of the nation which they had fought for. The Presbyterians were highly offended at this, and declared it with such violence as gave the army cause to increase their jealousies.

In June 1647, the army took the initiative and removed the King from his parliamentary guards at Holmby House in Northamptonshire. They went on to issue a declaration crystallising the New Model Army's sense of its divine worth: 'We were not a mere mercenary army hired to serve any arbitrary power of a state, but called forth...to the defence of the people's just right and liberties.' The Army had become a political player in its own right. It marched into London, deposed Holles and the Presbyterians, and in August 1647 put a wholly new set of terms to the King. The *Heads of the Proposals* demanded extensive political and religious reforms including changes to the franchise, decentralization of power to the localities, the proper accountability of ministers in Parliament, the dismantling of the ecclesiastical hierarchy, and greater religious toleration.

However, there were splits even within the New Model Army. Just as many of the rank and file had suspected the Presbyterians in Parliament of selling them out, so they were suspicious of the 'Grandees' negotiating with the King. They elected 'Agitators' to represent their grievances. As one contemporary wag put it:

> As the King at first called a Parliament he could not rule, and afterwards the parliament raised an army it could not rule, so the army had made agitators they cannot rule. What will in the end be the conclusion of this, God only knows.

Engraving depicting the triumph of Parliament (BAL, Ashmolean Museum, Oxford)

The army rank and file fears were fuelled by a radical group known as the Levellers. Clarendon, who was now safely ensconced in Jersey with the Prince of Wales, describes their appeal:

> These spoke insolently and confidently against the King and Parliament and the great officers of the army; professed as great malice against all the lords as against the King; and declared that all degrees of men should be levelled, and an equality should be established, both in titles and estates, throughout the kingdom.

In October 1647, the Levellers issued a counter-manifesto to the *Proposals*, known as the *Agreement of the People*, demanding a far more fundamental programme of political reform which placed popular sovereignty above any other political power. As the historian John Morrill explains, at the heart of their thinking was the contention that Parliament had become just as corrupt and tyrannical as the king: 'power had to be taken away from all future governments, to prevent both kingly or parliamentary tyranny.' The Long Parliament needed to be dissolved, full manhood suffrage introduced, elections held every two years, and complete religious toleration.

Such was the breadth of support for the Levellers that Cromwell, Fairfax and the other Grandees were forced to debate their ideas at a grand meeting of the Army Council at St Mary's Church in Putney. The 'Putney Debates' of October/November 1647 are a fascinating insight into the political thought of the period. At the root of the debates was a battle over the franchise: should it be open to all men (but never women) or limited only to property holders and independent tradesmen. Cromwell's son-in-law, the increasingly influential Henry Ireton, outlined to the Leveller Rainsborough the Grandees' objections to the *Agreement*:

> COMMISSARY-GENERAL HENRY IRETON – The exception that lies in it is this. It is said, they [votes] are to be distributed according to the number of the inhabitants: 'The people of England,' etc. And this does make me think that the meaning is, that every man that is an inhabitant is to be equally considered, and to have an equal voice in the election of those representers, the persons that are for the general representative; and if that be the meaning, then I have something to say against it.

> COLONEL THOMAS RAINSBOROUGH – I think that the poorest he that is in England hath a life to live, as the greatest he; and therefore truly, sir, I think it's clear, that every man that is to live under a government ought first by his own consent to put himself under that government; and I do think that the poorest man in England is not at all bound in a strict sense to that government that he hath not had a voice to put himself under; and I am confident that, when I have heard the reasons against it, something will be said to answer those reasons, insomuch that I should doubt whether he was an Englishman or no, that should doubt of these things.

But Ireton was convinced that universal suffrage would inevitably lead to the abolition of private property:

> IRETON – Give me leave to tell you, that if you make this the rule I think you must fly for refuge to an absolute natural right, and you must deny all civil right; and I am sure it will come to that in the consequence....For my part, I think it is no right at all. I think that no person hath a right to an interest or share in the disposing of the affairs of the kingdom, and in determining or choosing those that shall determine what laws we shall be ruled by here – no person hath a right to this, that hath not a permanent fixed interest in this kingdom, and those persons together are properly the represented of the kingdom, and consequently are [also] to make up the representers of this kingdom, who taken together do comprehend whatsoever is of real or permanent interest in the kingdom....This is the most fundamental constitution of this kingdom and [that] which if you do not allow, you allow none at all. This constitution hath limited and determined it that only those shall have voices in elections....And if

we shall go to take away this, we shall plainly go to take away all property and interest that any man hath either in land by inheritance, or in estate by possession, or anything else.

RAINSBOROUGH – Truly, sir, I am of the same opinion I was….I do hear nothing at all that can convince me, why any man that is born in England ought not to have his voice in election of burgesses….I do think that the main cause why Almighty God gave men reason, it was that they should make use of that reason, and that they should improve it for that end and purpose that God gave it them…I think there is nothing that God hath given a man that any [one] else can take from him. And therefore I say, that either it must be the law of God or the law of man that must prohibit the meanest man in the kingdom to have this benefit as well as the greatest. I do not find anything in the law of God, that a lord shall choose twenty burgesses, and a gentleman but two, or a poor man shall choose none: I find no such thing in the law of nature, nor in the law of nations. But I do find that all Englishmen must be subject to English laws, and I do verily believe that there is no man but will say that the foundation of all law lies in the people, and if [it lie] in the people, I am to seek for this exemption.

Every man born in England cannot, ought not, neither by the law of God nor the law of nature, to be exempted from the choice of those who are to make laws for him to live under, and for him, for aught I know, to lose his life under. And therefore I think there can be no great stick in this.

At the core of Ireton's hostility was his opposition to the notion of a natural right. For the Grandees, man was not born with an inalienable natural right to the vote:

IRETON – All the main thing that I speak for, is because I would have an eye to property. I hope we do not come to contend for victory – but let every man consider with himself that he do not go that way to take away all property. For here is the case of the most fundamental part of the constitution of the kingdom, which if you take away, you take away all by that. Here men of this and this quality are determined to be the electors of men to the parliament, and they are all those who have any permanent interest in the kingdom, and who, taken together, do comprehend the whole [permanent, local] interest of the kingdom….Now I wish we may all consider of what right you will challenge that all the people should have right to elections. Is it by the right of nature? If you will hold forth that as your ground, then I think you must deny all property too, and this is my reason. For thus: by that same right of nature (whatever it be) that you pretend, by which you can say, one man hath an equal right with another to the choosing of him that shall govern him – by the same right of nature, he hath the same [equal] right in any goods he sees – meat, drink, clothes – to take and use them for his sustenance….

RAINSBOROUGH – to say because a man pleads that every man hath a voice [by right of nature], that therefore it destroys [by] the same [argument all property – this is to forget the law of God]. That there's a property, the law of God says it; else why [hath] God made that law, 'Thou shalt not steal'? And for my part I am against any such thought, and, as for yourselves, I wish you would not make the world believe that we are for anarchy.

Nineteenth-century painting of St Mary's Church, Putney, by Hubert J. Medlycott scene of the Putney debates (BAL)

OLIVER CROMWELL – I know nothing but this, that they that are the most yielding have the greatest wisdom; but really, sir, this is not right as it should be. No man says that you have a mind to anarchy, but [that] the consequences of this rule tends to anarchy, must end in anarchy; for where is there any bound or limit set if you take away this [limit], that men that have no interest but the interest of breathing [shall have no voice in elections]? Therefore I am confident on't, we should not be so hot one with another.

Rainsborough goes on to press a more telling point. What on earth have they been fighting for if not political equality?

RAINSBOROUGH – To the thing itself – property [in the franchise]. I would fain know how it comes to be the property [of some men, and not of others]....And I would fain know what we have fought for. [For our laws and liberties?] And this is the old law of England – and that which enslaves the people of England – that they should be bound by laws in which they have no voice at all!

IRETON – I do not speak of not enlarging this [representation] at all, but of keeping this to the most fundamental constitution in this kingdom, that is, that no person that hath not a local and permanent interest in the kingdom should have an equal dependence in election [with those that have]. But if you go beyond this law, if you admit any man that hath a breath and being, I did show you how this will destroy property.

RAINSBOROUGH – I desire to know how this comes to be a property in some men, and not in others.

COLONEL [NATHANIEL] RICH – I confess [there is weight in] that objection that the commissary-general [i.e. Ireton] last insisted upon; for you have five to one in this kingdom that have no permanent interest. Some men [have] ten, some twenty servants, some more, some less. If the master and servant shall be equal elections, then clearly those that have no interest in the kingdom will make it their interest to choose those that have no interest. It may happen, that the majority may by law, not in a confusion, destroy property; there may be a law enacted, that there shall be an equality of goods and estates.

EDWARD SEXBY – I see that though liberty were our end, there is a degeneration from it. We have engaged in this kingdom and ventured our lives, and it was all for this: to recover our birthrights and privileges as Englishmen; and by the arguments urged there is none. There are many thousands of us soldiers that have ventured our lives; we have had little propriety in the kingdom as to our estates, yet we have had a birthright. But it seems now, except a man hath a fixed estate in this kingdom, he hath no right in this kingdom. I wonder we were so much deceived. If we had not a right to the kingdom, we were mere mercenary soldiers....I shall tell you in a word my resolution. I am resolved to give my birthright to none....I do think the poor and meaner of this kingdom – have been the means of the preservation of this kingdom, I say, in their stations, and really I think to their utmost possibility; and their lives have not been [held] dear for purchasing the good of the kingdom. [And now they demand the birthright for which they fought.] Those that act to this end are as free from anarchy and confusion as those that oppose it, and they have the law of God and the law of their conscience [with them].

IRETON – For my part, rather than I will make a disturbance to a good constitution of a kingdom wherein I may live in godliness and honesty, and peace and quietness, I will part with a great deal of my birthright....

Now let us consider where our difference lies. We all agree that you should have a representative to govern, and this representative to be as equal as you can [make it]. But the question is, whether this distribution can be made to all persons equally, or whether [only] amongst those equals that have the interest of England in them. That which I have declared [is] my opinion [still].

RAINSBOROUGH – Sir, I see that it is impossible to have liberty but all property must be taken away. If it be laid down for a rule, and if you will say it, it must be so. But I would fain know what the soldier hath fought for all this while? He hath fought to enslave himself, to give power to men of riches, men of estates, to make him a perpetual slave. We do find in all presses that go forth none must be pressed that are freehold men. When these gentlemen fall out among themselves they shall press the poor scrubs to come and kill [one another for] them.

The Leveller demands were simply too radical for the Grandees who called the debates to an inconclusive halt. The New Model Army was not going to turn into a debating society. Its discipline was needed now more than ever – Charles I had escaped.

VIII

Civil War to Revolution

| 1647 November | Fearing assassination, Charles flees from Hampton Court to the Isle of Wight |
| | |

| 1647 December | Charles agrees to introduce Presbyterianism in an alliance with the Scottish Covenanters known as the Engagement |

| 1648 January | Parliament's Vote of No Addresses to Charles |

| 1648 May | Royalist rebellion in Kent |

| 1648 June | Roundhead forces besiege Colchester |

| 1648 July | Scottish army of 'Engagers' led by the Duke of Hamilton invades England on behalf of King Charles |

| 1648 August | Cromwell hammers the Scottish 'Engagers' at the Battle of Preston. Fairfax crushes Royalist rebels holed up in Colchester |

| 1648 September | Treaty of Newport between King Charles and moderates in Parliament |

| 1648 October | Victorious Cromwell welcomed into Edinburgh |

| 1648 December | Pride's Purge eliminates moderate Parliamnetarians from the House of Commons. Charles is removed from Carisbrooke Castle to Hurst Castle on the south coast |

NOT FAR UP RIVER FROM PUTNEY LIES HAMPTON COURT PALACE. As the soldiers of the New Model Army debated natural rights and manhood suffrage at St Mary's, King Charles I lingered under house arrest in his old royal palace. His plan of playing Parliament off against Army, Presbyterians against Independents, had so far come to nought. Instead, he watched with growing concern the radical direction in which the army seemed to be heading. The politics of representative democracy and social equality preached by the Levellers left little room for the divine right of kings. Fearing the threat of assassination (whether credible or not), Charles made a calamitous decision. His steadfastly loyal Groom of the Bedchamber, Sir John Ashburnham, describes the moment when Charles decided to flee:

> Not many days after Mr Legge [another royal courtier] came to me from His Majesty (for He only was permitted to continue still near Him), and told me that His Majesty was resolved to escape from Hampton Court, and commanded me to contrive it for Him; to which I did most readily submit, and promised to do my duty therein; but desired to know whether He intended to go: he replied His Majesty left that thought to me. I did again ask him whether the King had yet thought of any place to go to. He told us that He inclined to go beyond the seas, and for his part he supposed Jersey a proper place for Him. I replied that I would willingly wait on Him to what place He pleased, but His deserting the Kingdom would (in my judgement) prove very disadvantageous to His affairs, not only as a thing scarce practicable in regard of the sudden pursuit would be made after Him, and the *preparation of a vessel to transport Him, being a work of more time than could be allowed, such Cautions being to be used for the obtaining of it, as His Majesty's Condition did require;* but also, that it would make desperate all His Party, and leave the whole dominion to His Enemies, who in His absence might possibly find some more reasonable pretence to govern the Kingdom by the Parliament He had settled, than they could have if He continued in it…

Ignoring the reservations, Charles together with Ashburnham and Legge fled through the lightly guarded gardens of Hampton Court on the night of 11 November 1647. They galloped south-west towards Southampton in the hope of catching a boat to Jersey. But the journey was a fiasco. They lacked a fresh change of horses and got hopelessly lost in the New Forest. By the time they reached the coast, Ashburnham was unable to find the ship and the escape to Jersey was no longer possible. In desperation and now fearful of capture, they crossed the Solent to seek sanctuary on the Isle of Wight, despite the fact that its governor, Colonel Robert Hammond, was a Roundhead. Unsurprisingly, Hammond informed Parliament and took Charles into genteel custody within the confines of Carisbrooke Castle. The Isle of Wight nobleman, Sir John Oglander, recorded in his diaries the King's unexpected arrival:

King Charles came into our Island, Sunday the 14th of November, 1647, to my great astonishment. For, as a great while I could not be brought to believe it, so when I was certain of it, I could do nothing but sigh and weep for two nights and a day. And the reason of my grief was that I verily believed he could not come into a worse place for himself, and where he could be more securely kept.

Charles I as prisoner in Carisbrooke Castle, contemporary woodcut (AA, BL)

Yet to have the King among one's social circle was certainly a welcome addition to Newport society:

> on the Monday myself and most of the Island gentlemen went to Carisbrooke Castle to him, where he used us all most graciously and asked the names of those he knew not and, when he asked my eldest son his name, he asked me whether it was my son....Now, when we had dined, we all went up to Carisbrooke Castle, where we had not stayed half an hour before His Majesty came to us and, after he had given every man his hand to kiss, he made this speech, but not in these words but, as well as my memory will give me leave, to this effect:
>
> 'Gentlemen, I must inform you that, for the preservation of my life, I was forced

from Hampton Court. For there were a people called Levellers that had both voted and resolved of my death, so that I could no longer dwell there in safety. And, desiring to be somewhat secure till some happy accommodation may be made between me and my Parliament, I have put myself in this place, for I desire not a drop more of Christian blood should be spilt, neither do I desire to be chargeable to any of you. I shall not desire so much as a capon from any of you, my resolution in coming being but to be secured till there may be some happy accommodation made.'

While His Majesty was in our Island I went (most commonly) once a week to see him, and I seldom went but His Majesty would talk with me, sometimes almost a quarter of an hour together, but all (since he chose imprisonment) openly.

The New Model Army and the Scottish Covenanters

Charles's predicament was bleak but once again the divisions amongst his enemies gave him hope. With the signing of the *Solemn League and Covenant* in September 1643, the English Roundheads had allied themselves with the Scottish Covenanters in an anti-royal pact. Yet just as Parliament had become increasingly wary of the religious and political radicalism of the New Model Army, so too had the Presbyterian Covenanters grown resentful of the army hot-heads. In fact, more so. One of their lead negotiators in London, Robert Baillie, was openly hostile to the army's religious zealots:

> The Independents have the least zeal to the truth of God of any men we know. Blasphemous heresies are now spread here more than ever in any part of the world; yet they are not only silent, but are patrons and pleaders for liberty almost to them all.

The fear was that given the army was in control of the political agenda if it negotiated a truce with the King, then the Covenanters' Presbyterian religion (for the defence of which they had gone to war in the first place) might well be under threat:

> These matters of England are so extremely desperate, that now twice they have made me sick: except God arise, all is gone there. The imprudence and cowardice of the better part of the City and Parliament, which was triple or sextuple the greater, has permitted a company of silly rascals, which calls themselves yet no more than fourteen thousand, horse and foot, to make themselves masters of the King, and parliament, and City, and by them of all England; so that now that disgraced parliament is but a committee to act all at their pleasure, and the City is ready to fright the parliament, at every first or second boast from the army. No human hope remains but in the King's unparalleled wilfulness, and the army's unmeasurable pride. As yet they are not agreed, and some writes they are not like to agree: for in our particular I expect certainly they will agree well enough, at what distance soever their affections and principles stand. Always if the finger of God in their spirits should so far dement them as to disagree, I would think there were yet some life in the play; for I know the body of

England are overwearily long ago of the parliament, and ever hated the sectaries, but much more now for this their unexpected treachery and oppression. On the other part, the King is much pitied and desired; so if they give him not contentment, he will overthrow them.

If he and they agree, our hands are bound: we will be able, in our present posture and humour of our highly distracted people, to do nothing; and whom shall we go to help, when none calls but the King? Parliament and City, as their masters command, are ready to declare against us if we should offer to arm: but if the King would call, I doubt not if rising of the best army ever we had, for the crushing of these serpents, enemies to God and man.

There was only one solution: the Covenanters needed to make their own peace with the King. From mid-1647, when King Charles was still imprisoned in Hampton Court, the Covenanters had begun a series of discreet negotiations. Clarendon describes their diplomatic advances:

No men were fuller of professions of duty, and a resolution to run all hazards, than the Scotch commissioners; who from the time they had delivered up the King [to Parliament in January 1647] resided at London with their usual confidence, and loudly complained of the presumption of the army in seizing upon the person of the King.

Woodcut depicting Charles I in negotiation with the Scottish Covenanters (BAL)

They insinuated themselves to all those who were thought to be most constant and inseparable from the interest of the crown, with passionate undertaking that their whole nation would be united to a man in any enterprise for his majesty's service. And now, from the time his majesty came to Hampton Court, they came to him with as much presumption as if they had carried him to Edinburgh. This was the more notorious, and was thought to signify the more, because their persons were known to be most odious to all the great officers in the army, and to those who now governed in the Parliament. And here the foundation of the Engagement was laid which was endeavoured to be performed the next year ensuing.

Seeing no hope of regaining his power through either Parliament or the Army, Charles decided to throw his lot in with the Scots. Isolated in Carisbrooke Castle, on 24 December 1647 he rejected Parliament's settlement of the *Four Bills* – an unattractive offer which would have stripped the King of all fiscal authority and power over Parliament – and two days later signed the *Engagement* with the Covenanters at Carisbrooke. Ashburnham offers the rationale:

> His Majesty totally despairing of any good either by Parliament or Army and in hopes to get into France, from whence He might wait advantages by the promised Army from Scotland, most heartily embraced the Treaty with the Scots Commissioners, and came in two days to a conclusion of all things; nothing being desired of the King but that as many of His English subjects as were willing to take the Covenant might do it, without being liable to punishment for it, but on their parts all imaginable Supplies that the Kingdom of Scotland could afford towards the restoring His Majesty to His just Rights were undertaken.

The *Engagement* declared that in return for an invasionary force, King Charles would introduce Presbyterianism for three years and outlaw the wilder sects of Independency:

> His Majesty giving belief to the professions of those who have entered into the League and Covenant, and that their intentions are real for preservation of His Majesty's person and authority according to their allegiance, and no ways to diminish his just power and greatness, His Majesty, so soon as he can with freedom, honour and safety be present in a free Parliament, is content to confirm the said League and Covenant by Act of Parliament in both kingdoms. His Majesty will likewise confirm by Act of Parliament in England, Presbyterial government, the directory for worship, and Assembly of Divines at Westminster for three years….and that a free debate and consultation be had with the Divines at Westminster, and with such as shall be sent from the Church of Scotland, whereby it may be determined by His Majesty and the two Houses how the Church government, after the said three years, shall be fully established as is most agreeable to the Word of God: that an effectual course shall be taken by Act of Parliament, and all other ways needful or expedient, for suppressing the opinions and practices of Anti-Trinitarians, Anabaptists, Antinomians, Arminians, Familists, Brownists, Separatists, Independents, Libertines, and Seekers, and generally for suppressing all blasphemy, heresy, schism, and all such scandalous doctrines and

practices as are contrary to the light of nature, or to the known principles of Christianity.

…upon the issuing of the said Declarations, that an army shall be sent from Scotland into England, for preservation and establishment of religion, for defence of His Majesty's person and authority, and restoring him to his government, to the just right of the Crown and his full revenues, for defence of the privileges of Parliament and liberties of the subject, for making a firm union between the kingdoms, under His Majesty and his posterity, and settling a lasting peace; in pursuance whereof the kingdom of Scotland will endeavour that there may be a free and full Parliament in England, and that His Majesty may be with them in honour, safety and freedom…. and that His Majesty shall contribute his utmost endeavours both at home and abroad for assisting the kingdom of Scotland in carrying on this war by sea and land, and for their supply by monies, arms, ammunition, and all other things requisite, as also for guarding the coasts of Scotland with ships, and protecting all Scottish merchants in the free exercise of trade and commerce with other nations; and His Majesty is very willing and doth authorise the Scots army to possess themselves of Berwick, Carlisle, Newcastle-upon-Tyne, Tynemouth, and Hartlepool, for to be places of retreat and magazine, and, when the peace of the kingdom is settled, the kingdom of Scotland shall remove their forces, and deliver back again the said towns and castles…

On hearing the news, Parliament and the Army went into apoplexy at this latest royal betrayal. Clarendon accuses Cromwell of inciting the dangerous new mood against the King:

Cromwell declared that the King was a man of great parts and a great understanding (faculties they had hitherto endeavoured to have him thought to be without) but that he was so great a dissembler, and so false a man, that he was not to be trusted. He also declared that whilst the King professed with all solemnity that he referred himself wholly to the Parliament and depended wholly upon their wisdom and counsel for the settlement and composing the distractions of the Kingdom, he had at the same time secret treaties with the Scots' commissioners how he might embroil the nation in a new war and destroy the Parliament. Cromwell concluded that they might no farther trouble themselves with sending messages to the King, or farther propositions, but that they might enter upon those counsels which were necessary towards the settlement of the Kingdom without having further recourse to the King.

On 17 January 1648, Parliament passed the *Vote of No Addresses*, breaking off all official negotiations with the King:

The Lords and Commons assembled in Parliament, after many addresses to His Majesty for the preventing and ending of this unnatural war raised by him against his Parliament and kingdom, having lately sent Four Bills to His Majesty which did contain only matter of safety and security to the Parliament and kingdom, referring the composure of all other differences to a personal treaty with His Majesty; and having received an absolute negative, do hold themselves obliged to use their utmost endeavours speedily to settle the present government in such a way as may bring the greatest security to this kingdom in the enjoyment of the laws and liberties thereof; and in

Charles I trying to escape through the bars of his window at Carisbrooke Castle, 1648 broadsheet (WA, British Library)

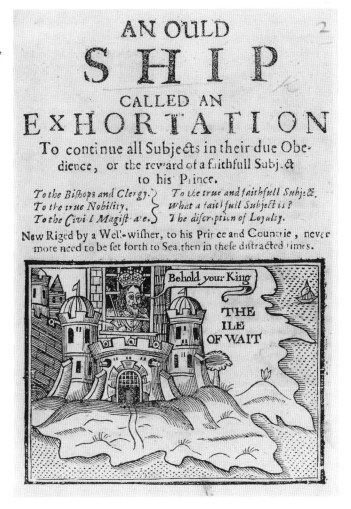

order thereunto, and that the House may receive no delays nor interruptions in so great and necessary a work, they have taken these resolutions, and passed these votes, viz.:

1. That the Lords and Commons do declare that they will make no further addresses or applications to the King.
2. That no application or addresses be made to the King by any person whatsoever, without the leave of both Houses.
3. That the person or persons that shall make breach of this order shall incur the penalties of high treason.
4. That the two Houses declare they will receive no more any message from the King; and do enjoin that no person whatsoever do presume to receive or bring any message from the King to both or either of the House of Parliament, or to any other person.

They were now focused on drawing up a political settlement that excluded Charles Stuart. It was not yet a settlement that excluded the institution of monarchy.

Flight and Fury

As the winter turned into the spring of 1648, war loomed on the horizon. In Scotland, the 'Engagers' (as they were known) began to mass troops under the flawed leadership of the veteran Caroline courtier, the Marquis of Hamilton. Charles meanwhile became more and more nervous. In March 1648, he attempted a series of escapes from Carisbrooke Castle, all of which were unsuccessful. Ashburnham describes the farcical nature of one attempted flight to France:

> What I had proposed to Him concerning His escape was very welcome, and in order thereto would have me wait for Him every night at the sea-side, till He discharged me, for most assuredly He would do his part, being confident of the assistance of one about Him, and having discovered (upon trial) that He could pass His body between the bars of the window of His Chamber, because He found there was room enough for His head (the rule being that where the head can pass the body may); but most unhappily He mistook the way of measure, for instead of putting forth His head sideways, He did it right forward; by which Error, when all things wee adjusted for His escape the second time, and that He thought to put in execution, what He thought so sure (His passage through the window) He stuck fast in it, and (as He was pleased to send me word) did strain so much in the attempt, as He was in great extremity, though with long and painful struggling He got back again, without any certain notice taken by any man, but by him who waited to have served Him when He had come down.

So began the legend of Charles attempting to squeeze himself through the bars of Carisbrooke. Clarendon was dismissive of Ashburnham's account – perhaps believing such stories did not reflect well on the King's dignity:

> Being in this readiness, the night was appointed, and Osborne [the King's gentleman-usher] was at the place where he was appointed to receive the King. But one of the soldiers informed Rolfe [Carisbrooke guard and Cromwell loyalist]...By this Rolfe concluded that Osborne was false, and directed the soldier to proceed and stand sentry in the same place to which he had been assigned. Rolfe, and some others trusted by him, were armed and stood very near with their pistols. At midnight the King came to the window, resolving to go out; but as he was putting himself out, he discerned more persons to stand thereabout than usually did so, and thereupon suspected that there was some discovery made. So he shut the window and retired to his bed. And this was all the ground of a discourse which then flew abroad, that the King had got half out at the window, and could neither draw his body after nor get his head back, and was so compelled to call out for help – which was a mere fiction.

True or not, the King was hopelessly marooned on the Isle of Wight, unable to assist a rebellion or to be rescued. It was a predicament he might have given slightly more thought to before the ill-fated dash from Hampton Court.

Across the country support was growing for the royalist position. People were tired of war. More specifically, they resented the heavy taxes imposed by Parliament to fund the New Model Army. These demands were felt particularly hard during years of bad harvest and disrupted trade. Many also longed for the old rhythms of the Church of England rather than the barren preaching and gutted churches of the Puritan revolution.

Many Englishmen wanted a return to the popular festivals and communal celebrations that the Roundheads had outlawed. Clarendon enthusiastically recounts the mood:

> If a universal discontent and murmuring of the three nations, and almost as general a detestation both of Parliament and army, and a most passionate desire that all their follies and madness might be forgotten in restoring the King to all they had taken from him and in the settling that blessed government they had deprived themselves of, could have contributed to his majesty's recovery, never people were better disposed to erect and repair again the building they had so maliciously thrown and pulled down. In England there was a general discontent amongst all sorts of men. Many officers and soldiers who had served the Parliament from the beginning of the war, and given too great testimonies of their courage and fidelity, and had been disbanded upon the making of the new model, looked upon the present army with contempt, as those who reaped the harvest and reward of their labours, and spake of them and against them in all places accordingly. The nobility and gentry, who had advanced the credit and reputation of the Parliament by concurring with it against the King, found themselves totally neglected, and the most inferior people preferred to all places of trust and profit.

Conversely, but not surprising given his views, Edmund Ludlow saw the resentment arise against Parliament because of a lack of action against the King:

> Much time being spent since the Parliament had voted no more addresses to be made to the King, nor any messages received from him, and yet nothing done towards bringing the King to a trial, or the settling of affairs without him; many of the people who had waited patiently hitherto, finding themselves as far from a settlement as ever, concluded that they should never have it, nor any ease from their burdens and taxes, without an accommodation with the King; and therefore entered into a combination through England, Scotland, and Ireland, to restore him to his authority.

Yet as Ludlow goes on to show, there was now a new, more deadly hostility to the King in parliamentary and military circles. Charles's decision to enter a military alliance with the Scots and set the country back on the road to war opened up more fundamental questions about the wisdom of having so much political power focused in one man:

> The Commonwealths-men declared that monarchy was neither good in itself, nor for us. That it was not desirable in itself, they urged from the 8th chapter and 8th verse of the first Book of Samuel, where the rejecting of the Judges, and the choice of a King, was charged upon the Israelites by God himself as a rejection of him. And that it was

no way conducing to the interest of this nation, was endeavoured to be proved by the infinite mischiefs and oppressions we had suffered under it, and by it: that indeed our ancestors had consented to be governed by a single person, but with this proviso, that he should govern according to the direction of the law, which he always bound himself by oath to perform: that the King had broken this oath, and thereby dissolved our allegiance; protection and obedience being reciprocal: that having appealed to the sword for the decision of the things in dispute, and thereby caused the effusion of a deluge of the peoples blood, it seemed to be a duty incumbent upon the representatives of the people to call him to an account for the same; and then to proceed to the establishment of an equal commonwealth founded upon the consent of the people, and providing for the rights and liberties of all men.

While these were truly radical sentiments, it is interesting to note that they are founded on a fundamentally conservative principle that the King could be deposed not for abrogating new powers but for failing to fulfil his traditional coronation oaths. Other members of the army had less high-flown ideals. They simply wanted revenge against the man who had brought so much bloodshed into their lives. As skirmishes began to break out in April 1648, the New Model Army held an extraordinary prayer meeting at Windsor Castle. There they decided that if God granted them victory, it was their duty to bring King Charles to account – personally:

[The Lord] did direct our steps, and presently we were led, and helped to a clear agreement amongst ourselves, not any dissenting, that it was the duty of our day, with the forces we had, to go out and fight against those potent enemies, which that year in all places appeared against us, with an humble confidence in the name of the Lord only, that we should destroy them; also enabling us then, after serious seeking his face, to come to a very clear and joint resolution, on many grounds at large then debated amongst us, that it was our duty, if ever the Lord brought us back again in peace, to call Charles Stuart, that man of blood, to an account, for that blood he had shed, and mischief he had done, to his utmost, against the Lord's cause and people in these poor nations: and how the Lord led and prospered us in all our undertakings this year, in this way, cutting his work short in righteousness, making it a year of mercy equal, if not transcendent to any since these wars began, and making it worthy of remembrance by every gracious soul, who was wise to observe the Lord and operations of his hands.

The scene was now set for the short and bloody 'Second Civil War.'

The Second Civil War

The second English Civil War, which was little more than a desperate royal uprising, erupted in late March in Pembroke. Soon large parts of Wales, which was always a stronghold of royalist and Anglican sentiment, were in revolt against their dictatorial Puritan masters. The rebellion spread to Kent, to Berwick and Carlisle in the north, and even onto the naval fleet harboured in the Downs. The New Model Army reacted with brutal efficiency. Fairfax headed south-east to deal with the Kent rebels, while Cromwell marched west to suppress Wales and confront the suspected Scottish invasion. Fairfax's army made a gory progress through the Kentish towns taking Dover, Rochester and Maidstone. The royalist ringleaders eluded his grasp, retreating behind the high walls of Colchester, but their sanctuary soon turned to grim incarceration when Fairfax besieged the town with more than 5,000 troops. Conditions inside were appalling as Fairfax cut the water supply and destroyed the surrounding suburbs. He refused to let women and children leave. A trapped royalist gives an account of their desperate attempts to stave off hunger:

> It was thought most convenient to keep those horse, which were fitting, for the Soldiers to eat; so they were again drawn into the Castle yard, with order that not any Officer whatsoever should conceal his Horses, but cause them to be brought into the field, upon the forfeiture of them to immediate slaughter; and the third part of every Troop drawn out and disposed to the Commissary to be killed, and some to be immediately distributed, and the rest powdered; which the Soldiers very willingly submitted to, and as cheerfully fed upon them, rather than deliver themselves to their Enemies, upon any base or dishonourable terms, which expressions of theirs were so common and public, as that the Enemy hearing of our falling to Horse-flesh, heard also of that resolution of the Soldiery, which did something startle them; for before they hoped for, and expected, our daily submission to a Treaty for Rendition.
>
> Now upon the last search that was made in the Townsmen's houses and shops for all things edible, there was very little Corn found, as in some houses not above a peck, and in some two, some none, or any Flesh hardly, yet was there a good quantity of spice and Oil; which so far as it would hold out, proved very useful with the Horse-flesh; some starch also was found, which was preserved, and made very good puddings.

By the end of August 1648, the besieged royalists could see no chance of reinforcements and capitulated. There followed an orgy of destruction as the Roundheads poured into the buckled town:

> And having thus possessed themselves of this House, (as it is their custom in all other places, the first thing thought on is plunder) they fell to searching the House, and those things that were in it moveable though little of worth, or convenience they took away; which could be little more then bedsteads, and stools, and the like. That house having been divers times before, and indeed the first in the Kingdom, as is believed plundered: But finding themselves no better rewarded for their service, that they might be more notorious in their villainy, broke up the vault wherein the ancestors of that Family were usually Interred, under the pretence of searching for money, and finding them not yet quit dissolved, the corpses of the Lady *Lucas*, and the Lady *Killigrew*, (as I received it from eye witnesses) wrapped in Lead; they tore open that

coffin, beyond what ever was known or read of before, or amongst the most inhumane barbarous thoughts, dismembered their trunks, throwing a leg in one corner of the vault, and arm in another, and were so Impudent in this so and worse than brutish act, as to bear away the hair of their heads in their Hats as a triumphant bravado in honour to their villainy....Is not that Commonwealth happy that must receive a reformation from such Saints? Who have these ten years been practising acts, absolutely monstrous to even nature itself: Beyond parallel, precedent, or political complement of the most subtle Machiavellian, or bloody Tyrants in the world.

As his soldiers embarked on their plunder, Fairfax showed he was not in a forgiving mood. Clarendon recounts the martial law meted out to the royalist ringleaders:

> They sent to Fairfax, to treat about the delivery of the town upon reasonable conditions; but he refused to treat, or to give any conditions, if they would not render to mercy all the officers and gentlemen.
>
> They were required presently to send a list of all their names to the General, which they presently did. Within a short time after, a guard was sent to bring Sir Charles Lucas and Sir George Lisle to the General, who being sat with his council of war, they were carried in and, in a very short discourse, told that it was necessary, for the example of others, and that the peace of the kingdom might be no more disturbed in that manner, that some military justice should be executed. Therefore that council had determined that they should be presently shot to death, for which they were advised to prepare themselves.
>
> Sir Charles Lucas was their first work, who fell dead. Upon this George Lisle ran to him, embraced and kissed him, and then stood upon and looked those who were to execute him in the face. Thinking they stood at too great a distance, he spoke to them to come nearer. One of them said 'I'll warrant you, sir, we'll hit you,' to which he answered, smiling, 'Friends, I have been nearer you when you have missed me.' Thereupon they all fired upon him, and did their work home, so that he fell down dead of many wounds without speaking another word.

Such summary executions were novel in the war. It testified to a bitter determination to bring six years of conflict to an end.

In the north of England, Cromwell enjoyed similar success. Having crushed the royalists in Wales, Cromwell marched north to confront Hamilton's army of Engagers who had crossed the border and joined with a Cavalier force led by Sir Marmaduke Langdale. On 17 August 1648, at Ribbleton Moor on the outskirts of Preston, Cromwell caught up with the Royalists with devastating results. A powerful cavalry charge by the Ironsides was followed up with an infantry push. Despite brave resistance, the Royalists were driven back to Preston. In a disastrous series of orders and counter-orders, they collapsed under the onslaught. More than 1,000 were killed and a staggering 4,000 taken prisoner. It took a further two days to finish off the force. But at Warrington on 19 August, the unenthusiastic Scottish army finally surrendered. Cromwell wrote back to the House of Commons in glory:

You see by computation about two-thousand of the enemy slain; betwixt eight and nine thousand prisoners, besides what are lurking in hedges and private places, which the country daily bring in or destroy. Where Langdale and his broken forces are, I know not, but they are exceedingly shattered.

Surely, Sir, this is nothing but the hand of God, and wherever anything in this world is exalted, or exalts itself, God will pull it down, for this is the day wherein He alone will be exalted. It is not fit for me to give advice, nor to say a word what use should be made of this, more than to pray you, and all that acknowledge God, that they would exalt Him, and not hate His people, who are as the apple of His eye, and for whom even Kings shall be reproved; and that you would take courage to do the work of the Lord, in fulfilling the end of your magistracy, in seeking the peace and welfare of the people of this Land, that all that will live quietly and peaceable may have countenance from you, and they that are implacable and will not leave troubling the Land may speedily be destroyed out of the land. And if you take courage in this, God will bless you and good men will stand by you, and God will have glory, and the Land will have happiness by you in despite of all your enemies. Which shall be the prayer of,

[Warrington, 20 August, 1648]
> Your most humble and faithful servant,
> O. CROMWELL.

Woodcut of a Leveller tract expressing the militancy of the New Model Army rank and file (BAL)

The Endgame

With the New Model Army mopping up the remnants of royalism in the north of England, Parliament seized the opportunity for one last attempt at negotiation with the King. In early September 1648, in total disavowal of the *Vote of No Addresses*, a selection of parliamentary commissioners travelled to Newport on the Isle of Wight to speak directly to Charles. They were, according to Clarendon, shocked at the state of the 48-year-old monarch:

> They who had not seen the King since the time that he had left Hampton Court, found his countenance extremely altered. From the time that his own servants had been taken from him he would never suffer his hair to be cut, nor cared to have any new clothes, so that his aspect and appearance was very different from what it had used to be. Otherwise his health was good, and he was much more cheerful in his discourses towards all men than could have been imagined, after such mortification of all kinds. He was not at all dejected in his spirits, but carried himself with the same majesty he had used to do. His hair was all grey, which, making all others very sad, made it thought that he had sorrow in his countenance, which appeared only by that shadow.

Terrified by the forces the civil war had unleashed, the Parliamentarians were desperate for some kind of negotiated settlement:

> The truth is, there were amongst the commissioners many who had been carried with the violence of the stream, and would have been glad of those concessions which the King would very cheerfully gave granted; an act of indemnity and oblivion being what they were principally concerned in. Of all the rest, who were more passionate for the militia and against the church, there was no man, except Sir Harry Vane, who did not desire that a peace might be established by that treaty. For, as all the other lords desired, in their own natures and affections, no more than that their transgressions might never more be called to remembrance, so the Lord Saye himself well foresaw what would become of his peerage if the treaty proved ineffectual and the army should make its own model of the government. Therefore he did all he could to work upon the king to yield to what was proposed to him, and afterwards upon the Parliament to be content with what his majesty had yielded.

Charles foolishly interpreted their eagerness as weakness. He still, even at this late stage, did not realise the total poverty of his position. The negotiations ground on remorselessly. In the end the sticking point was religion:

> The first proposition being thus consented to as they could wish, they delivered their second, concerning religion and the church. This comprehended the utter abolishing episcopacy, and all jurisdiction exercised by archbishops, bishops, deans and chapters, and the alienating their lands, which should be sold to the use and benefit of the commonwealth. The Covenant was to be presented to his majesty to take himself, and to

impose upon all others. The Common Prayer and public liturgy of the church were to be abolished and taken away; and the reformation of religion according to the Covenant, in such manner as both Houses had or should agree, after consultation with divines, should be settled by Act of Parliament. This pregnant proposition, containing so many monstrous particulars, sufficiently warned his majesty how impossible it would be to give them satisfaction in all.

If Charles thought the commissioners were not offering enough, there was an equal body in Parliament and the New Model Army who thought they were going too far. Edmund Ludlow dismissed the Newport Treaty, wanting no more to do with Charles Stuart, that 'man of blood':

I could not consent to the counsels of those who were contented to leave the guilt of so much blood upon the nation, and thereby to draw down the just vengeance of God upon us all; when it was most evident that the war had been occasioned by the invasion of our rights, and open breach of our laws and constitution on the King's part.

The Commissioners that were appointed to manage the treaty with the King, returned with the King's answer, containing neither a positive grant, nor an absolute denial. As to the bishops, he still retained his principle of their Divine right, and therefore declared that he could not dispense with the abolition of them; but for present satisfaction, hoping by giving ground to gain a better opportunity to serve them, he consented that those who had bought their lands should have a lease of them for some years: and for satisfaction for the blood that had been shed, he was willing that six should be excepted; but withal care was taken, that they should be such as were far enough from the reach of justice. By another article, the militia was to remain in the Parliament for ten years: thereby implying, if I mistake not, that the right of granting it was in the King, and consequently that we had done him wrong in contending with him for it. By such ways and means did some men endeavour to abuse the nation.

Under the guidance of Henry Ireton, the Army now proposed a different solution. The *Army Remonstrance* was presented to Parliament on 20 November 1648. It demanded an end to the Newport negotiatons, the dissolution of the Long Parliament and a reformed franchise. It also called for the trial of King Charles I on the charge of high treason. Clarendon describes the new mood:

It was with great impudence very vehemently urged that they ought to begin with him who had been the cause of all the miseries and mischiefs which had befallen the kingdom, and whom they had already divested of all power and authority to govern them for the future. They had already had near two years' experience that the nation might be very happily governed without any recourse to him: and they had already declared—in which the House of Peers had concurred with them – that the king had been the cause of all the blood which had been spilt. Therefore they thought it was fit that such a man of blood should be brought to justice, that he might undergo the penalty that was due for his tyranny and murders; that the people expected this at their hands; and that, having the principle malefactor in their hands, he might not escape the punishment that was due to him.

Yet there was still enough royal support in Parliament to hinder this solution. Ludlow recalls how the Army solved the impasse:

> Some of the principal officers of the army came to London, with expectation that things would be brought to this issue; and consulting with some members of Parliament and others, it was concluded after a full and free debate, that the measures taken by the Parliament [Newport negotiations] were contrary to the trust reposed in them, and tending to contract the guilt of the blood that had been shed upon themselves, and the nation: that it was therefore the duty of the army to endeavour to put a stop to such proceedings; having engaged in the war, not simply as mercenaries, but out of judgment and conscience, being convinced that the cause in which they were engaged was just. Being come to this resolution, three of the members of the House and three of the officers of the army withdrew into a private room, to consider of the best means to attain the ends of our said resolution, where we agreed that the army should be drawn up the next morning, and guards placed in Westminster Hall, the Court of Requests, and the Lobby; that none might be permitted to pass into the House but such as had continued faithfully to the publick interest. To this end we went over the names of all the members one by one, giving the truest characters we could of their inclinations, wherein I presume we were not mistaken in many. Col. Pride commanded the guard that attended at the Parliament-doors, having a list of those members who were to be excluded, preventing them from entering into the House.

On 6 December 1648, Colonel Pride stood outside the Commons and refused entry to any MP suspected of Presbyterian leanings. One exiled politician unhappily recalls the purge:

> Wednesday the 6 of December 1648 before eight in the morning, the army sent a party of horse and foot to beset all passages and avenues to the two houses of parliament to frighten away the members; yet many members of us repairing to the House, were seized upon, and carried prisoners by the soldiers into the queen's court; nothing being objected against us; nor no authority vouched for it; at last the number shut up prisoners in the queen's court amounted to 41....the coaches carried us all to Master Duke's alehouse in *Hell*, and there thrust us in to spend the night without any accommodation of beds, etc. only Colonel Hewson came to us, and offered it as a courtesy, that some of the eldest should be suffered to lie at home that night, engaging to render themselves the next morning by 9 of the clock at Colonel Hewson's lodgings in Whitehall, which was refused, it not being thought fit we should so far own an usurped authority. All this is done in pursuance of the army's last *Remonstrance* and *Declaration*, and in subversion of the king, and his posterity, parliament, city, and kingdom; the utter extirpation of all law, government, and religion: and the converting of our well-regulated monarchy into a military anarchy, with a popular parliament of the meanest of the commons, only at the beck of the army.

The so-called 'Rump Parliament' set in motion the trial of the King. Few among the Rump were committed republicans. Most were either driven by religious zeal

Playing card ridiculing the 'Rump Parliament', seventeenth-century (WA)

to cleanse the nation of the 'man of blood' or simply distrusted Charles, seeing no end to the war with him still alive. It was more a question of political necessity than a triumph of republican ideology. In typically weasel words, Cromwell summed up the mood of the army Grandees:

> Mr. Speaker, if any man whatsoever had carried on this design of deposing the King and disinheriting his posterity, or if any man had yet such a design, he should be the greatest traitor and rebel in the world. But since the Providence of God hath cast this upon us, I cannot but submit to Providence, though I am not yet provided to give you my advice.

Charles meanwhile had been transported from Carisbrooke Castle to Hurst Castle on the south coast. It was, as his attendant Thomas Herbert describes, a bleak destination:

> The wind and tide favouring, they crossed that narrow sea in three hours, and landed at Hurst Castle erected by order of King Henry VIII upon a spot of earth a good way into the sea, and joined to the firm land by a narrow neck of sand which is covered over with small loose stones and pebbles, and upon both sides the sea beats, so as at spring tides and stormy weather the land passage is formidable and hazardous. The Castle has very thick stone walls, and the platforms are regular, and both have several culverines and sakers mounted, which if their shot doth not reach such ships as pass that narrow strait that is much frequented, they threaten them; nevertheless a dismal receptacle or place for so great a Monarch....His Majesty was very slenderly accommodated at this place. The Room he usually eat in, was neither large nor lightsome; at Noon-day (in that winter season) requiring candles; and at night he had his wax lamp set (as formerly) in a silver bason, which illuminated his Bedchamber.

The trappings of monarchy, which the King had always previously enjoyed while in custody, were withdrawn. He was now a prisoner of the state. At Hurst Castle, he must have realised how far his futile negotiations, his endless scheming, his foolish escapes had brought him. Charles was on the road to the scaffold.

IX

Tyrant, Traitor, Murderer and Public Enemy

1648 *10 December*	The Rump Parliament reinstates the Vote of No Addresses and annuls the Newport proposals	**1649** *10 January*	Provincial judge John Bradshaw is appointed President of the High Court of Justice
1648 *23 December*	Parliament orders Charles's trial and the King is taken to Windsor	**1649** *13 January*	Charles is taken to London
1649 *1 January*	Parliamentary ordinance proposes a special court for Charles's trial	**1649** *20 January*	The trial of the King begins
1649 *4 January*	The Rump Parliament decrees itself the supreme authority in the country	**1649** *27 January*	Charles is condemned to death by execution
1649 *8 January*	The High Court of Justice discusses procedure for Charles's trial	**1649** *30 January*	King Charles I is executed outside the Banqueting House, Whitehall

ON 1 JANUARY 1649, THE DEPLETED HOUSE OF COMMONS PASSED AN ACT TO ERECT A HIGH COURT OF JUSTICE TO TRY KING CHARLES FOR TREASON:

> Whereas it is notorious, that Charles Stuart, the now King of England, not content with those many encroachments which his predecessors had made upon the people in their Rights and Freedoms, hath had a wicked design totally to subvert the ancient and fundamental Laws and Liberties of this Nation, and in their trade to introduce an Arbitrary and Tyrannical Government, and that besides all other evil Ways and Means to bring this design to pass. He hath prosecuted it with fire and sword levyed, and maintained a cruel War in the Land against the Parliament and Kingdom, whereby the Country has been miserably wasted, the public treasure exhausted, trade decayed thousands of people murdered, and other infinite mischiefs committed for all which high and treasonable offences the said Charles Stuart might long since justly have been brought to exemplary and condign punishment.
>
> For prevention therefore of the like or greater inconveniences, and to the end no chief Officer or magistrate whatsoever, may hereafter presume Traitorously and maliciously to imagine or contrive the enslaving or destroying of the English Nation and to expect impunity for so doing: Be it ordained and enacted by the Commons in Parliament, and it is hereby ordained and enacted by the Authority thereof, That [the following persons] shall be and are hereby appointed and required to be Commissioners and Judges for the hearing, trying and adjudging of the said Charles Stuart and the said Commissioners or any twenty or more of them, shall be and are hereby authorised and constituted a High Court of Justice....for the charging of him the said Charles Stuart with the crimes and treasons above mentioned, and for the receiving of his personal answer thereunto, and for the examination of witnesses upon oath, which the court hath hereby authority to administer, or otherwise, and taking any other evidence concerning the same, and thereupon, or in default of such answer, to proceed to final sentence to execute or cause to be executed speedily and impartially.

Now under the *de facto* control of the New Model Army, Parliament set up a kangaroo court to murder a king. Its purpose was to validate the sentence of execution already decided upon by Cromwell and to provide some semblance of legitimacy to this unprecedented act. The House of Lords was bypassed, the Scottish Parliament ignored, and the rule of law abrogated as Cromwell along with his son-in-law Ireton pressed on with the final solution to the civil war. One hundred and thirty-five commissioners were nominated to try the King in the sweeping Gothic environs of Westminster Hall. Among the chosen were Edmund Ludlow and Colonel Hutchinson. Lucy Hutchinson describes how her husband,

Charles I before the High Court of Justice at Whitehall, 27 January 1649, contemporary engraving (BAL)

TYRANT, TRAITOR, MURDERER AND PUBLIC ENEMY

Very much against his own will, was put in; but looking upon himself as called hereunto, he durst not refuse it, as holding himself obliged by the covenant of God and the public trust of his country reposed in him, although he was not ignorant of the danger he run as the condition of things then were.

Numerous commissioners refused to go through with the trial – not least the New Model Army general Sir Thomas Fairfax who carefully excused himself from the court. Interestingly, another who dropped out of the trial was the republican ideologist Algernon Sydney who held deep reservations about the legality of the proceedings:

> I did positively oppose Cromwell, Bradshaw, and others who would have the trial to go on, and drew my reasons from these two points. First the King could not be tried by no court [sic], secondly that no man could be tried by that court. This being alleged in vain, and Cromwell using these formal words, 'I tell you we will cut off his head with the crown on it,' I replied, 'You may take your own course, I cannot stop you, but I will keep myself clear from having any hand in this business', immediately went out of the room and never returned.

The bullet-proof hat of the trial judge President Bradshaw (BAL, Ashmolean Museum, Oxford)

The President of the court was named as John Bradshaw – an obscure provincial judge with a solid Puritan pedigree and willing to carry out Ireton's every whim. Three Lord Chief Justices as well as the parliamentarian lawyer Bulstrode Whitelocke had all refused the poisoned chalice. As the trial date loomed, Charles was transferred from Hurst Castle to Windsor Castle and then to London, where he stayed in the Westminster house of Sir Robert Cotton during his trial.

The Trial

On 20 January 1649, the trial of King Charles I began. Barely half the appointed commissioners turned up for the case. Fearing assassination, Bradshaw wore a bullet-proof hat throughout the proceedings. Charles on the other hand looked his regal best dressed in black with a sumptuous silver star denoting the Order of the Garter embroidered on his cloak. Despite his waned complexion and grey hair, he adopted a pose of supreme insouciance to those around him. As the official report records, President Bradshaw started the proceedings:

> *Lord President.* Charles Stuart, King of England, the commons of England assembled in Parliament being deeply sensible of the calamities that have been brought upon this nation, which is fixed upon you as the principal author of it, have resolved to make

inquisition for blood; and according to that debt and duty they owe to justice, to god, the kingdom, and themselves, and according to the fundamental power that rests in themselves, they have resolved to bring you to Trial and Judgement: and for that purpose have constituted this High Court of Justice, before which you are brought.

This said, Mr Cook, Solicitor for the Commonwealth, standing with a bar on the right hand side of the prisoner, offered to speak: but the King having a staff in his hand, held it up, and laid it upon the said Mr. Cook's shoulder two or three times, bidding him hold.

As Charles tapped John Cook on the shoulder, the silver head of his cane fell to the floor. No one picked it up and Charles the fallen monarch was forced to do so. It was taken as an ominous sign by his retinue of troubled royalists. Cook went on to read the charge which included the familiar allegations of tyranny, usurping the rights and liberties of the people, levying war, and shedding innocent blood. Bradshaw asked for Charles's response. The King refused to answer and instead immediately went for the court's Achilles' heel. He disputed its fundamental right to try him, the King of England, on the charge of treason. There was no possible way a king could commit treason against his own people:

King. Now I would know by what authority, I mean lawful; there are many unlawful authorities in this world, thieves and robbers by the highways; but I would know by what authority I was brought from thence [the Isle of Wight], and carried from place to place, and I know not what: and when I know what lawful authority, I should answer. Remember, I am your King, your lawful King, and what sins you bring upon your heads, and the judgement of God upon this land; think well upon it, I say, think well upon it, before you go further from one sin to a greater: therefore let me know by what lawful authority I am seated here, and I shall not be unwilling to answer. In the meantime, I shall not betray my trust; I have a trust committed to me by god, by old and lawful descent; I will not betray it, to answer you a new unlawful authority, therefore resolve me that, and you shall hear more of me.

Displaying his nervous inexperience, Bradshaw defended the court's validity on the spurious grounds of the King's elective duties:

Lord President. If you had been pleased and had observed what had been hinted to you by the Court at your first coming hither, you would have known by what authority; which authority requires you, in the name of the people of England, of which you are elected King, to answer them.

King. No Sir, I deny that.

Lord President. If you acknowledge not the authority of the court, they must proceed.

King. I do tell them so; England was never an elective kingdom for near these thousand years; therefore let me know by what authority I am called hither: I do stand more for the liberty of my people than any here that come to my pretended judges; and therefore let me know by what lawful authority I am seated here, and I will answer it; otherwise I will not answer it.

Charles was into his stride and he pounded away at the court's shaky foundations. As the King pointed out, he wasn't even being made to answer to Parliament. Rather an illegal, *ad hoc* assembly of dubious commissioners:

> *King.* I do not come here as submitting to the Court: I will stand as much for the privilege of the House of Commons, rightly understood as any man whatsoever. I see no House of Lords here that might constitute a Parliament; and the King too should have been. Is this the bringing of the King to his Parliament? Is this the bringing an end to the Treaty in the public faith of the world? Let me see a legal authority warranted by the constitutions of the kingdom, and I will answer.

The increasingly exasperated Bradshaw tried to press on with the trial:

> *Lord President.* Sir, you have propounded a question, and have been answered. Seeing you will not answer, the Court will consider how to proceed: in the meantime, those that brought you hither, are to take charge of you back again. This court desires to know, whether this will be all the answer you give, or no.

> *King.* Sir, I would desire that you would give me, and all the world, satisfaction in this. Let me tell you, it is not a slight thing you are about. I am sworn to keep the peace, by that duty I owe to God and my country, and I will do it to the last breath of my body: and therefore you shall do well to satisfy first God, and then the country, by what authority you do it: if you do it by an usurped authority you cannot answer. There is a god in Heaven, that will call you, and all that give you power, to account. Satisfy me in that, and I will answer; otherwise I betray my trust, and the liberties of the people: and therefore think of that, and I will answer; otherwise I betray my trust, and the liberties of the people: and therefore think of that, and then I shall be willing. For I do avow, that it is a great sin to withstand lawful authority, as it is to submit to a tyrannical, or in other ways unlawful authority; and therefore satisfy me that you shall receive my answer.

Receiving no plea from the King, Bradshaw adjourned the court. On Monday 22 January, Charles was brought back into Westminster Hall to answer the charge. Once again, Charles denied the court's jurisdiction and emphasised his divine right as a monarch to be judged by God and none other. He also placed himself on the side of his subjects, protesting that no one could be safe if such an arbitrary use of the law as the establishment of this court went unopposed:

> *King.* When I was here last, it is very true, I made that question; truly if it were only my own particular case, I would have satisfied myself with the protestation I made the last time I was here against the legality of this Court, and that a king cannot be tried by any superior jurisdiction on earth. But it is not my case alone, it is the freedom and liberty of the people of England; and do you pretend what you will, I stand more for their liberties. For if power without law may make laws, may alter the fundamental laws of the kingdom, I do not know what subject he is in England, that can be sure of his life, or anything that he calls his own: therefore when that I came here, I did expect particular persons to know by what law, what authority you did proceed

against me here. And therefore I am a little to seek what to say to you in this particular, because the affirmative is to be proved, the negative often is very hard to do: but since I cannot persuade you to do it, I shall tell you my reasons as short as I can. My reasons why in conscience and duty I owe to God first, and my people next, for the preservation of their lives, liberties and estates, I conceive I cannot answer this, till I be satisfied of the legality of it. All proceedings against any man whatsoever—

Lord President. Sir, I must interrupt you, which I would not do, but that what you do is not agreeable to the proceedings of any court of justice: you are about to enter into argument, dispute concerning the authority of this Court, before whom you appear as a prisoner, and are charged as a high delinquent: if you take upon you to dispute the authority of the Court, we may not do it, nor will any court give way unto it…

King. Sir, by your favour, I do not know the forms of law and reason, though I am no lawyer professed; but I know as much law as any gentleman in England; and therefore (under favour) I do plead for the liberties of the people of England more than you do…

Bradshaw returned fire arguing that the law, something the King had previously shown little respect for, was undoubtedly on Parliament's side:

Lord President. Sir, I must interrupt you, you may not be permitted: you speak of law and reason; it is fit there should be law and reason, and there is both against you. Sir, the vote of the Commons of England assembled in Parliament, it is the reason of the kingdom, and they are these that have given to that law, according to which you should have ruled and reigned. Sir, you are not to dispute our authority, you are told it again by the Court.…neither you nor any man are permitted to dispute that point; you are concluded, you may not demure to the jurisdiction of the Court: if you do, I must let you know, that they over-rule your demurrer; they sit here by the authority of the commons of England, and all your predecessors and you are responsible to them.

King. I deny that; show me one precedent.

Lord President. Sir, you ought not to interrupt while the Court is speaking to you. This point is not to be debated by you, neither will the Court permit you to do it: if you offer it by way of demurrer to the jurisdiction of the Court, they have considered of their jurisdiction, they do affirm their own jurisdiction.

King. I say, sir, by your favour, that the commons of England was never a Court of Judicature; I would know how they came to be so.

Lord President. Sir, you are not permitted to go on in that speech and these discourses.

Then the clerk of the court read as followeth:

"Charles Stuart King of England, you have been accused on behalf of the people of England of high treason, and other high crimes; the Court have determined that you will answer the same."

King. I will answer the same as soon as I know by what authority you sent this.

Lord President. If this be all that you will say, then, Gentlemen, you that brought the prisoner hither, take charge of him back again.

Charles demanded once more to explain his reasons for refusing the court's jurisdictions but was now forcibly prevented by the rattled Bradshaw:

Lord President. Sir, you are not to have liberty to use this language. How great a friend you have been to the laws and liberties of the people, let all England and the world to judge.

King. Sir, under favour, it was the liberty, freedom, and laws of the subject that ever I took–defended myself with arms; I never took up arms against the people, but for the laws.

Lord President. The command of the Court must be obeyed; no answer will be given to the charge.

King. Well, Sir!

Charles had in fact drafted a speech which he planned to deliver on that day outlining his theological and legal objections to the court. It was subsequently printed by the King's allies. At its intellectual core is the contention that no property, liberty or livelihood would be safe if such a wholly unconstitutional court was allowed to try a king:

the duty I owe to god in the preservation of the true liberty of my people will not suffer me at this time to be silent: for, how can any free-born subject of England call life or anything he possesses his own, if power without right daily make new, and abrogate the old fundamental laws of the land which I now take to be the present case?…there is no proceeding just against any man, but what is warranted, either by god's laws or the municipal laws of the country where he lives. Now I am most confident of this day's proceeding cannot be warranted by God's laws; for, on the contrary, the authority of obedience unto Kings is clearly warranted, and strictly commanded in both the Old and New Testament, which, if denied, I am ready instantly to prove.

Thus you see that I speak not for my own right alone, as I am your King, but also for the true liberty of all my subjects, which consists not in the power of government, but in living under such laws, such a government, as may give themselves the best assurance of their lives and property of their goods…

Besides all this, the peace of the kingdom is not the least in my thoughts; and what hope of settlement is there, so long as power reigns without rule or law, changing the whole frame of that government under which this kingdom hath flourished for many hundreds of years? (nor will I say what will fall out in case this lawless, unjust proceeding against me do go on) and believe it, the commons of England will not thank you for this change; for they will remember how happy they have been of late years under the reigns of Queen Elizabeth, of the King my father, and myself, until the beginning of these unhappy troubles, and will have no cause to doubt, that they shall never be so happy under any new: and by this time it will be too sensibly evident, that the arms I took up were only to defend the fundamental laws of this kingdom against those who have supposed my power hath totally changed the ancient government.

Charles could write as many eloquent and intelligent speeches as he liked. But he was now excluded from the court proceedings which ground on relentlessly without him. President Bradshaw had decided that since Charles had refused to enter a plea, he was necessarily guilty. Yet to salve their consciences and to generate some modicum of public support, the ever-declining number of commissioners embarked on an examination of witnesses. Among those giving evidence was J. B. Harwood, a glover turned Cavalier soldier from the County of York:

> And this deponent further said, 'That there was then there the Earl of Lindsey's Regiment, who had their Colours given them, and that the said Earl of Lindsey was then also proclaimed there, The King's General, and that it was proclaimed then there likewise in the King's name, at the Head of every Regiment, that the said Forces should fight against all that came to oppose the King, or any of his followers, and in particular, against the Earl of Essex, the Lord Brook, and divers others, and they the said Earl of Essex, and Lord Brook, and divers others, were then proclaimed Traitors, and that the same proclamations were printed and dispersed by the officers of the Regiments throughout every Regiment.'
>
> And this deponent further said, 'That in or about the month of October 1642, he did see the King at Edgehill in Warwickshire, where he, sitting on horse-back while his army was drawn up before him, did speak to the colonel of every Regiment that passed by him, that he would have them speak to their soldiers to encourage them to stand to it, and to fight against the Lord of Essex, the Lord Brook, Sir William Waller, and Sir William Balfour.'
>
> And this Deponent said, 'That he did see many slain at the fight at Edgehill, and that afterwards he did see a list brought unto Oxford, of the men which were slain in that fight, by which it was reported that there were slain 6,559 men.'

Other witnesses pointed to the King's presence at Naseby and Newbury. There was no cross-examining of evidence by the incarcerated defendant. After hearing testimony from the final witnesses, the remaining forty-five commissioners went into closed session to draw up the inevitable sentence against the king.

The Sentence

Charles was brought back to Westminster Hall on 27 January 1649 to learn his fate. The King immediately entered into another futile exchange with President Bradshaw concerning the court's legitimacy. Perhaps at last realising the gravity of the moment, Charles this time suggested he would be happy to be tried by a court more representative of Parliament. But the moment for compromise was over. Charles was ordered silent as the Clerk of the Court read out the charge, the verdict and the sentence:

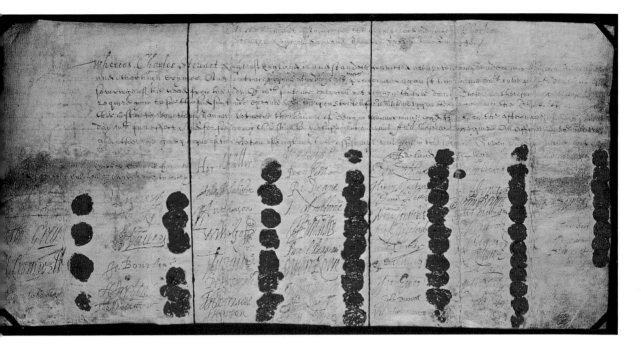

The death warrant of Charles I with regicide signatures. Those of Bradshaw and Cromwell can be seen in the first column (BAL, Houses of Parliament)

Whereas the Commons of England assembled in Parliament have by their late Act…authorised and constituted us an High Court of Justice for the trying and judging of the said Charles Stuart for the crimes and treasons in the Act mentioned…a Charge of High Treason and other high crimes, was in the behalf of the people of England, exhibited against him, and read openly unto him, wherein he was and therein trusted with a limited Power to govern by and according to the Law of the Land, and not otherwise, and by his Trust, Oath and Office, being obliged to use the power committed to him, for the good and benefit of the People, and for the preservation of their rights and liberties, yet nevertheless out of a wicked design to erect and uphold in himself an unlimited and tyrannical power to rule according to his Will, and to overthrow the Rights and Liberties of the People, and to take away and make void the foundations thereof, and of all redress and remedy of misgovernment, which by the fundamental constitutions of this kingdom were reserved on the Peoples behalf in the Right and Power of frequent and successive Parliaments…he, the said Charles Stuart, for accomplishment of such his designs, and for the protecting of himself and his adherents in his and their wicked practices, to the same end, hath traitorously and maliciously levied War against the present Parliament, and People therein represented…and that he hath thereby caused and procured many of the thousands of free People of this Nation to be slain, and by Divisions, Parties and Insurrections within this Land, by Invasions from foreign Parts, endeavoured and procured by him, and by many other evil ways and means, he, the said Charles Stuart, hath not only maintained and carried on the said War both by Sea and Land, but also hath renewed, or caused to be renewed, the said War against the Parliament, and good People of this Nation in this present year 1648[9] in several Counties and Places in this kingdom in the charge specified.

...and for accomplishment of the said designs and that he hath been and is the occasioner, author, and continuer of the said unnatural, cruel, and bloody wars, and therein guilty of High Treason and of Murders, Rapines, Burnings, Spoils, Desolations, Damage and Mischief to this Nation acted and committed in the said War and occasioned thereby. For all which Treasons and Crimes this court doth adjudge that he, the said Charles Stuart, as a Tyrant, Traitor, Murderer and public Enemy to the good people of this Nation shall be put to Death by severing the head from his Body.

The dye had been cast: the King was guilt of treason against his people and his country. He would be executed as a traitor. Charles rose to answer the sentence:

His Majesty then said:
The King. Will you hear me a word, Sir?
The President. Sir, you are not to be heard after the sentence.
The King. No, Sir?
The President. No, Sir, by your favour, Sir. Guard, withdraw your prisoner.
The King. I may speak after Sentence. By your favour, Sir, I may speak after Sentence, ever. By your favour – hold. The sentence, Sir, – I say, Sir, I do, – I am not suffered for to speak. Expect what other justice other people will have.

The King was bustled out of Westminster Hall plaintively demanding his voice be heard. He was taken through the streets not to Cotton's house but to Whitehall Palace and then the secure location of St James's Palace. Despite the jeering crowds and aggressive soldiers, according to his attendant Thomas Herbert, the King assumed an air of serene martyrdom:

Nothing of the fear of death, or indignities offered seemed a terror, or provoked him into impatience, nor uttered he a reproachful word reflecting upon any of his judges...or against any Member of the House, or officer of the Army; so wonderful was his patience, though his spirit was great, and might otherwise have expressed his resentments upon several occasions.

Charles spent the following two days preparing for death: praying, receiving courtiers and saying goodbye to his children. His final words to his third son Henry, Duke of Gloucester are among the most macabre. Lifting his youngest son onto his knee, he said:

'Sweetheart, now they will cut off thy father's head.' Upon which words the child looked very steadfastly upon him. 'Mark, child, what I say, they will cut off my head and perhaps make thee a king. But mark what I say; you must not be a king so long as your brothers Charles and James do live. For they will cut off your brothers' heads,

The children of Charles I showing Princess Elizabeth, James, Duke of York, and Henry, Duke of Gloucester, by John Hoskins (BAL, Fitzwilliam Museum, University of Cambridge)

when they can catch them, and cut off thy head too, at the last.' At which the child sighing said, 'I will be torn to pieces first.' Which falling unexpectedly from one so young it made the King rejoice exceedingly.

Henry's sister Princess Elizabeth later recorded her last moments with the King:

He wished me not to grieve and torment myself for him, for that would be a glorious death he should die, it being for the Laws and liberties of this land and for maintaining the true Protestant religion. He told me that he had forgiven all his enemies and hoped God would forgive them also, and commanded us and all the rest of my brothers and sisters to forgive them. He bid me tell my mother that his thoughts had never strayed from her and that his love would be the same to the last. With all he commanded me and my brother to be obedient to her. And bid me send my blessing to the rest of my brothers and sisters, with commendation to all his friends…

The regicides meanwhile were busy drawing up the death warrant. They snubbed all international pleas for clemency. The time and place of the execution had already been decided and with the publication of the official warrant came a dubious legality to the act.

At the High Court of Justice for the trying and judging of Charles Stuart, King of England, Jan. 29, Annno Domini 1648[9]

Whereas Charles Stuart, King of England, is, and standeth convicted, attainted and condemned of high treason, and other high crimes; and sentence upon Saturday last was pronounced against him by this court, to be put to death by the severing of his head from his body; of which sentence, execution yet remaineth to be done; these are therefore to will and require you to see the said sentence executed in the open street before Whitehall, upon the morrow, being the thirtieth day of this instant month of January, between the hours of ten in the morning and five in the afternoon of the same day, with full effect. And for so doing this shall be your sufficient warrant. And these are to require all officers, soldiers, and others, the good people of this nation of England, to be assisting unto you of this service.

Yet again there was a trailing off of commissioners as the execution day approached with many refusing to put their names to the warrant. Cromwell had forcibly to guide the hand of one commissioner, Richard Ingoldsby, onto the page. In fact, the future Lord Protector's nerves were shot to pieces: he giggled maniacally, flicked ink at other signatories, and exhibited signs of general hysteria. Sending a king to his death was obviously more stressful than he imagined. Among those who had less difficulty sanctioning Charles's execution was Colonel Hutchinson. He had, according to his wife, sought God's guidance:

and finding no check, but a confirmation in his conscience that it was his duty to act as he did, he, upon serious debate, both privately and in his addresses to God, and in conference with conscientious, upright unbiased persons, proceeded to sign the sentence against the King. Although he did not then believe it might one day come to be again disputed among men, yet both he and others thought they could not refuse it without giving up the people of God, whom they had led forth and engaged themselves unto by the oath of God, into the hands of God's and their enemies; and therefore he cast himself upon God's protection, acting according to the dictates of a conscience which he had sought the Lord to guide…

The Execution

King Charles spent his final night in St James's Palace – today the official residence of the Prince of Wales and future Charles III. On the morning of 30 January 1649, he rose early at 5 a.m. It was a fiercely cold day with the River Thames still frozen solid. Fearing the assembled crowds might suspect he was shivering from fear, Charles asked Thomas Herbert to dress him warmly for his coming martyrdom:

Charles I at Whitehall, 30 January 1649, by Ernest Crofts (BAL, Forbes magazine collection, New York)

'Herbert, this is my second Marriage Day; I would be as trim today as may be; for before night I hope to be espoused by the blessed Jesus.' He then appointed what clothes he would wear; 'Let me have a shirt on more than ordinary,' said the King, 'by reason the season is so sharp as probably will make me shake, which some observers imagine proceeds from fear. I would have no such imputation. I fear not death! Death is not terrible to me. I bless my god I am prepared.'

After five hours of scrupulous dressing followed by the taking of the Holy Sacrament with the loyal Laudian cleric Bishop Juxon, a guard led by Colonel Hacker arrived for the King. To the sound of a beating drum, Charles, Herbert and Juxon were marched by a troop of soldiers from St James's Palace through St James's Park to Whitehall. The King was taken to his old bed-chamber in Whitehall Palace:

> where, after a little Repose, the Bishop went to Prayer; which, being done, his Majesty bid Mr. *Herbert* bring him some Bread and Wine, which being brought, the King broke the Manchet, and eat a Mouthful of it, and drank a small Glassful of Claret-Wine, and then was sometime in private with the Bishop, expecting when *Hacker* would the third and last time give warning. Mean time his majesty told Mr. *Herbert* which Satin night-cap he would use, which being provided, and the King at private prayer, Mr *Herbert* addressed himself to the Bishop, and told him, the King had ordered him to have a White Satin night-cap ready, but was not able to endure the sight of that Violence they upon the Scaffold would offer the King. The Good Bishop bid him then give him the Cap, and wait at the end of the Banqueting-House, near the Scaffold, to take care of the King's Body; for (said he) that, and his Internment, will be our last Office.
>
> Colonel *Hacker* came soon after to the Bed-Chamber-Door, and gave his last signal; the Bishop and Mr. *Herbert*, weeping, fell upon their Knees, and the King gave them his Hand to kiss, and helped the Bishop up, for he was aged. Colonel *Hacker* attending still at the Chamber-Door, the King took notice of it, and said, *Open the Door*, and bade *Hacker* go, he would follow.

At 1.30 p.m. King Charles left his bed-chamber and proceeded along Whitehall Palace to Banqueting House which had been the scene of so many joyous royal revels in the 1630s.

> A Guard was made all along the Galleries and the Banqueting-House; but behind the Soldiers abundance of Men and Women crowded in, though with some Peril to their Persons, to behold the saddest sight *England* ever saw. And as his Majesty passed by, with a cheerful Look, heard them pray for him, the Soldiers not rebuking any of them; by their silence and dejected Faces seeming afflicted rather than insulting. There was a Passage broken through the Wall by which the King passed unto the Scaffold...

He walked through the window of Banqueting House (removed for the occasion) and onto the scaffold. John Rushworth describes the scene:

The scaffold was hung round with black, and the floor covered with black, and the axe and block laid in the middle of the scaffold. There were divers companies of Foot and Horse on every side of the scaffold, and the multitudes of people that came to be spectators were very great…

Broadsheet showing Charles I's speech from the scaffold (AA)

Standing around the scaffold were numerous soldiers, Bishop Juxon, Parliamentarian reporters, the two heavily disguised executioners, as well as a coffin draped in black velvet and a block waiting to receive the King's head. The heaving crowd of ghoulish spectators were kept suitably back from the scaffold to hear any of the King's final words. Nonetheless Charles was determined to say his peace. Rushworth recounts how he began by blaming Parliament for the nation's ills:

> I think it is my duty to God first, and to my Country, for to clear myself both as an honest man, a good king, and a good Christian. I shall begin first with my innocence. In truth, I think it is not very needful for me to insist long upon this, for all the world knows I never did begin the war with the two Houses of Parliament, and I call God to witness (to whom I must shortly make an account) that I never did intend to encroach upon their privileges. They began upon me. It is the militia they began upon, they confessed that the militia was mine, but they thought it fit to have it from me. And to be short, if anyone will look but to the dates of the commissions, their commissions and mine, and likewise to the declarations, will see clearly that they began these unhappy troubles, not I. So that as to the guilt of these enormous Crimes that are laid against me, I hope in God, that God will clear me of it, I will not, I'm in Charity. God forbid that I would lay it on the two houses of parliament, there is no necessity of either. I hope they are free of this guilt for I believe that ill instruments between them and me, has been the chief cause of all this bloodshed, so that by way of speaking, as I find myself clear of this, I hope (and pray God) that they may too.

However, Charles accepted he too had been at fault. Most shamefully by acceding to the execution of the Earl of Strafford:

> Yet for all this God forbid that I should be so ill a Christian, as not to say that God's Judgements are just upon me many times he does pay justice by an unjust Sentence, that is ordinary. I only say this, that an unjust sentence [*meaning Strafford*] that I suffered to take effect, is punished now by an unjust Sentence upon me, that is, so far I have said to show you that I am an innocent man.

He went on to assert that the health of his subjects had been his only concern as King:

> For the People, and truly I desire their liberty and freedom, as much as anybody whomsoever, but I must tell you, that their liberty and freedom consist in having of Government, those laws by which their life and their goods may be most their own. It is not for having share in Government, Sirs; that is nothing pertaining to them. A subject and a sovereign are clean different things, and therefore, until they do that, I mean, that you do put the people in that liberty as I say, certainly they will never enjoy themselves. Sirs, it is for this that now I am come here. If I would have given way to an arbitrary way, for to have all laws changed according to the Power of the Sword, I needed not to have come here, and therefore I tell you, (and I pray God it be laid not to your Charge), that I am the Martyr of the people.

But at the centre of his scaffold oration was a restatement of his commitment to

Two contemporary depictions of the execution, by Jan Weesop and Gonzales Cocques. At the bottom left of the Weesop, Charles is led to the platform; at the bottom right, mourners soak their handkerchiefs in the blood of the dead King. (BAL; BAL, Museé de Picardie, Amiens)

Executioner with the King's severed head. (WA)

Carnifex Maiestatis Regis Angliæ

the Protestant religion and the Church of England. He denied as he always had throughout the wars any intention to subvert the true religion of England:

> In truth Sirs, my conscience in Religion, I think is very well known to the world, and therefore I declare before you all, that I die a Christian according to the profession of the Church of England as I found it left to me by my Father, and this honest man [*meaning Bishop* Juxon] I think will witness it.

At 2 p.m., the King kneeled down and readied himself for his final and most finely performed act in the entire civil war drama:

> Then the King speaking to the Executioner, said, 'I shall say but very short prayers, and then thrust out my hands.' Then the King called to Dr Juxon for his night-cap, and having put it on, he said to the Executioner, 'Does my hair trouble you.' Who desired him to put it all under his cap, which the King did accordingly by the help of the Executioner and the Bishop. Then the King turning to Dr Juxon, said, 'I have a good cause and a gracious God on my side.'

> *Dr Juxon.* 'There is but one stage more. This stage is turbulent and troublesome, it is a short one. But you may consider it will soon carry you a very great way, it will carry you from earth to heaven, and there you shall find to your great joy the prize. You haste to a crown of glory.'

The King. 'I go from a corruptible to an incorruptible Crown, where no disturbance can be.'

Dr Juxon. 'You are exchanged from a temporal to an eternal Crown, a good exchange.'

Then the King took off his cloak and his George [his Garter insignia], giving his George to Dr Juxon, saying, 'Remember,' (it is thought for the Prince) and some other ceremonies [were] past. After which the King stooping down, laid his neck upon the block. And after a little pause, stretching forth his hands, the Executioner at one blow severed his head form his body.

Aftershocks

If only Charles Stuart had betrayed such steadfastness, such command of the moment and character during the civil war as he did facing his death the outcome might have been very different. Nothing became him so much as his execution. Buried at St George's Chapel, Windsor in a snow storm, he became the legendary 'White King' who had laid down his life for Church and country. The cult of King

'The White King': Edwardian depiction of Charles I's coffin being carried through the snow to St George's Chapel, Windsor Castle, by Ernest Crofts (BAL, City of Bristol Museum and Art Gallery)

Victorian painting of the burial of Charles I, Martyr (BAL)

Charles I, Martyr grew steadily, abetted by the swift publication of *Eikon Basilike or the Portraiture of His Sacred Majesty in his Solitudes and Sufferings*. Written most probably by John Gauden, the Bishop of Worcester, it presented an image of Charles as a selfless martyr vainly fighting for the Church and common man cruelly set about by rogues and knaves. Within a year of the execution, some thirty-five editions were in circulation.

The profundity of executing a king took days to register. As the historian Thomas Carlyle wrote in the nineteenth century: 'The truth is, no modern reader can conceive the then atrocity, ferocity, unspeakability of this fact. First, after long reading in the old dead Pamphlets does one see the magnitude of it. To be equalled, nay to be preferred think some, in point of horror, to "the Crucifixion of Christ."' It was unprecedented, unspeakable, extraordinary. The reaction of the ardent Yorkshire royalist Alice Thornton expresses a sense of searing grief mixed with anger:

The apotheosis of the King: Royalist engraving of Charles I's ascension to Heaven (BAL)

The iconography of martyrdom: contemporary Royalist engravings (BAL)

Let all true Christians mourn for the fall of this stately cedar, who was the chief support of the church of God. A holy, pious prince, who fought God's battles against His enemies, being a nursing father, a good Josiah to his three kingdoms; who, for the defence of the true catholic religion of Jesus Christ his Lord, and for the defence of the noble laws of this kingdom of England, the protestant faith, and the privileges of the parliament and subject, ruling them in peace and happiness many years, he laid down his life; being sacrificed by the iniquities of his subjects; their sins pulled down his ruin on him and our selves…Oh! How we may take up justly those bitter lamentations of Jeremiah, the anointed of the Lord, the joy of our hearts, the light of our eyes is taken in their pits, the crown is fallen from our heads; woe unto us that we have sinned, let every soul gird itself with sackcloth, and lament the displeasure of God which has smitten our head, and wounded the defence of this our English church, our Solomon.

The execution disturbed royalists across Europe. In a letter to Lord Hatton sent from Holland, his correspondent describes how:

The very relation…of that monstrous fact in England upon the person of the King struck one woman dead upon the first hearing it, and another lies yet so ill that it is thought she will not recover.

When the King's severed head was held aloft by the executioner in Whitehall, no cheer arose from crowd. There was instead a low, audible groan. Despite widespread understanding for the necessity of the execution, there was little outward enthusiasm for the bloody act even among the godly. In Essex, the Puritan minister Ralph Josselin recorded his reaction in his meticulous diary:

Feb. 4 1649. I was much troubled with the black providence of putting the King to death; my tears were restrained at the passage about his death; the Lord in mercy lay it not as sin to the charge of the kingdom, but do in mercy do us good by the same; the small pox on some families of the town spreadeth not, to God be the glory thereof; this week I could do nothing neither in my Hebrew, nor in my reconciler.

The death of the king talked much of; very many men of the weaker sort of Christianity in divers places passionate concerning it, but so ungroundedly, that it would make any to bleed to observe it; the Lord hath some great things to do; fear and tremble at it, oh England.

Many were just fearful of the future. Terrified of what God might bring on their heads for such an unnatural assault upon the great chain of being. And they had a right to be worried: the execution accelerated a radical new chartering of ideas never since equalled in British history.

A World Turned Upside Down

1649 *March*	Gerard Winstanley's Diggers or 'True Levellers' begin planting crops on St George's Hill, Surrey, in order to turn the earth into 'a common treasury'	**1650** *May*	Parliament passes an Act against 'Incest, Adultery and Fornication'
1649 *May*	A Leveller revolt in the Army is suppressed by Cromwell and three militants are executed at Burford	**1650** *August*	Parliament passes an Act against 'Atheistical, Blasphemous and Execrable Opinions'
1649 *September*	Parliament abolishes compulsory attendance at parish churches		
1649 *November*	Ranter 'hysteria' begins to sweep London as both City authorities and many inhabitants, believing often spurious and exaggerated reports, fear blaspheming and promiscuous sectaries		

AS THE KING'S SEVERED HEAD THUDDED ONTO THE SCAFFOLD BOARDS, THE MENTAL WORLD OF SEVENTEENTH-CENTURY ENGLAND FELL APART. With the end of monarchy came the re-examination of every established tenet of religion, politics, and society. The early 1650s saw an extraordinary culmination of the intellectual anarchy thrown up by the civil war years.

Religion

With the abolition of episcopacy in 1646, the fabric of the Church of England had been torn apart. One contemporary described a new world disfigured by religious anarchy and plagued by fanatics:

> Enemies of the church…abuse the precious saints of God with these and other reproaches…Oh, these are the men that would turn the world upside down, that make the nation full of tumults and uproars, that work all the disturbance in church and state. It is fit such men and such congregations be suppressed…that we may have truth and peace and government again.

Many feared the country would be engulfed by a tide of irreligion and ungodliness. One royalist, Ephraim Pagitt, a minister in the heart of London, railed against the heretics unleashed by the collapse of church hierarchy:

> They come! But whence come they, from the schools of the Prophets? No, but many of them from mechanic trades: as one from a stable from currying his horses, another from his stall from cobbling his shoes…These take upon themselves to reveal the secrets of the most high, to open and shut heaven, to save souls…Alas, what heresies have we not? And most of those are subdivided into many sects: as there are about twenty sorts of Anabaptists, fourteen set down by Alstedius, and the rest by Bullinger; sundry sorts of Familists, Brownists, and of others: every day begets a new opinion, it faring with them, as with the ancient Hereticks, who having once forsaken the truth, wandered from one error to another, they agreeing only in this one thing, to do mischief to the Church of God.

With no bishops to govern the nation's religion, eccentric heresies and strange sects multiplied. Pagitt, who was reviled in his own pulpit by those he attacked, continued:

> With illuminated Anabaptists, who blaspheme the baptism of Children, and these heretics, whom in time past we burned, we may hear now in our pulpits seducing people. We have also Donatistical Brownists, who like the Pharisees of old, separate themselves from other men, counting all men prophane that are not of their conventi-

THE
World turn'd upfidedown:

OR

A briefe defcription of the ridiculous Fafhions
of thefe dulbacted Times.

By T. J. a well-willer to King, Parliament and Kingdom.

'The World Turned Upside Down': title page of a pamphlet, 1647 (BAL, BL)

cles. We have also Independents, who dream that they have a perfect model of Church government, which Almighty God kept secret from the patriarchs, priests, prophets, apostles, and Doctors of the Church, and now lately revealed unto them. We have also Antinomians, who whereas the papists leave out one commandment of the ten, they null the whole Law, not allowing it to be a rule of life. This opinion simple people swallow down, having, as they suppose, found a new way to heaven. We have Arminians, an after-brood of Pelagius. We have Sabbatarians, who affirm the old Jewish Sabbath to be kept, and not the Lords day. We have also Antisabbatarians, who would have no special Sabbath day at all, affirming every day to be a Sabbath to a Christian man. We have Traskites, who affirm many Jewish ceremonies to be observed by Christians. We have Arians, who deny the deity of Christ. We have Antitrinitarians, who blaspheme the holy Trinity. We have Millenaries, who dream that we must live with Christ 1000 years here on earth before the Resurrection. We have Hetheringtonians, who hold a hodge-podge of many heresies. We have an Atheistical sect, who affirm that men's souls sleep with their bodies. We have Socinians, who teach that Christ died, not to satisfy for our sins, but to give us an example of patience, with other abominable errors.

It was the Presbyterians in Parliament and Scotland who had been charged with replacing the episcopal order of archbishops, bishops, deans and archdeacons. They were appalled at the tide of sectarianism unleashed by war. The men and women whom Pagitt labelled Brownists, Hetheringtonians, Traskites and Arians – who sought to worship God according to their own conscience and interpretation of the Scriptures – were sub-sects of the Presbyterian's old foe, the 'Independents'. The Presbyterians' authority was embodied in the Westminster Assembly, a church council appointed by the Long Parliament in 1643 to reform the English Church. This synod implemented Presbyterian reforms of the prayer book by composing a *Directory for the Public Worship of God* and the Church of England's articles of faith by drawing up the Presbyterian *Westminster Confession*. More widely, Presbyterians and Independents argued about the limits of church government, and whether contrary religious opinions could be tolerated. Thomas Edwards, who had been so shocked by the heterodoxy of the New Model Army, was outraged by the prospect of tolerating what he considered to be religious error:

> How do sects and schisms increase and grow daily, sectaries doing even what they will, committing insolencies and outrages, not only against the truth of God and the peace of the Church, but the civil state also, going up and down counties, causing riots, yea tumults and disturbances in the public assemblies! How do persons cast out of other countries for their errors, not only live here, but gather churches, preach publicly their opinions! What swarms are there of all sorts of illiterate mechanic preachers, yea of women and boy preachers! What a number of meetings of sectaries in this city, eleven at least in one parish! What liberty of preaching, printing of all errors, or for a toleration of all, and against the Directory, Covenant, monthly fast, Presbyteriall government, and all ordinances of Parliament in reference to religion, and most of these persons either never questioned at all, or if questioned, abusing those in a high manner who question them, coming off one way or other, and afterwards going on in spreading their errors more then before, or if committed by some below, whereby they are hindered from preaching and dipping, then brought off and released by some above (of which they brag and boast) yea many Sectaries countenanced, employed and preferred to special places both of profit, honour and trust, and that which is saddest of all (and yet too true) orthodox worthy persons who being in places of power, for preventing mischiefs and evils questioning some sectaries for their unlawful meetings and false doctrines, have been looked upon ever after with an evil eye, and opportunities watched to molest and displace them. In a word, there hath not been to this day any exemplary restraint of the Sectaries.

Allegorical engraving of anarchy unleashed by civil war (BAL)

Thomas Edwards's hysteria was no doubt prone to exaggeration, but the sectarian menace was considerable: by the mid-1640s, there were thirty to forty separatist congregations in London. Though the total population was 250,000, members of this small but vocal minority were notorious advocates of their own cause. The breakdown in episcopal order had rendered censorship of the country's presses impossible and the sects were able to propagate their views with impunity. The amount of published material soared: 22 new titles appeared in 1640, 2000 in 1641 and, by 1660, around 3 new titles appeared every day. While books were formerly weighty tomes, suitable only for personal libraries and learned reading, pamphlets and broadsides appeared, written in easy, accessible English often shouted through the streets for the illiterate majority. The civil war saw competing newspapers, often published weekly, which presented religious separatists both as notorious rebels against God and champions of new, insightful forms of worship.

The Retreat from Politics

The early Commonwealth also witnessed an acceleration of the radical ideas that had first surfaced at the Putney Debates. After the Debates, many Independents felt betrayed by the Grandees' crushing of free thinking. The Leveller leaders, men such as John Lilburne, Richard Overton and William Walwyn, formulated petitions and declarations to help the movement retain some momentum. On 15 November 1647, seven regiments received permission to assemble on Corkbush Field in Ware, Hertfordshire. Regiments belonging to Colonel Thomas Harrison and John Lilburne's brother also attended, with Leveller manifestos pinned to their hats. Fairfax's loyal secretary, John Rushworth, records the incident:

> Monday the 15th instant, according to appointment, the rendezvous of the first brigade of the army was held in Corkbush Field between Hertford and Ware…it may not be forgot, that upon the general's coming into the field, Colonel Eyre, Major Scot, and others, were observed insinuating divers seditious principles unto the soldiers, incensing them against the general and general officers; upon which order was given to the commitment of Colonel Eyre and others into the marshal's hands, Major Scot was committed to the custody of Lieutenant Chillenden, and sent up to the parliament, he being a member of the House of Commons. Some inferior persons were likewise committed for dispersing factious papers, as *The Agreement of the People*, etc. among the private soldiers, and finding those people who pretend most for the freedom of the people, had dispersed divers of those papers amongst Colonel Lilburne's regiment of foot, the most mutinous regiment in the army, strict command was given for them, to tear them, and cast them away, which was done; and Captain-Lieutenant Bray, who was the only officer above a lieutenant left among them, the rest being driven away by the mutinous soldiers, and one of the wounded, was taken from the head of that regiment, and committed to custody: it being alleged, that he had led on the soldiers to that rendezvous, contrary to orders. And afterwards, a council of war

being called in the field, divers mutineers, for examples sake, were drawn forth, three of them were tried and condemned to death; and one of them whose turn it fell to by lot, was shot to death at the head of the regiment, and others are in hold to be tried.

Colonel Rainsborough and some others, presented a petition, and the *Agreement of the People*, to his excellency, at his first coming. Colonel Harrison's regiment, who had papers in their hats, with this motto, *England's freedom*, and *Soldiers' rights*, when they understood their error, by the general's severe reproof, of their so doing, tore them, and expressed their resolution to be obedient to his excellency's commands.

With Cromwell's help (who was also present with Fairfax on this occasion), other meetings at Windsor and Kingston passed without incident, but Cromwell was convinced of the Levellers' threat. When John Lilburne was examined before the Council of State in March 1649, the Levellers had still not been crushed. During the trial, Lilburne was sent to an adjoining room from which he could hear Cromwell addressing the Council with furious frustration:

> 'I tell you, sir,' Cromwell declared, thumping the table, 'you have no other way to deal with these men but to break them or they will break you; yea and bring all the guilt of the blood and treasure shed and spent in this kingdom upon your heads and shoulders, and frustrate and make void all that work that, with so many years' industry, toil, and pains, you have done, and so render you to all rational men in the world as the most contemptiblest generation of silly, low-spirited men in the earth, to be broken and routed by such a despicable, contemptible generation of men as they are, and therefore, sir, I tell you again, you are necessitated to break them.'

Colonel John Lilburne, leader of the Levellers (WA)

Lilburne was sent to the Tower (where he spent so much time he eventually christened one of his daughters 'Tower'), but the Levellers were not finally broken until several months later. Though the Army had not been paid, Cromwell intended an Irish expedition, and two regiments infiltrated by Levellers mutinied. On 13 May 1649, as the mutineers were camped at Burford, Oxfordshire, Cromwell launched a surprise night attack, killing several mutineers and imprisoning the rest in Burford Church for four days. Three of the ringleaders were executed and with that sudden act of classic Cromwellian brutality Leveller dissent evaporated. The news-sheet, *The Moderate*, was sympathetic to the Levellers and reported the execution with compassionate scrutiny:

> Burford, May 19…This day Cornet Thompson was brought into the churchyard (the place of execution). Death was a great terror to him, as unto most. Some say he had hopes of a pardon, and therefore delivered something reflecting upon the legality of his engagement, and the just hand of God upon him; but if he had, they failed him. Corporal Perkins was the next; the place of death, and sight of his executioners, was so far from altering his countenance, or daunting his spirit, that he seemed to smile upon both, and account it a great mercy that he was to die for this quarrel, and casting his eyes up to His Father and afterwards to his fellow prisoners (who stood upon the church leads to see the execution) set his back against the wall, and bid the executioners shoot, and so died as gallantly, as he lived religiously. After him Master John Church was brought to the stake, he was as much supported by God, in this great agony, as the latter, for after he had pulled off his doublet, he stretched out his arms, and bid the soldiers do their duties, looking them in the face, till they gave fire upon him, without the least kind of fear or terror. Thus was death, the end of his present joy, and beginning of his future eternal felicity. Cornet Denne was brought to the place of execution. He said, he was more worthy of death than life and showed himself somewhat penitent, for being an occasion of this engagement; but though he said this to save his life, yet the last two executed, would not have said it, though they were sure thereby to gain their pardon.

The crushing of the Levellers did not quash the broader discontent towards a Commonwealth government which was not delivering full religious emancipation. With a political settlement dashed in the grounds of Burford Church, some men and women turned their backs on immediately human, political solutions, arguing that Christ Himself would complete the task which some Levellers had hoped for. These 'Fifth Monarchists' were millenarian enthusiasts who, having read the biblical prophecies of Revelation and the Book of Daniel, expected the imminent establishment of Christ's Kingdom, the fifth monarchy, on earth. In 1649, they petitioned Parliament with their beliefs:

> Your petitioners acknowledge themselves unspeakably engaged to the God of heaven and earth, for his great mercy to us, in giving you hearts to offer yourselves so willingly among the people, in the late great undertakings of this nation, against the enemies of the peace thereof, and blessing your faithful endeavours with such glorious

and wonderful successes: whereby, as the Lord hath put great honour upon you, crowning your valour with victory, and making you the warlike glory of the world; so He hath no less put great obligations upon you all, to exalt Him that hath exalted you, and to lift up his glory in the world, where He hath given you a name so great and glorious…Therefore our daily prayer shall be for yourselves and your noble army, that you may never stumble at the stumbling stone, nor take that honour to yourselves, that is due to Christ, nor be instrumental for the setting up of a mere natural and worldly government, like that of heathen Rome and Athens (as too many late overtures have caused us to fear) whereby the public interest of you (whom God hath honoured so highly, as to begin the great work of smiting the image on the feet) may show yourselves thankful to Him, that hath given you victory through our Lord Jesus Christ, may honour His Son, and comfort his saints, in whom He reigns spiritually, and by whom He will reign visibly over all the nations of the world.

Unlike 'a mere natural and worldly government', Fifth Monarchists sought to establish 'an habitation of justice, and mountain of holiness':

> 1…A kingdom and dominion, which the church is to exercise on the earth, 2. that extends to all persons and things universally, which is to be externally and visibly administered, 3. by such laws and officers, as Jesus Christ our mediator hath appointed in his kingdom. 4. It shall put down all worldly rule and authority (so far as relates to the worldly constitution thereof) though in the hands of Christians: 5. and is to be expected about this time we live in. 6. This kingdom shall not be erected by human power and authority, but Christ by his spirit shall call and gather a people, and form them into several less families, churches and corporations; and when they are multiplied, they shall rule the world by general assemblies; or church-parliaments, of such officers of Christ, and representatives of the churches, as they shall choose and delegate, which they shall do, till Christ come in person.

Many feared the fifth monarchy was upon them when on 29 March 1652 a solar eclipse threw the country into total darkness. One astrologer saw the events of 'Mirk Monday' full of portent:

> The Fifth Monarchy of the World is coming, and the effects of the Eclipse make way for him…His Rise will be great, his Coronation glorious, and he shall rule all Nations in the world…This is the Monarchy that I expect; yet I expect it not in the effect of this Eclipse, for this shall only make way for the Fifth Monarchy; and when you see all Europe together by the ears, when you see kings mad, and their subjects stubborn, then think of these things, and know that he that shall come, will come, and will not tarry.

Diggers and Ranters

Rather than embrace the biblical literalism of Fifth Monarchists, other Levellers styled themselves as 'True-Levellers' or 'Diggers'. They sought to restore Christ's kingdom to its inhabitants by farming common land and living in self-sufficient communes. Led by Gerard Winstanley, the Diggers established their first community on St George's Hill, Surrey in March 1649. Another nine would follow, complete with home-grown crops and cottages. Winstanley justified his groups' actions in the face of local opposition and harassment:

In the beginning of time, the great creator Reason made the earth to be a common treasury, to preserve beasts, birds, fishes and man, the lord that was to govern this creation: for man had domination given to him, over the beasts, birds and fishes; but not one word was spoken in the beginning, that one branch of mankind should rule over another.

And the reason is this, every single man, male and female, is a perfect creature of himself; and the same spirit that made the globe dwells in man to govern the globe; so that the flesh of man being subject to reason, his maker, hath him to be his teacher and ruler within himself, therefore needs not run abroad after any teacher and ruler without him; for he needs not that any man should teach him, for the same anointing that ruled the Son of Man teacheth him all things.

But since human flesh (that king of beasts) began to delight himself in the objects of the creation, more than in the spirit reason and righteousness, who manifests himself to be the indweller in the five senses of hearing, seeing, tasting, smelling, feeling; then he fell into blindness of mind and weakness of heart, and runs abroad for a teacher and ruler. And so selfish imagination, taking possession of the five senses and ruling as king in the room of reason therein, and working with covetousness, did set up one man to teach and rule over another; and thereby the spirit was killed and man was brought into bondage, and became a greater slave to such of his own kind, than the beasts of the field were to him.

And hereupon the earth (which was made to be a common treasury of relief for all, both beasts and men) was hedged into enclosures by the teachers and rulers, and the others were made servants and slaves: and that earth, that is within this creation made a common storehouse for all, is bought and sold and kept in the hands of a few, whereby the great creator is mightily dishonoured, as if he were a respecter of persons, delighting in the comfortable livelihood of some, and rejoicing in the miserable poverty and straits of others. From the beginning it was not so.

Winstanley refused to refer to St George's Hill by its proper name as many radicals didn't recognise the false saints of a false church:

Secondly, in that we begin to dig upon George Hill to eat our bread together by righteous labour and sweat of our brows, it was showed us by vision in dreams and out of dreams that that should be the place we should begin upon. And though that earth in view of flesh may be very barren, yet we should trust the spirit for a blessing. And that not only this common or heath should be taken in and manured by the people, but all the commons and waste ground in England and in the whole world shall be taken in by the people in righteousness, not owning any property; but taking the earth to be a common treasury, as it was first made for all.

Thirdly, it is showed us that all the prophecies, visions and revelations of scriptures, of prophets and apostles, concerning the calling of the Jews, the restoration of Israel, and making of that people the inheritors of the whole earth, doth all seat themselves in this work of making the earth a common treasury…

Fourthly, this work to make the earth a common treasury was showed us by voice in trance and out of trance, which words were these, 'Work together, eat bread together, declare this all abroad.' Which voice was heard three times. And in obedience to the spirit we have declared this by word of mouth, as occasion was offered. Secondly, we have declared it by writing, which others may read. Thirdly, we have now began to declare it by action, in digging up the common land and casting in seed, that we may eat our bread together in righteousness. And every one that comes to work shall eat the fruit of their own labours, one having as much freedom in the fruit of the earth as another…

Fifthly, that which does encourage us to go on in this work is this: we find the streaming out of love in our hearts towards all, to enemies as well as friends; we would have none live in beggary, poverty or sorrow, but that everyone might enjoy the benefit of his creation: we have peace in our hearts and quiet rejoicing in our work, and filled with sweet content, though we have but a dish of roots and bread for our food.

Above and opposite: 'Three Grand Enemies to Church and State': engravings depicting the proliferation of religious sects (British Library; BAL)

Though the Diggers were not successful, the ideas they promoted lived on among other sectaries and radicals. In the early 1650s, religious eccentrics were struck by visions, endowed with self-proclaimed divine authority (and sometimes even divinity itself), and attempted to live the Bible in the world around them. The first of these were the Ranters. Gerard Winstanley had already complained of those who came to his communities and took up 'the Ranting practice' in 1649. He regarded them as layabouts prone to promiscuity, drunkenness and blasphemy. However, they soon found spokesmen ready to justify such behaviour theologically. One of the most notorious was Laurence Clarkson, a self-styled 'Captain of the Rant'. Though it is unlikely he was involved in Winstanley's Digging, he cunningly traced his spiritual evolution towards the belief that sin itself did not exist. He dismissed his previous 'orthodox' conception of God, the Devil, Heaven and Hell, and continued:

> This was the height of my knowledge under the Bishops' Government, and I am persuaded was the height of all Episcopal ministers then living…After this I travelled into the Church of the Presbyterians…for herein consisted the difference of the Presbyterian and Episcopal, only in a few superstitious rites and ceremonies…But I

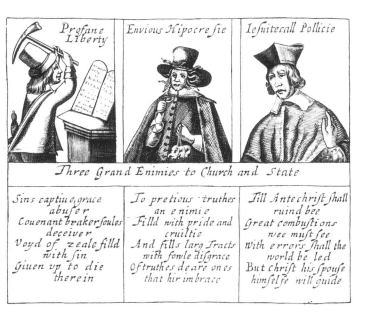

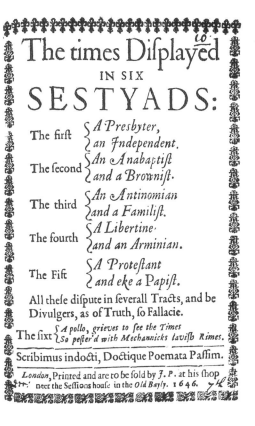

must return to the time then…in which I did endeavour to become one of those that God saw no sin, and in some measure I began to be comforted therewith; but how, or which way to continue in the same I could not tell, having as yet but little understanding in the Scripture I was silent, only still enquiring after the highest pitch of light then held forth in London…Fourthly, take notice in this Sect I continued a certain time, for Church it was none, in that it was but part form, and part none…Now after I had continued half a year, more or less the Ministers began to envy me for my doctrine, it being free grace, so contrary to theirs, and that…more [of] their people came from their own parish to hear me…Now dipping being a command of Christ, I judged them rebels that did profess the name of Christ, and not submit their bodies to the ordinance of Christ, and that Christ requires obedience from none but such as was capable of being taught, and therefore no children, but men and women, ought to receive the ordinance of baptism…Then, sixthly, I took my journey into the society of those people called Seekers, who worshipped God only by prayer and preaching…As all along in this my travel I was subject to that sin, and yet as saint-like, as though sin were a burden to me…I concluded there was none could live without sin in this world; for notwithstanding I had great knowledge in the things of God, yet I found my heart was not right to what I pretended, but full of lust and vainglory of this world…Seventhly, I took my progress into the wilderness…with many more words I affirmed that there was no sin, but as man esteemed it sin, and therefore none can be free from sin, till in purity it can be acted as no sin, for I judged that pure to me, which to dark understandings was impure, for to the pure all things, yea all acts were pure…I was moved to write to the world what my principle was, so brought to public view a book called *The Single Eye* so that men and women came from many parts to see my face, and hear my knowledge in these things, being restless till they were made free.

Clarkson published *A Single Eye All Light, No Darkness; or, Light and Darkness One* in October 1650. It collided moral categories 'so that', Clarkson wrote, 'Devil is God, Hell is Heaven, Sin Holiness, Damnation Salvation' because all things were a single unity, the same sides of one universal coin: 'my love my dove is but one, thou one, not two, but only one, my love: Love is God, and God is Love'. By drawing upon God's own title of Exodus 3:14 ('And God said unto Moses I AM THAT I AM: and he said, Thus thou shalt say unto the children of Israel, I AM hath sent me to you'), some Ranters saw themselves mingling with God Himself. Abiezer Coppe, who was reputed to preach naked and swear profusely, took this to an extreme:

> Only I must let you know, that I long to be utterly undone, and that the pride of my fleshly glory is stained: and that I, either am, or would be nothing, and see the Lord all, in all, in me. I am, or would be nothing. But by the grace of God, I am what I am, and what I am in I am, that I am so I am in the Spirit.

The Ranters caused hysteria during the early 1650s. News-sheets and broadsides splashed on stories of the obscene sanctimony and rampant promiscuity which this self-deifying theology could justify. Ranters were often pictured in taverns, feasting and drinking, after which they would have sex with one another in blasphemous abandon. They would often sing perverse hymns and pornographic ballads to accompany their merry-making, of which this is one example that was allegedly sung to amorous Ranter women:

> *You that can revel day and night,*
> *To enjoy the fruits of Loves Delight,*
> *With whomsoever you can acquire,*
> *To quench the flames of Cupid's fire,*
> *You must mark this, that when you meet*
> *(In garden, orchard, field or street)*
> *With feeble brethren that scarce can*
> *Perform the duty of a man,*
> *Let them not sally from your lap*
> *Till you salute them with the clap;*
> *Dear sisters, you may freely do't*
> *As easy as to stir a foot*
> *But if you cannot, tell me now,*
> *And I myself will teach you how.*
> *When you meet lusty men of strength,*
> *That will not bate a jot of length,*
> *Oh hug them hard, and suck them in,*
> *Until they do even burst your skin,*
> *Spread forth the crannies of those rocks*
> *That lie beneath your Holland smocks;*
> *Stretch out your limbs, sigh, heave and strain,*
> *Till you have opened every vein:*
> *That so Loves gentle juice that flows*
> *Like dewy nectar, out of those*
> *That press you down may run a tilt,*
> *Into your wombs, and not be spilt*
> *Do this (dear sisters) and hereby*
> *You shall increase and multiply,*
> *And in some 20 years you'll spread*
> *Further than Jacob's children did.*
> *But (like the saints) I pray be sure*
> *Your speeches all be fine and pure;*
> *Let Gospel words, and sweet expressions,*
> *Divine narrations, and confessions,*
> *Be in your mouths, though lusty t-ses,*
> *Are stoutly knocking at your asses.*

Repression and the Quakers

Though such reported activities were often the result of hearsay and exaggeration, many believed the allegations. Parliament certainly did and in May 1650 passed 'An Act for Suppressing the Detestable Sins of Incest, Adultery and Fornication':

> For the suppressing of the abominable and crying sins of incest, adultery and fornication, wherewith this land is much defiled, and Almighty God highly displeased, be it enacted by the authority of this present Parliament, that if any person or persons whatsoever, shall…have the carnal knowledge of the body of his or her grandfather or grandmother, father or mother, brother or sister, son or daughter, or grandchild, father's brother or sister, mother's brother or sister, father's wife, mother's husband, son's wife, daughter's husband, wife's mother or daughter, husband's father or son; all and every such offences are hereby adjudged incest: and every such offence shall be, and is hereby adjudged felony; and every person offending therein, and confessing the same, or being thereof convicted by verdict upon indictment or presentment, before any judge or justices at the assize or sessions of the peace, shall suffer death as in a case of felony, without benefit of clergy.

'A Quaker Meeting', by Egbert Heemskerk (BAL)

The Quaker's Dream, a broadsheet from 1655 (BAL)

The Quaker's Dream, a broadsheet from 1655 (BAL)

Later that year, the Commonwealth also sanctioned 'An Act Against Several Atheistical, Blasphemous and Execrable Opinions, Derogatory to the Honour of God, and Destructive to Humane Society' which clearly had the Ranters in its sights:

> To Parliament holding it to be their duty, by all good ways and means to propagate the Gospel in this Commonwealth, to advance religion in all sincerity, godliness, and honesty, have made several ordinances and laws for the good and furtherance of reformation; in doctrine and manners, and in order to the suppressing of prophaneness, wickedness, superstition and formality, that God may be truly glorified, and all might in well-doing be encouraged. But notwithstanding this their care, finding to their

great grief and astonishment, that there are divers men and women who have lately discovered themselves to be most monstrous in their opinions, and loose in all wicked and abominable practices...not only to the notorious corrupting and disordering, but even to the dissolution of all humane society.

But the Blasphemy Acts did nothing to stop other groups emerging who were scurrilously branded 'Ranter' by their opponents. The Quakers, established by George Fox in the early 1650s, was one such group. They searched for the 'inner light' within a believer rather than any external or independent manifestation of spiritual election. The Puritan preacher Richard Baxter considered Quakers just as bad as Ranters:

The Quakers who were but the Ranters turned from horrid prophaneness and blasphemy to a life of extreme austerity on the other side. Their doctrines were mostly the same with Ranters': they make the light which every man hath within him to be his sufficient rule, and consequently the scripture and ministry are set light by. They speak much for the dwelling and working of the spirit in us, but little of justification and the pardon of sin, and our reconciliation of God through Jesus Christ. They pretend their dependence on the spirit's conduct against set times of prayer, and against sacraments, and against their due esteem of scripture and ministry. They will not have the scripture called the word of God ; their principal zeal lieth in railing at the ministers as hirelings, deceivers, false prophets, etc., and in refusing to swear before a magistrate , or to put off their hat to any, or to say 'You' instead of 'Thou' or 'Thee' which are their words to all. At first they did use to fall into tremblings and vomitings in their meetings, and pretended to be violently acted by the spirit, but now that is ceased; they only meet, and he that pretendeth to be moved by the spirit speaketh, and sometime they say nothing, but sit an hour or more in silence and then depart. One while divers of them went naked through divers chief towns and cities of the land, as a prophetical act; some of them have famished themselves and drowned themselves in melancholy, and others undertaken by the power the spirit to raise them, as Susan Pearson did at Claines near Worcester, where they took a man out of his grave that had made away with himself, and commanded him to arise and live, but to their shame...James Naylor acted the part of Christ at Bristol, according to much of the history of the Gospel, and was long laid in Bridewell for it, and his tongue bored as a blasphemer by the Parliament.

With an 'inner light' prompting so many to such public acts of personal faith, it is no surprise that denominational labels, such as 'Ranter' or 'Quaker', soon became inadequate categories for expressing the variety and diversity of religious opinions which people held. In 1651, *A List of Some of the Grand Blasphemers and Blasphemies Which Was Given to the Committee for Religion* compiled an intriguing constellation of eccentrics:

I.   John Robins said, That he was God Almighty; he was committed to New-prison at Clerkenwell, 1651.

II   Thomas Tidford said, That John Robins was God the Father, and the Father of our Lord Jesus Christ; he was summoned to the Gatehouse, 1651.

III.   Richard King said, His wife was with child of him that should be the Saviour of all those that shall be saved, was committed to the New-prison, 1651.

IV.   Thomas Kerby said, That Cain (who murdered his Brother Abel) was the third person in the Trinity; he was committed to the Gatehouse, 1651.

V.   Elizabeth Sorrell said, That those of her society had power to raise the dead; she was committed to the Gatehouse, 1651.

VI.   Joshua Garment, clapping his hands, and filliping with his fingers, said, That was preaching of the Gospel. Committed to the New-prison, 1651.

VII.   Elizabeth Haygood, being uncivil and playing the fool, said, That was preaching the Gospel, which was foolishness; she was committed to the New-prison, 1651…

XIX.   A Goldsmith that did live in the Strand, and after in the City, and then at Eltham; who called his name Theau au John Tany, the High Priest, &c. published in print, that all religion is a lie, a deceit, and a cheat, 1651,

'Theau au John Tany, the High Priest' was one Thomas Tany, also once mistaken for a Quaker in a news-book which reported his antics in more detail:

> A hair-brained fellow or Quaker, who calls himself Theareau John, and useth now and then to live in Tents, which he erects sometimes at Lambeth, and sometimes at Greenwich, saying, he is to gather the dispersed Jews, and carry them to the Holy-Land. This man came in an antique habit, with a long rusty sword by his side to the room at the Parliament House door, where a toy taking him in the head, he suddenly fell a slashing of the by-standers, cutting the clothes of some; and in that fury, he ran with his sword drawn and bounced with his foot at the house door, to have forced and entered it; but being laid hold on, he was sent in, and coming to the Bar, he stood covered; but the sergeant was commanded to take off his hat. He was there asked divers questions, and afterwards committed to the Gatehouse. He was formerly committed to Newgate for blasphemy; and last week, at Lambeth, he openly, with great solemnity burnt a sword, a great saddle, a pair of pistols, and the Bible together, declaring them the three grand idols of England.

Tany's antics defied sectarian labelling, not least as he laid claim to the crowns of France, Rome, Naples and Sicily. As Parliament heard, he declared religion was a lie, a cheat and a deceit. In one of his pamphlets, noted for their mystically attuned puns and repeated exclamations of divine insight, he stated these opinions with a boldness that gave way to eccentric use of fake Hebrew, in which even Tany admitted he could see no sense:

> Now you Persecutors, you dwell in forms, and know the form of the thing is not the true thing, for the true light it is not in any man's form, or formed, or forming; but it is Truth in its own root, unforming your Independency, your Anabaptism, and your Antinomianism, and your Presbyterianism, and your Judaism, and all the rest of these base, beggarly packed cloaks of knavery, under which so many wolfish devils walk, devouring one another, and this is religion, which whilst you are devouring one another you must have Christs cloak to cover all your villainy, under what kind of

devouring soever. Now know that all Religion is a lie, and a cheat, a deceit; for there is but one Truth & that is Love, & that devoureth, not neither destroyeth any man, but lives in its own fire, fed with its own heat, beholding all beauteous, desiring no part, but unto all alike, alike unto all: Love it is *Salma Ori am*, that is, it is the adornative beauty of select virtue…if truly viewed in your lying colours you are clearly deciphered out, for know, they or that which accuseth it, is a Devil; a deceived Spirit, for if you were in light, then you were in Love, then no accusation but Love, and that acting in mercy; for the reducement of them that are deceived and in darkness *Sabeannus alla Sam ardiby notyd nomis peleg ory*, the English is, the safe light accuseth not, but it is the non resident that flieteth crying, *Segad*, that word hold the full import.

Such individual eccentricity defied the sectarian categories used during the 1640s to classify religious radicalism. Yet such antics were rare and its practitioners were usually imprisoned, emigrated or died. Tany himself was lost at sea, attempting to return the Jews to England in a rowing boat. Though the Ranters caused widespread hysteria and the Quakers were destined to become a powerfully subversive movement, the authorities of the Commonwealth were more concerned with another religion. Across the Irish sea, the Roman Catholic religion was still practised with impunity. In late 1649, Oliver Cromwell sailed west to settle the unfinished business started by the Irish Rebellion of 1641.

XI

The Lord Protector

1649 *February*	Prince Charles, the future Charles II, is proclaimed King in Scotland	**1651** *September*	Scots and Royalists defeated at Battle of Worcester. Charles II escapes to France
1649 *August*	Cromwell lands in Dublin to suppress the Irish Confederates	**1653** *April*	Cromwell dissolves the Rump Parliament
1649 *September*	Cromwell storms Drogheda with terrible results	**1653** *July*	Nominated or Barebones Parliament meets
1649 *October*	Cromwell leaves Ireland for England	**1653** *December*	Barebones Parliament is dissolved. Cromwell becomes Lord Protector.
1650 *July*	Cromwell invades Scotland		
1650 *September*	Cromwell defeats Scots at the Battle of Dunbar		

THE ENGLISH ELEMENT OF THE CIVIL WAR MAY HAVE COME TO AN END WITH THE EXECUTION OF KING CHARLES I, BUT IN IRELAND AND SCOTLAND THE CONFLICT STILL RAGED. In a speech to the General Council which now governed the republican Commonwealth, Oliver Cromwell set out his priorities:

Truly, notwithstanding you have brought this work to this issue, yet it seems your work is not at an end. You have yet another enemy to encounter with, and friends to stand by, the interest you have fought for yet further to make good; to the end you may be able to resist those that have been heretofore your enemies, and are still your enemies, and are more enraged, and are not warned by those examples and those witnesses that God hath witnessed for you. But they are removed at a further distance, joined together in strong combination to revive the work here again – that is certainly in the kingdom of Scotland [and] in the kingdom of Ireland. In the kingdom of Scotland, you cannot too well take notice of what is done nor of this: that there is a very angry, hateful spirit there against your army, as an army of sectaries, which you see all their papers do declare their quarrel to be against. And although God hath used us as instruments for their good, yet hitherto they are not sensible of it, but they are angry that God brought them His mercy at such an hand; and this their anger (though without any quarrelling of ours with them) will return into their own bosoms; for God did do the work without us, and they that are displeased with the instruments, their anger reaches to God and not [only] to them.

In the next place we are to consider Ireland. All the Papists and the King's party – I cannot say all the Papists, but the greater party of them – are in a very strong combination against you, and they have made an union with those apostate forces that were under Insiquene [Baron of Inchiquin, royalist commander] and the Confederate Catholics of Ireland, and all that party are in a very strong combination against you…these are all agreed and ready in conjunction to root out the English interest in Ireland, and to set up the Prince of Wales his interest there likewise, and to endeavour as soon as they can, to attempt upon our interest in Leinster and Ulster and Connaught…And truly this is really believed: if we do not endeavour to make good our interest there, and that timely, we shall not only have (as I said before) our interest rooted out there, but they will in a very short time be able to land forces in England, and to put us to trouble here. I confess I have had these thoughts with myself, that perhaps may be carnal and foolish. I had rather be overrun with a Cavalierish interest than a Scotch interest; I had rather be overrun with a Scotch interest, than an Irish interest; and I think of all this is most dangerous.

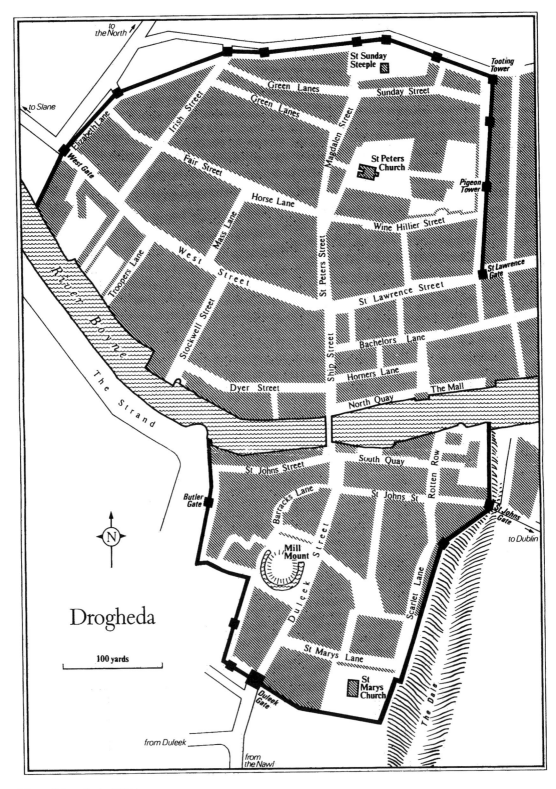

Map of Drogheda (WA)

Ireland

Ireland had been ravaged by a complicated sectarian war since the rebellion of October 1641. A force of indigenous Irish Catholics (known as the Confederates) had allied with Old English Catholic families in a struggle against the New English and Ulster Scots Protestant settlers. Throughout the 1640s the King's forces had tried intermittently to suppress the Confederates. But in the late 1640s the royalists led by King Charles's Lord Lieutenant the Earl of Ormond joined up with the Confederate rebels. However, differences over strategy and how best to challenge the Protestant forces of the English Parliament produced a hopelessly divided alliance.

The Commonwealth, on the other hand, was united in its determination to conclude the unfinished business of Ireland. The 1641 Irish Rebellion held prime position in the Protestant pantheon of Catholic crimes. The murderous Irish papists had never been fully recompensed for their indiscriminate slaughter of Protestant settlers. For someone as religiously driven as Cromwell, this was an unforgivable omission. There was the equally pressing point that a large part of the New Model Army funding had been secured from the City on the promise of Irish land. The City institutions were now calling in their debts.

On 13 August 1649, Cromwell set sail for Ireland with 10,000 war-hardened troops. He headed for Dublin which Colonel Michael Jones had recently captured from Ormond's royalist force. Cromwell's intention was to march north from Dublin and retake the Confederate lands for Parliament. Ormond posted the English Catholic commander Sir Arthur Aston at Drogheda with orders to halt Cromwell's advance. Aston had only 2,200 infantry troops and equally small cavalry numbers, but he was confident of victory: 'He who could take Drogheda could take Hell.' Prophetic words.

Cromwell quickly besieged the town and then officially demanded its surrender. Aston refused. On 10 September 1649, Cromwell ordered a day-long bombardment that saw over 200 cannonballs career into the crumbling city walls. Edmund Ludlow, who would later be posted to Ireland as a Cromwellian governor, describes the scene as garnered from first-hand accounts:

> The Lieutenant-General [Cromwell] well knowing the importance of this action, resolved to put all upon it; and having commanded some guns to be loaded with bullets of half a pound, and fired upon the enemy's horse, who were drawn up somewhat in view; himself with a reserve of foot marched up to the breach, which giving fresh courage to our men, they made a second attack with more vigour than before: whereupon the enemy's foot being abandoned by their horse, whom our shot had forced to retire, began to break and shift for themselves; which ours perceiving, followed them so close, that they overtook them at the bridge that lay cross the river, and separated that part where the action was from the principal part of the town; and

preventing them from drawing up the bridge, entred pell-mell with them into the place.

With the walls breached, Cromwell's men unleashed hell. Cromwell describes the moment with unhealthy relish:

Eighteenth-century engraving showing Cromwell besieging Drogheda (BAL)

And after a very hot dispute, the enemy having both horse and foot, and we only foot, within the wall, they gave ground, and our men became masters both of their retrenchments and the church; which indeed, although they made our entrance the more difficult, yet they proved of excellent use to us, so that the enemy could not annoy us with their horse, but thereby we had advantage to make good the ground, that so we might let in our own horse, which accordingly was done, though with much difficulty.

The enemy retreated, divers of them into the Mill-Mount: a place very strong and of difficult access, being exceedingly high, having a good graft, and strongly palisa-doed. The Governor, Sir Arthur Ashton, and divers considerable Officers being there, our men getting up to them, were ordered by me to put them all to the sword. And indeed, being in the heat of action, I forbade them to spare any that were in arms in the town, and, I think, that night they put to the sword about 2,000 men, divers of the officers and soldiers being fled over the Bridge into the other part of the Town, where about one hundred of them possessed St. Peter's church-steeple, some the west gate, and others a strong round tower next the gate called St. Sunday's. These being summoned to yield to mercy, refused, whereupon I ordered the steeple of St. Peter's Church to be fired, where one of them was heard to say in the midst of the flames: 'God damn me, God confound me; I burn, I burn.'

The next day, the other two towers were summoned, in one of which was about six or seven score; but they refused to yield themselves, and we knowing that hunger must compel them, set only good guards to secure them from running away until their stomachs were come down. From one of the said towers, notwithstanding their condition, they killed and wounded some of our men. When they submitted, their officers were knocked on the head, and every tenth man of the soldiers killed, and the rest shipped for the Barbadoes. The soldiers in the other tower were all spared, as to their lives only, and shipped likewise for the Barbadoes.

Nineteenth-century painting of the siege at Drogheda (BAL, Fine Art Society, London)

Cromwell goes on to justify this butchery on grounds of sectarian vengeance and the less credible hope of avoiding future bloodshed:

> I am persuaded that this is a righteous judgment of God upon these barbarous wretches, who have imbrued their hands in so much innocent blood; and that it will tend to prevent the effusion of blood for the future, which are the satisfactory grounds to such actions, which otherwise cannot but work remorse and regret.

Among the dead was the governor, Sir Arthur Aston. Ludlow describes his undignified end:

> Their works and fort were also stormed and taken, and those that defended them put to the sword also, and amongst them Sir Arthur Ashton, governor of the place. A great dispute there was amongst the soldiers for his artificial leg, which was reported to be of gold, but it proved to be but of wood, his girdle being found to be the better booty wherein two hundred pieces of gold were found quilted. The slaughter was continued all that day and the next; which extraordinary severity I presume was used, to discourage others from making opposition.

Historians have remained divided over the 'legality' of Cromwell's actions in Drogheda. According to the customs of war of the time, the fact he had summoned the town and it had refused to surrender meant he was within his rights to kill the defiant soldiers. However, it was a fairly strict interpretation of the rules and the fact that nearly 4,000 Confederate troops lost their lives certainly points to a wholesale slaughter. The execution of the officers and one soldier in ten also indicates an unnecessarily savage resolution to the siege. Equally controversial is whether other Irish towns then surrendered because of the killing or in fact fought harder against Cromwell having heard of the Drogheda atrocities. What is not in doubt is that the Lieutenant General's actions in Wexford were far less excusable.

By early October, Cromwell's army had reached southern Ireland. His next target was Wexford where the Confederates received arms from abroad and maintained diplomatic links with foreign Catholic powers. After a few days skirmishing, the Confederate cause was betrayed by Captain James Stafford who allowed the parliamentarian forces in. In a letter to the Speaker of the House of Commons, Cromwell describes the ensuing carnage:

> And which they were come into the market-place, the enemy making a stiff resistance, our forces brake them, and then put all to the sword that came in their way. Two boatfuls of the enemy attempting to escape, being overprest with numbers, sank whereby were drowned near three-hundred of them. I believe, in all, there was lost of the enemy not many less than two-thousand; and I believe not twenty of yours killed from first to last of the siege.
>
> And indeed it hath not without cause been deeply set upon our hearts, that, we intending better to this place than so great a ruin, hoping the town might be of more use to you and your army, yet God would not have it so; but, by an unexpected providence, in His righteous justice, brought a just judgment upon them, causing them to

*Cromwell as conqueror of Ireland, 1650
(National Library of Ireland)*

*Portrait of Cromwell from the Roll of Accounts for
Ireland, 1649–56 (Public Records Office, London)*

become a prey to the soldier, who in their piracies had made preys of so many families, and made with their bloods to answer the cruelties which they had exercised
upon the lives of divers poor Protestants....

The soldiers got a very good booty in this place, and had they not had opportunity
to carry their goods over the river, which we besieged it, it would have been much
more. I could have wished for their own good, and the good of the garrison, they had
been more moderate. Some things which were not easily portable, we hope we shall
make use of to your behoof. There are great quantities of iron, hides, tallow, salt,
pipe- and barrel-staves, which are under commissioners' hands, to be secured. We
believe there are near a hundred cannon in the fort, and elsewhere in and about the
two...

This town is now so in your power, that [of] the former inhabitants, I believe scarce
one in twenty can challenge any property in their houses. Most of them are run away,
and many of them killed in this service. And it were to be wished, that an honest
people would come and plant here, where are very good houses, and other accommo-
dations fitted to their hands, and may by your favour be made of encouragement to
them, as also a seat of good trade, both inward and outward, and of marvellous great

advantage in the point of the herring and other fishing. The town is pleasantly seated and strong, having a rampart of earth within the wall, near fifteen foot thick.

Thus it hath pleased God to give into your hands this other mercy, for which, as for all, we pray God may have all the glory. Indeed your instruments are poor and weak, and can do nothing but through believing, and that is the gift of God also.

The bloodbath in Wexford was the Protestant payback for the Irish Rebellion of 1641. Cromwell happily set loose his dogs of war on an Irish race he regarded as backward and fallen. As Christopher Hill described it, 'The native Irish were treated much as the original settlers of New England treated the Indians.' Cromwell's progress through the rest of Ireland was brutal and tortuous. Despite suffering massive losses, he captured Ross, Cork, Kildare, Kilkenny and Clonmel – where almost 2,500 of his men died in a cleverly executed Confederate counter-attack. By May 1650, the main body of resistance was crushed and Cromwell felt able to sail back to England. On his return, he was greeted with a Horation ode by Andrew Marvell:

> The forward youth that would appear
> Must now forsake his muses dear,
>   Nor in the shadows sing
>   His numbers languishing.
> 'Tis time to leave the books in dust,
> And oil the unused armour's rust:
>   Removing from the wall
>   The corslet of the hall.
> So restless Cromwell could not cease
> In the inglorious arts of peace,   10
>   But through adventurous war
>   Urged his active star.
> And, like the three-forked lightning, first
> Breaking the clouds where it was nursed,
>   Did thorough his own side
>   His fiery way divide.
> (For 'tis all one to courage high
> The emulous or enemy:
>   And with such to enclose
>   Is more than to oppose.)   20
> Then burning through the air he went.
> And palaces and temples rent:
>   And Caesar's head at last
>   Did through his laurels blast.
> 'Tis madness to resist or blame
> The force of angry heaven's flame:
>   And, if we would speak true,
>   Much to the man is due,

Who, from his private gardens, where
He lived reserved and austere,   30
   As if his highest plot
   To plant the bergamot,
Could by industrious valour climb
To ruin the great work of time,
   And cast the kingdom old
   Into another mould.
Though justice against fate complain,
And plead the ancient rights in vain:
   But those do hold or break
   As men are strong or weak…   40

   So when they did design
   The Capitol's first line,
A bleeding head where they begun,
Did fright the architects to run;   70
   And yet in that the State
   Foresaw its happy fate.
And now the Irish are ashamed
To see themselves in one year tamed:
   So much one man can do,
   That does both act and know…

The Pict no shelter now shall find
Within his pari-coloured mind,
   But from this valour sad
   Shrink underneath the plaid:
Happy, if in the tufted brake
The English hunter him mistake,   110
   Nor lay his hounds in near
   The Caledonian deer.
But thou, the Wars' and Fortune's son,
March indefatigably on,
   And for the last effect
   Still keep thy sword erect:
Besides the force it has to fright
The spirits of the shady night,
   The same arts that did gain
   A power, must it maintain.   120

It was indeed the Pict who Cromwell had his eye on.

Scotland

In February 1649, the nineteen-year-old Prince of Wales had been proclaimed King Charles II in Scotland. Under the strong maternal influence of his mother Henrietta-Maria, the young Charles II had already declared himself an ardent believer in the divine right of kings and shown strong inklings towards Catholicism. But by agreeing to sign the Covenant and commit himself to Presbyterianism, Charles secured the backing of a Scottish army in his campaign to reclaim the English throne. It was an early taste of the political cynicism that would come to define his monarchy. The English Parliament was furious. Ludlow describes the mood:

> But the enemy which most threatened the disturbance of the Parliament, was that of Scotland, where all interests were united in opposition to the present authority in England. They had also many who favoured their design in our nation, as well Presbyterians as Cavaliers: the former of these were most bold and active, upon presumption of more favour in case of ill success. The Parliament being sensible of these things, published a declaration, shewing that they had no design to impose upon the nation of Scotland any thing contrary to their inclination: that they would leave them to choose what government they thought most convenient for themselves, provided they would suffer the English nation to live under that establishment which they had chosen: that it evidently appeared that the Scots were acted by a spirit of domination and rule; and that nothing might be wanting to compel us to submit to their imposition, they had espoused the interests of that family, which they themselves had declared guilty of much precious blood, and resolved to force the same upon England...

In July 1650, Cromwell's army crossed the Tweed – the scene of so much cross-border activity over the previous thirteen years – and headed towards Edinburgh where the Scottish general David Leslie kept a 22,000 strong force behind the castle's giant fortifications. Ludlow recounts how Leslie played a debilitating cat and mouse game with Cromwell's army, tying them down them in fruitless marches across the Borders.

> the Scots would not hazard all by the decision of a battle, hoping to tire us out with frequent skirmishes and harassing our men, relying much upon the unsuitableness of the climate to our constitutions, especially if they should detain us in the field till winter. Their counsels succeeded according to their desires, and our army through hard duty, scarcity of provisions, and the rigour of the season, grew very sickly, and diminished daily, so that they were necessitated to draw off to receive supplies from our shipping, which could not come nearer to them than Dunbar, distant from Edinburgh about twenty miles.

The Scots had also adopted a scorched earth policy which meant Cromwell's army had to obtain its supplies from England, mostly via the port of Dunbar. On 1 September 1650, Cromwell's demoralised army was forced to retreat to Dunbar with a Scottish army following close behind. Captain John Hodgson describes the beleaguered scene:

> We staid until about ten o'clock, had been at prayer in several regiments, sent away our wagons and carriages towards Dunbar, and not long afterwards marched, a poor, shattered, hungry, discouraged army; and the Scots pursued very close, that our rear-guard had much ado to secure our poor weak foot that was not able to march up.
>
> We drew near Dunbar towards night, and the Scot ready to fall upon our rear: two guns played upon them, and so they drew off, and left us that night, having got us into a pound as they reckoned. The next morning was very tempestuous, and they had blocked up our way for England. A great clough was betwixt the armies, and it could

Victorian painting of Cromwell victorious at Dunbar (BAL, Imperial Defence College, Camberley)

be no less than a mile of ground betwixt their right wing, near Roxburgh house, and their left wing: they had a great mountain behind them, which was prejudicial, as God ordered it. Our poor army drew up about swamps and bogs, not far from Dunbar, and could not pitch a tent all day. About nine o'clock at night we had a council of war called; and, debating the case what to do, many of the colonels were for shipping the foot, and the horse to force their passage; but honest Lambert [Parliamentarian Major-General] was against them in all that matter, he being active the day before in observing the disadvantage the Scots might meet with in the posture they were drawn up in, and gave us reasons, and great encouragements to fight; first we had great experience of the goodness of God to us, while we kept close together: and if we parted we lost all: we had great advantage of them in their drawing up; if we beat their right wing, we hazarded their whole army, for they would be all in confusion, in regard they had not great ground to traverse their regiments betwixt the mountain and the clough.

Fearing annihilation, the Parliamentarians chose to turn and fight. Rather than await Leslie's advance the following day, they decided that at the break of dawn on 3 September they would charge the Scots. Thomas Carlyle, in his collection of Cromwell's letters and speeches, gives a sublime account of the ensuing Battle of Dunbar:

And so the soldiers stand to their arms, or lie within instant reach of their arms, all night; being upon an engagement very difficult indeed. The night is wild and wet; – the Harvest Moon wades deep among clouds of sleet and hail. Whoever has a heart for prayer, let him pray now, for the wrestle of death is at hand. Pray, – and withal keep his powder dry! And be ready for extremities, and quit himself like a man! – Thus they pass the night; making that Dunbar Peninsula and Brock Rivulet long memorable to me. We English have some tents; the Scots have none. The hoarse sea moans bodeful, swinging low and heavy against these whinstone bays; the sea and the tempests are abroad, all else asleep but we, – and there is One that rides on the wings of the wind.

Towards three in the morning the Scotch foot, extinguish their matches, all but two in a company; cower under the corn-shocks, seeking some imperfect shelter and sleep. Be wakeful, ye English; watch, and pray, and keep your powder dry. About four o'clock comes order to my pudding-headed Yorkshire friend [Hodgson] that his regiment must mount and march straightway; his and various other regiments march pouring swiftly to the left to Brocksmouth House, to the Pass over the Brock. With overpowering force let us storm the Scots right wing there; beat that, and all is beaten. Major Hodgson riding along, heard, he says, 'a Cornet praying in the night;' a company of poor men, I think, making worship there, under the void Heaven, before battle joined. And the Heavens, in their mercy, I think, have opened us a way of deliverance! – The Moon gleams out, hard and blue, riding among hail-clouds; and over St. Abb's Head a streak of dawn is rising.

And now is the hour when the attack should be, and no Lambert is yet here, he is ordering the line far to the right yet; and Oliver occasionally, in Hodgson's hearing, is impatient for him. The Scots too, on this wing, are awake; thinking to surprise us;

there is their trumpet sounding, we heard it once; and Lambert, who was to lead the attack, is not here. The Lord General is impatient; – behold Lambert at last! The trumpets peal, shattering with fierce clangor Night's silence; the cannons awaken along all the Line: 'The Lord of Hosts! The Lord of Hosts!' On, my brave ones, on! –

The dispute 'on this right wing was hot and stiff, for there three quarters of an hour.' Plenty of fire, from field pieces, snap-hances, matchlocks, entertains the Scotch main-battle across the Brock; – poor stiffened men, roused from the corn-shocks with their matches all out! But here on the right, their horse, 'with lancers in the front rank,' charge desperately; drive us back across the hollow of the Rivulet; – back a little; but the Lord gives us courage, and we storm home again, horse and foot, upon them, with a shock like torn do tempests; break them, beat them, drive them all adrift. 'Some fled towards Copperspath, but most across their own foot.' Poor men, it was a terrible awakening for them: field-pieces and charge of foot across the Brocksburn; and now here is their own horse in mad panic trampling them to death. Above three thousand killed upon the place: 'I never saw such a charge of foot and horse,' says one; nor did I. Oliver was still near to Yorkshire Hodgson when the shock succeeded; Hodgson heard him say, 'They run! I profess they run!' And over St. Abb's Head and the German Ocean, just then, bursts the first gleam of the level Sun upon us, 'and I heard Nol [Cromwell] say, in the words of the Psalmist, "Let God arise, let His enemies be scattered."'

Hodgson takes up the story:

I heard him say, 'I profess they run!' and then was the Scots' army all in disorder and running, both right wing and left, and main battle. They had routed one another after we had done their work on their right wing; and we, coming up to the top of the hill with the straggling parties that had been engaged, kept them from bodying: and so the foot threw down their arms and fled towards Dunbar, our pinfold, and there they were surrounded and taken. The horse fled what way they could get, ours pursued towards Haddington; and the General made a halt, and sung the hundred and seventeenth psalm; and by that time they had done, their party was increased, and advancing; the Scots ran, and were no more heard of that fight. The commander of our army was busy in securing prisoners, and the whole bag and baggage; and, afterwards, we returned to bless God in our tents, like Issachar, for the great salvation afforded to us that day.

With 3,000 Scots killed and 10,000 taken prisoner, Dunbar was a staggering victory for Cromwell – perhaps his greatest. But the Scottish challenge was not quashed. Over the course of the next year, Cromwell fought a long campaign against the Covenanter–Royalist forces involving a siege of Edinburgh Castle and a pitched battle against Leslie near Stirling. Realising his options were becoming increasingly limited in Scotland, Charles II dashed south hoping to incite a popular uprising. He made for the loyal royalist town of Worcester. But the country did not rise for Charles and more worryingly Cromwell was not far behind. On 3 September 1651, the civil wars came to an end when an invincible Cromwell effortlessly crushed the royalist and Scottish forces. While the Earl of Cleveland bravely led some last-ditch charges against the overwhelming parliamentary force, Charles II fled the battlefield for France – pausing on the way to hide in an oak tree to avoid search parties. With the royalist threat finally neutered, Cromwell was now free to implement his godly Commonwealth across the three kingdoms.

Charles II hidden in the Oak Tree, nineteenth-century engraving (BAL)

Cromwellian Settlement

The civil wars of the 1640s began partly because Charles I tried to stamp unitary policies across three kingdoms. Lacking any political sensitivity, he governed from Whitehall three separate kingdoms with antagonistic religious and political priorities. Cromwell who had battled against these policies now followed the same path – and achieved it. The reluctantly admiring Clarendon put it thus:

> What he once resolved, in which he was not rash, he would not be dissuaded from, nor endure any contradiction of his power and authority; but extorted obedience from them who were not willing to yield it....To reduce three nations, which perfectly hated him, to an entire obedience, to all his dictates; to awe and govern those nations by an army that was indevoted to him, and wished his ruin, was an instance of a very prodigious address.

In Ireland the Cromwellian settlement was most thorough. All Irish estates east of Shannon were to be cleared of their Catholic landowners. Irish landholders were evicted en masse and were ordered to cross the Shannon or face death. Parliamentary soldiers and commercial investors took up the best estates in this massive transfer of wealth and property. But famine and plague swept the land, prompting Richard Lawrence to remark, 'a man might travel twenty or thirty miles and not see a living creature, either man, beast or bird.' Arbitrary executions were a regular occurrence and it was estimated that nearly 12,000 Irish, mainly children, were transported to the West Indies as slaves. Cromwell's vengeful policies in Ireland cemented sectarian antagonism between Catholic and Protestant, native and settler, that has not healed to this day. Meanwhile Scotland, which had initially gone to war against Charles I to protect its independence, was forced into a union with England that saw its precious autonomy progressively whittled away.

In England, Cromwell's godly authoritarianism knew no limits. After victory at Dunbar, the Lord General had written to Parliament in even more aggressive terms than usual:

> This is the great hand of the Lord, and worthy of the consideration of all those who take into their hands the instruments of a foolish shepherd, to wit, meddling with worldly policies, and mixtures of earthly power, to set up that which they call the kingdom of Christ, which is neither it, nor, if it were it, would such means be found effectual to that end; and will also do it. This is humbly offered for their sakes who have lately too much turned aside, that they might return again to preach Jesus Christ, according to the simplicity of the Gospel; and then no doubt they will discern and find your protection and encouragement.

On 20 April 1653, Cromwell moved against the Commonwealth. He denounced the sitting MPs of the 'Rump Parliament' as whore-masters and drunkards, and dissolved the assembly: 'You have sat too long here for any good you have been doing. Depart, I say, and let us have done with you. In the name of God, go!' 'Thus' remarked the veteran parliamentarian Bulstrode Whitelocke, 'was this great parliament which had done so great things…this assembly famous through the world for its actions, undertakings and successes, wholly at this time routed.' In its place Cromwell ordained the Nominated or Barebones Parliament (so-called after one of its more Puritan members, Praisegod Barebones) which he hoped would oversee a reign of Saintly rule. Yet fearful of its radicalism, he soon suppressed that body and decided the simplest thing was to rule himself as Lord Protector with a Council of State. In 1655 the military dictatorship was normalised when the country was divided into eleven regions, each under the governance of a major-general.

Lucy Hutchinson, who had been such a militant supporters of Cromwell and the cause, was furious at his betrayal of the revolution:

> First he calls a Parliament out of his own pocket, himself nominating a sort of godly men for every county, who meeting and not agreeing, part of them, in the name of

Cromwell dissolves the 'Rump Parliament', April 1653, contemporary engraving (AA)

the people, gave up the sovereignty to him, who shortly after makes up several sorts of mock parliaments, but not finding one of them absolutely for his turn, turned them off again…He weeded, in a few months' time, above a 150 godly officers out of the army, with whom many of the religious soldiers went off, and in their room abundance of the King's dissolute soldiers were entertained; and the army was almost changed from that godly religious army, whose valour God had crowned with triumph, into the dissolute army they had beaten, bearing yet a better name…His court was full of sin and vanity, and the more abominable, because they had not yet quite cast away the name of God, but profaned it by taking it in vain upon them. True religion was now almost lost, even among the religious party, and hypocrisy became an epidemical disease, to the sad grief of Colonel Hutchinson and all true-heartened Christians and Englishmen…The Cavaliers, in policy, who saw that while Cromwell reduced all by the exercise of tyrannical power under another name, there was a door opened for the restoring of their party, fell much in with Cromwell, and heightened all his disorders; who at last exercised such an arbitrary power that the whole land grew weary of him, while he set up a company of silly mean fellows, called major-generals, as governors in every county, who ruled according to their wills, by no law but what seemed good in their own eyes, imprisoning men and obstructing the course of justice between man and man and perverting right through partiality, acquitting some that were guilty, and punishing some that were innocent as guilty.

*Two versions of Cromwell's signature.
The first is dated 5 July 1655. Note the
shakiness of the second, dated 26 July
1658, less than six weeks before
Cromwell's death (WA)*

*Cromwell as military leader, contemporary
engraving (BL)*

Following Cromwell's assumption of the Protectorate, Colonel Hutchinson
resigned from the Council of State.

There were those more willing to defend Cromwell and his will to power. The
most fluent, the most brilliant was the blind poet John Milton. Appointed Latin (or
Foreign) Secretary to the Council of State during the Commonwealth, he composed furious responses to royalist propaganda. As early as 1644 he was writing
some of the most inspiring works of the civil war. In *Areopagitica*, he gave voice to
Puritan hopes for a risen English nation free of religious and political tyranny:

> Methinks I see in my mind a noble and puissant nation rousing herself like a strong
> man after sleep, and shaking her invincible locks: methinks I see her as an eagle mew-
> ing her mighty youth, and kindling her undazzled eyes at the full midday beam; purg-
> ing and unscaling her long-abused sight at the fountain itself of heavenly radiance;
> while the whole noise of timorous and flocking birds, with those also that love the
> twilight, flutter about, amazed at what she means, and in their envious gabble would
> prognosticate a year of sects and schisms.

In *To The Lord General Cromwell*, Milton was even more emphatic:

> Cromwell, our chief of men, who through a cloud
>   Not of war only, but detractions rude,

Guided by faith and matchless fortitude
　　To peace and truth thy glorious way hast ploughed,
And on the neck of crowned fortune proud
　　Hast reared God's trophies and his work pursued,
　　While Darwen stream with blood of Scots imbrued,
　　And Dunbar field resounds thy praises loud,
And Worcester's laureate wreath; yet much remains
To conquer still; peace hath her victories
No less renowned than war, new foes arise
Threatening to bind our souls with secular chains:
　　Help us to save free conscience from the paw
　　Of hireling wolves whose gospel is their maw.

*John Milton, secretary
and ardent supporter of
Cromwell, 1629 (NPG)*

Cromwell had indeed transformed the country. The England of the 1650s Protectorate was a foreign country to its Caroline forebear: the King was executed by order of Parliament on a public scaffold at Whitehall; his kingdom was declared a republic; the House of Lords was abolished; episcopacy was destroyed; all manner of religious worship and belief was tolerated; the press went uncensored; religious and political movements organised common people in a way that had no equal until the nineteenth century. In public debate, mass petition and popular print, many traditionally sacrosanct principles were disputed: political equality, private property, marriage, even the Bible.

'The Genealogy of the Anti-Christ Oliver Cromwell': venomous Royalist propaganda (BAL, Bibliotheque Nationale, Paris)

'The Emblem of England's Distractions', engraving 1658 (BAL)

Amidst the turbulence of the times great changes were under way. The Commons claimed greater authority than the Lords and prerogative courts were abolished so that royal power could never again be exercised through arbitrary whim rather than due political process. The Court of High Commission was never restored meaning bishops were no longer able to impose their ecclesiastical will across the country; the Court of Star Chamber was never replaced so preventing central government dictating the law to local Justices of the Peace. Decentralisation was matched by consolidation. The events of the Civil War gave England national sovereignty over the British Isles: the great parliamentary armies of the 1640s and 1650s, which conquered Wales, the north and the south-west, as well as Ireland and Scotland, gave London, in particular, sovereignty over all. This was only consolidated by the war state Cromwell initiated by his military campaigns against Spain and Holland. Thus was the great struggle against Charles I's tyranny and personal rule concluded.

By the mid-1650s, the combination of foreign military setbacks, crushing taxes and the petty interference of Puritan governance made Cromwell an increasingly unloved Lord Protector. John Milton was not the only who could write verse. Among the most popular of the day was this ditty:

1 The army is come up, hay hoe,
The army is come up, hay hoe!
    to London it is brought,
    and who would have thought
It ever would have proved so?
    for the independents
are superintendents
Our kingdom and City also.
Then O fine Oliver, O brave, O rare Oliver, O, Dainty Oliver,
O gallant Oliver, O!...

3 For Oliver is all in all,
For Oliver is all in all,
    and Oliver is here,
    and Oliver is there,
And Oliver is at Whitehall.
    And Oliver notes all,
and Oliver votes all,
And claps his hand upon his bilboe.
Then O fine Oliver, O brave Oliver, &c.

Now Oliver must be he,
Now Oliver must be he,
for Oliver's nose
  is the Lancaster rose,

And thence comes his sovereignty.
  For Oliver teaches,
  and Oliver preaches,
And prayeth upon his tip-toe.
Then O fine Oliver, O rare Oliver, &c....

6 But doe you not hear? what news?
But doe you not hear? what news?
    The Prince they say
    will come this way,
And the Scots will him not refuse.
    I wish he may enter
    this Land to the Center,
And win it, and give a right blow.
Then O base Oliver, O s——— Oliver, O,
Stinking Oliver, O Traitor Oliver, O, Damned Oliver, O!

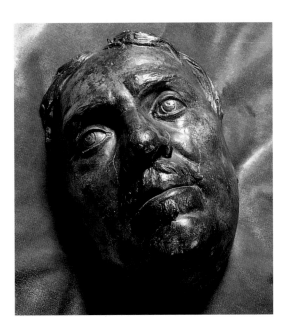

Death mask of Oliver Cromwell
(BAL, Chequers, Buckinghamshire)

Crown of Oliver Cromwell 1658
(obverse) (gold) (BAL, Fitzwilliam
Museum, University of Cambridge)

Chartering the Protectorate; Surviving the Restoration

In 1658, Cromwell's extraordinary energy finally failed him. The death of his favourite daughter Elizabeth in August 1658 seemed visibly to weaken the Lord Protector and on his lucky day of 3 September, the anniversary of his victories at

Dunbar and Worcester, he died of pneumonia. His hapless son Richard ('Tumbledown Dick') briefly took over the reigns of Lord Protector, but it wasn't long before King Charles II was sailing into Dover.

Managing 'regime changes', as they are now euphemistically titled, is among the more valuable skills a public figure can acquire. Many of the narrators of this story faced highly treacherous times from the late 1640s through to the Restoration in 1660. Committed supporters of Parliament and the Puritan cause had been appalled by Cromwell's actions in dissolving Parliament and setting up his dictatorship. Edmund Ludlow, the loyal Roundhead commander from Wiltshire, watched in horror at his old ally's usurpations. He began circulating anti-Cromwell pamphlets and was briefly imprisoned. When the Commonwealth momentarily returned in 1659 following the death of Cromwell and the overthrow of his son Richard, Ludlow was elected to Parliament. Yet Ludlow had signed Charles I's death warrant, and with the restoration of the martyred king's son Ludlow wisely chose exile on the tranquil shores of Lake Geneva. As we have seen, the Hutchinsons were equally critical of Cromwell's Protectorate. Unfortunately, Colonel Hutchinson like Ludlow was a regicide and it wasn't long before the Restoration authorities incarcerated him. It was his death in jail in 1664 that spurred Lucy Hutchinson to pen her *Memoirs*, designed to instruct his children in their late father's great role during the Puritan revolution.

Richard Baxter, the Kidderminster Puritan and Roundhead minister, was barred from preaching and subsequently imprisoned for libelling the church. His persecution ended with the 1688 Glorious Revolution and he outlasted the Stuart dynasty to pass away at the ripe age of 76 in 1691. Sir Simond D'Ewes, the antiquarian MP who witnessed the attempted arrest of the five members and later split from his Cavalier brother, was not so lucky. Distrusted by the New Model Army for his political moderation, he was exiled from Parliament in Pride's Purge and retreated to his estate in Suffolk where he died in 1650. Another victim of family divisions was Sir Ralph Verney. To his father's great shame, Ralph had declared for Parliament while Sir Edmund rode to his death as the King's standard bearer at Edgehill. Yet Ralph had entered the war because of his devotion to the Church of England and in 1643 he refused to sign the Solemn League and Covenant with the Scots. Instead, Verney went into exile in France and had his lands confiscated as a suspected royalist. When he returned in 1653, Cromwell imprisoned and fined him. With the Restoration, he was awarded a baronetcy by Charles II but retreated from court to live at the family seat in Claydon, Buckinghamshire until his death in 1696. His fellow royalist Edward Hyde, Earl of Clarendon, returned in triumph in 1660 as Charles II's Lord Chancellor. He worked hard to rebuild the Church of England and systematically refused any moves towards religious toleration. But in the mid-1660s he fell victim to court politics and fearing prosecution for treason fled England for France. Based in Rouen he spent the remaining years of his life writing the *History of the Great*

Rebellion. That other eloquent royalist, Sir Philip Warwick, spent the 1650s in England suffering only the occasional imprisonment. At the Restoration his loyalty to the Stuarts was rewarded with a knighthood. Returned as MP for Westminster, he too opposed all moves towards religious toleration and died of natural causes in 1683 aged 74. The great trimmer of the day Bulstrode Whitelocke enjoyed a similarly painless Restoration. Despite being President of the Council of State in the late 1650s, his acceptance of Charles II's return ensured suitable leniency from the Stuart monarchy. He was defended by various royalist friends and retired unmolested to Chilton Park in Wiltshire where he lived until his death in 1675.

The last word should, of course, belong to a witness to the events of those tumultuous years. At the Restoration, the great diarist John Evelyn returned from his twenty years of travel. What he saw in London that day lifted his heart and many others across the three kingdoms:

> This day [29 May 1660] came in his Majestie Charles the 2d to London after a sad, and long Exile, and Calamitous Suffering both of the King and Church: being 17 yeares: This was also his Birthday [thereafter to be celebrated as Oak-Apple Day] and with a triumph of above 2000 horse and foote, brandishing their swords and shouting with unexpressable joy: The wayes strew'd with flowers, the bell ringing, the streetes hung with Tapissry, fountaines running with wine: The Mayor, Aldermen, all the Companies in their liver[ie]s, Chaines of Gold, banners; Lords and nobles, Cloth of Silver, gold and vellvet every body clad in, the windows and balconies all set with Ladys, Trumpets, Musick, and [myriads] of people flocking the streets....I stood in the Strand and beheld it, and blessed God: And all this without one drop of bloud, and by that very Army, which rebell'd against him but it was the Lords doing for such a Restauration was never seene in the mention of any history, antient or modern, nor so joyfull a day.

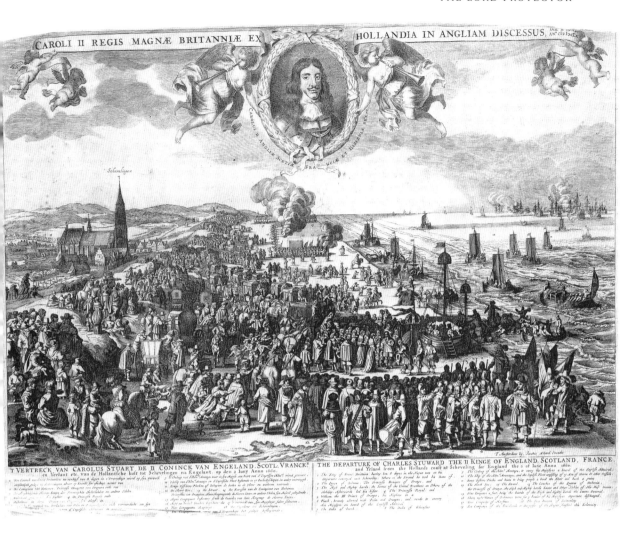

Departure of Charles II from Holland for England, 2 June 1660. Engraving by J. Alland (AA)

Bibliography

PRIMARY

Anon, *The Year of Wonders; or, The Glorious Rising of the Fifth Monarch* (London, 1652)

Anon, *A List of Some of the Grand Blasphemers and Blasphemies, Which Was Given to the Committee for Religion* (London, 1654)

Ashburnham, J., *A Narrative of His Attendance on King Charles* (Baldwin and Craddock, London, 1830)

Baillie, R., *The Letters and Journals of Robert Baillie*, ed. David Laing, 3 vols (Bannatyne Club, Edinburgh, 1841-2)

Baxter, R., *Reliquiae Baxterianae*, ed. M. Sylvester (Parkhurst, London, 1696)

Bruce, J., *The Quarrel Between the Earl of Manchester and Oliver Cromwell: An Episode of the English Civil War* (Camden Society, London, 1875)

Bruce, J., and W. Douglas Hamilton, eds, *Calendar of State Papers, Domestic Series, Charles I*, 22 vols (Longman, London, 1858-1893)

Bunyan, J., *Grace Abounding to the Chief of Sinners* (George Larkin, London, 1666)

Bulstrode, R., *Memoirs* (Charles Rivington, London, 1721)

Calverley-Trevelyan, Sir W., ed., *Letters from Roundhead Officers Written From Scotland and Chiefly Addressed to Captain Adam Byrnes* (Bannatyne Club, Edinburgh, 1856)

Charles I, *Eikon Basilike* (J Grismond, London, 1649)

Cholmley, Sir H., *Memoirs* (London, 1787)

Clarke, W., *The Clarke Papers*, ed. C. H. Firth (Camden Society, London, 1891–1901)

Clifford, D. J. H., *The Diaries of Lady Anne Clifford* (Sutton, Stroud, 1990)

Cromwell, O., *Writings and Speeches*, ed. W.C. Abbott, 4 vols (Harvard University Press, Cambridge MA, 1937–47)

Cromwell, O., *Cromwell*, ed. Thomas Carlyle (Chapman and Hall, London, 1845)

Dering, E., *The Diaries and Papers of Sir Edward Dering*, ed. M.F. Bond (HMSO, London, 1976)

Dor, R. N., *The Letter Books of Sir William Brereton* (The Record Society of Lancashire and Cheshire, Chester, 1984)

Edwards, T., *Gangraena: or A Catalogue and Discovery of Many of the Errours, Heresies, Blasphemies and Pernicious Practices of the Sectaries of this Time, Vented and Acted in England in these Last Four Years*, 3 parts (Ralph Smith, London, 1646)

Evelyn, J., *The Diary of John Evelyn*, ed. E.S. de Beer, 6 vols (Clarendon Press, Oxford, 1955)

D'Ewes, Sir S., *The Journal of Sir Simonds D'Ewes from the Beginning of the Long Parliament to the Opening of the Trial of the Earl of Strafford*, ed. Wallace Notestein (Yale University Press, New Haven, 1923)

Fairfax, Sir Thomas, *Short Memorials* (R Chiswell, London, 1699)

Fanshawe, H. C., ed., *The Memoirs of Ann, Lady Fanshawe* (John Lane, London, 1907)

Fea, A., *Memoirs of the Martyr King* (John Lane, London, 1905)

Feilding, C., *Royalist Father and Roundhead Son: The Memoirs of the First and Second Earls of Denbigh, 1600–1675* (Methuen, London, 1915)

Fox, G., *The Journal*, ed. Nigel Smith (Thomas Northcott, London, 1694)

Fyfe, J. G., ed., *Scottish Diaries and Memoirs 1550–1746* (Eneas Mackay, Stirling, 1928)

Green, M. A. E., ed., *The Diary of John Rous, 1625–1642* (Camden Society, London, 1856)

Herbert, Sir Thomas, *Memoirs* (George Nicol, London, 1839)

Hodgson, John, *The Autobiography of Captain John Hodgson of Coley Hall, near Halifax* (Brighouse, 1882)

Hutchinson, J., *Memoirs of Colonel Hutchinson*, ed. N. H. Keeble (Phoenix, London, 2000)

Hyde, E., *History of the Great Rebellion* (Oxford University Press, Oxford, 1967)

Hyde, E., *Selections From 'The History of the Great Rebellion' and 'The Life by Himself'* (Oxford University Press, Oxford, 1978)

Jackson, C., ed., *The Autobiography of Mrs Alice Thornton* (Surtees Society, Durham, 1875)

Jansson, M., ed., *Two Diaries of the Long Parliament* (Sutton, Stroud, 1984)

Josselin, R., *The Diary of Ralph Josselin 1616–1683*, ed. A. Macfarlane (Oxford University Press, London, 1976)

Knyvett, T., *The Knyvett Letters*, 1620–44, ed. B. Schofield (Norfolk Record Society, Norfolk, 1949)

Laud, W., *The History of the Troubles and Tryal of the Most Reverend Father in God, and Blessed Martyr, William Laud, Lord Arch-Bishop of Canterbury*, 2 vols (Chiswell, London, 1695–1700)

Lilly, William, *Annus Tenebrosus; or, The Dark Year* (London, 1652)

Loftis, J., ed., *Memoirs of Anne, Lady Halket and Anne, Lady Fanshawe* (Clarendon Press, Oxford, 1981)

Ludlow, E., *The Memoirs of Edmund Ludlow*, ed. C.H. Firth, 2 vols (Clarendon Press, Oxford, 1894) Sir Samuel Luke, *Journal* (Oxfordshire Record Society, Oxfordshire, 1947; 1950; 1952–3)

Milton, John, *Complete Shorter Poems*, ed. John Carey, 2nd edn (Longman, London, 1997)

Oglander, Sir J., *A Royalist's Notebook* (Constable & Co., London, 1936)

Pagitt, Ephraim, *The Mysticall Wolfe* (London, 1645)

Pagitt, Ephraim, *Heresiography: or, A Description of the Heretickes and Sectaries of these Latter Times*, 1st edn (London, 1645)

Parliament, Houses of, *A List of Some of the Grand Blasphemers and Blasphemies Which Was Given In to the Committee for Religion* (London, 1654)

Parliament, Houses of, *Parliamentary History of England from the Earliest Period to the Year 1803*, 36 vols (London, 1806–20)

Parsons, D., *Diary of Sir Henry Slingsby* (London, 1836)

Raymond, Thomas, *Autobiography of Thomas Raymond and Memoirs of the Family of Guise of Elmore, Gloucestershire*, ed. G. Davies (Camden Third Series, London, 1917)

Rushworth, J., *Historical Collections* (London, 1706, abr.)

Sprigge, J., *Angliae Rediviva* (Partridge, London, 1647)

Storey, M., *Two East Anglian Diaries…1641–1729* (Suffolk Records Society, Woodbridge, 1994)

Tany, Thomas, *The Nations Right in Magna Charta Discussed With the Thing Called Parliament. With Other Writings of Thomas Tany 'Theauraujohn'*, ed. Andrew Hopton (Aporia, London, 1988)

Tucker, N. and P. Young, eds, *Military Memoirs of the Civil War by Richard Atkins and John Gwyn* (Longman, London, 1967)

Verney, F. P. and Verney, M. M., eds, *Memoirs of the Verney Family During the Seventeenth Century*, vol. I (Longman, London, 1904)

Wallington, N., *Historical Notes* (London, 1869)

Walwyn, W., *The Writings of William Walwyn*, eds J. McMichael and B. Taft (University of Georgia Press, London, 1989)

Warwick, P., *Memoirs of the Reign of King Charles I, with A Continuation to the Happy Restoration of Charles II* (London, 1701)

Wentworth, Sir Thomas, *Articles of Impeachment of the Earl of Strafford, by the House of Commons, and Sundry Speeches Relating Thereto: Together With 'The Two Last Speeches of Thomas Wentworth, Late Earl of Strafford'* (London, 1641)

Whitelocke, B., ed. R. Spalding, *The Diary of Bulstrode Whitelocke* (Oxford University Press, Oxford, 1990)

Whitelocke, B., *Memorials of the English Affairs 1625–1660* (Oxford University Press, Oxford, 1853)

Winstanley, G., *Winstanley: The Law of Freedom and other Writings*, ed. C. Hill (Penguin Books, London, 1973)

Wood, A., *The Life and Times of Anthony Wood*, ed. A. Clark, 5 vols (Oxford University Press, London, 1961)

Wright, T., ed., *The Autobiography of Joseph Lister, of Bradford in Yorkshire* (London, 1862)

SECONDARY

Adair, J., *By the Sword Divided* (Century, London, 1983)

Ashton, Robert, *The English Civil War: Conservatism and Revolution, 1603–1649* (Weidenfeld and Nicolson, London, 1978)

Carlton, C., *Going to the Wars* (Routledge, London, 1992)

Carruthers, B., *The English Civil Wars* (Cassell, London, 2000)

Edwards, G., *The Last Days of Charles I* (Sutton, Stroud, 1999)

Forster, R., *Modern Ireland* (Penguin Books, London, 1989)

Gardiner, S. R., *History of England from the Accession of James I. to the Outbreak of the Civil War 1603–1642*, 10 vols (Longmans, Green & Co., London, 1883–4)

Gaunt, Peter, *The British Wars, 1637–51* (Routledge, London, 1997)

Gregg, P., *King Charles I* (JM Dent, London, 1981)

Hibbert, C., *Cavaliers and Roundheads* (HarperCollins, London, 1994)

Hill, C., *God's Englishman: Oliver Cromwell and the English Revolution* (Penguin Classic, London, 2000)

Hill, C., *The World Turned Upside Down* (Temple Smith, London, 1972)

Hill, C., *Milton and the English Revolution* (Faber, London, 1977)

Hill, C., *Some Intellectual Consequences of the English Revolution* (Weidenfeld and Nicolson, London,1980)

Holmes, R. and P. Young, *The English Civil War* (Wordsworth edition, Ware, 2000)

Kishlansky, M., *A Monarchy Transformed: Britain 1603–1714* (Penguin Books, London, 1997)

McGregor, J. F. and B. Reay, eds, *Radical Religion in the English Revolution* (Oxford University Press, Oxford, 1984)

Morrill, J., *The Revolt of the Provinces* (Longman, London, 1980)

Morrill, J., *The Nature of the English Revolution* (Longman, London, 1993)

Ollard, R., *The Image of the King* (Phoenix, London, 2000)

Russell, C., *The Causes of the English Civil War* (Clarendon Press, Oxford, 1991)

Seaver, P., *Wallington's World: A Puritan Artisan in Seventeenth-Century London* (Methuen, London, 1985)

Wedgwood, C.V., *The King's Peace 1637–1641* (Penguin Books, London, 1983)

Wedgwood, C.V., *The King's War 1641–1647* (Penguin Books, London, 1983)

Woolrych, A., *Battles of the English Civil War* (Pimlico, London, 1991)

Worden, B., *Roundhead Reputations* (Allen Lane, London, 2001)

Worden, B., *Stuart England* (Phaidon Press, Oxford, 1986)

Young, P., *Naseby 1645: The Campaign and the Battle* (Century, London, 1985)

Young, P., *Edgehill 1642: The Campaign and the Battle* (Windrush, Moreton-in-Marsh, 1995)

Young, P., *Marston Moor 1644: The Campaign and the Battle* (Windrush, Moreton-in-Marsh, 1997)

COLLECTIONS OF EDITED DOCUMENTS

Bruce, J (ed.), *The Verney Papers* (Camden Society, London, 1953)

Fassnidge, J., *Civil War Documents*, 4 vols (Longman Resources Unit, York, 1984)

Firth, C. H. and R. S. Rait, *Acts and Ordinances of the Interregnum, 1642-1660*, 3 vols (HMSO, London, 1911)

Gardiner, S. R., *Constitutional Documents of the Puritan Revolution*, 3rd edn (Longman, London, 1906)

Haller, W., ed., *Tracts on Liberty in the Puritan Revolution*, 3 vols (Columbia University Press, New York, 1934)

Haller, W., and G. Davies, eds, *The Leveller Tracts* (Columbia University Press, New York, 1964)

Hogan, J., ed., *Letters and Papers Relating to the Irish Rebellion* (Irish Manuscripts Commission, Dublin, 1930)

Hughes, A., ed., *Seventeenth-century England: A Changing Culture* (Open University Press, London, 1980)

Kenyon, J. P., ed., *The Stuart Constitution* (Cambridge University Press, Cambridge, 1986)

Lamont, W. M., and S. Oldfield, eds, *Politics, Religion and Literature in the Seventeenth Century* (Routledge, London, 1975)

Lindley, K., ed., *The English Civil War and Revolution: A Sourcebook* (Routledge, London, 1998)

Lockyer, R., *The Trial of Charles I* (Folio Society, London, 1959)

Prall, S., ed., *The Puritan Revolution...A Documentary History* (Routledge & Keegan Paul, London, 1968)

Raymond, J., *Making the News: An Anthology of the Newsbooks of Revolutionary England, 1641–1660* (Windrush, Moreton-in-Marsh,1993)

Smith, Nigel, ed., *A Collection of Ranter Writings from the Seventeenth Century* (Junction, London, 1983)

Underhill, E. B., ed., *Tracts on Liberty of Conscience and Persecution 1614–1661* (Knollys Society, London, 1846)

Wolfe, D. M. et al, eds, *Leveller Manifestoes of the Puritan Revolution* (Thomas Nelson and Son, New York, 1944)

Woodhouse, A. S. P., ed., *Puritanism and Liberty: Being the Army Debates, 1647–9* (JM Dent and Sons, London1938)

Index

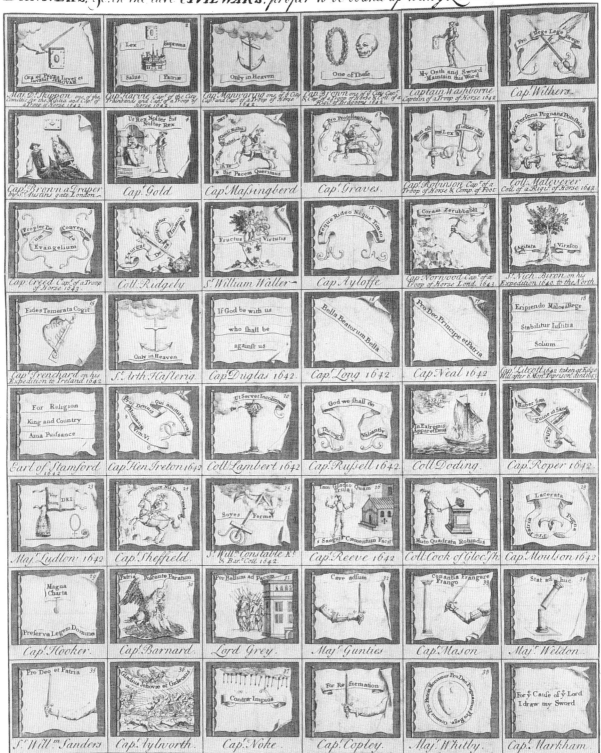

1. Pray and Fight, let Jehovah help & He will help. 2. The Supream Law is the Welfare of y Country. 3. For the King, Law, & Flock. 4. As our King, so be our King. 5. Our Eyes are Fixd on This 5 ...
Thus Seek we peace. 6. For the Protestants. 7. No Law is more Safe. 8. The King is y Person Fighting in his own power. 9. Word of God, Law of y People. 9. For God, the Gospel, & the Covenant.
10. Let God arise, & let his Enemies be dispersed. 11. The Fruit of Virtue. 12. I neither Laugh, nor Fear. 13. Before Zerubbabel. 14. Being Shaken I grow Stronger. 15. Faith being broken compels ...
16. The Warrs are the Warrs, of y Saints. 17. For God, the Prince, & the Country. 18. By taking away y Wicked, from the King, y Throne is Establish'd in Justice. 19. He that Looses, for Matters of God is a ...
... sinner for Human things, Force by force. 20. That it may be keep safe. 21. God appears in Extremity. 22. Made red with blood, to stop y Shedding of blood. 23. The Word of God. 24. Nothing ...
... to be disposed of of God being our Captain. 25. Be firm. 26. Both by y Sword & Trowell, Blood makes y Church Yard. 27. I change Square things into Round. 28. I torn in Fighting, for the Country.
29. Greats Charter. 1. Lord Preserve the Law. 30. The Country requiring Him to be ready. 31. By Warr to Peace. 32. Be ware I am ready. 33. I Break such as indeavour to break. 34. It Stands the ...
35. For God & the Country. 36. The Sword of the Lord & Gideon. 37. Against the Wicked. 38. Wee pray for the Country, Let us die for God, Wee Fight for the King. Note For the Benefit of the
English Reader The Latin Motto's are translated.